Wake Up! The Lord is Returning

By Alf Droy

ISBN 0-9531440-1-1

Web site **http://www.wakeupnow.com**
Email **alf@droy.freeserve.co.uk**

Printed in England
By El Shaddai Publishers

First Edition published in July 2001
Second Edition published in February 2002

CONTENTS

FOREWORDS

Wake Up! The Lord is Returning is a scholarly yet reader friendly presentation of a vital aspect of the Christian faith. You will be challenged as you explore the author's insights and examine your own personal understanding of God's purpose at this time in history.

Dr David Yonggi Cho, Senior pastor Yoido Full Gospel Church, Seoul, Korea.

Over the last seven years since I have enjoyed friendship with Alf, he has always shown a great zest for life together with a desire to communicate the uniqueness and grace of Jesus Christ. His thoroughly researched book has information which most of us would not be able easily to compile. Alf's writing therefore should bring us to consider carefully our understanding of God's world, his eternal purpose that he has accomplished in Christ and the importance of the coming again of Jesus. I trust that reading ***'Wake up! The Lord is Returning.'*** will stimulate increased confidence in God as well as a sober assessment of the responsibilities of following the Lord Jesus Christ in our present world situation. Together with Alf I look forward to a demonstration of the justice and righteousness that can only be found in Jesus himself.

D Coak Senior pastor City Church Cambridge

When I wrote the foreword for the first edition of Alf's Droy's book, ***Wake Up! The Lord is Returning***, we were coming to the end of 1999 and talk of Y2K filled the air. Would the human millennium be the time of the Lord's Return? At the time Alf's vision challenged that thought process and also the triumphalist, dominion theology of many believers. However, one wondered if Alf's revelations were inspired, or the outworking of an over-active imagination! But I was forced to face the issue head on; how and when will the Great Tribulation be triggered off, and the Lord return to 'Rapture' His bride, before establishing His Kingdom?

I was calling an old colleague from a national newspaper about 2 pm on Tuesday September 11th 2001. The first words he said were "We're keeping an eye out for low flying aircraft". I wondered to what he was alluding, and then seconds later I heard him say "My God!!!" He was watching the second aircraft plough into the World Trade Centre. It was only 3 or 4 hours later that my mind began to fully take in the enormity of that one-hour and recall the close parallels with the words from "***Wake Up***". The difference between the two editions is that now the reader can weigh Alf's conclusions against actual events. Alf has recorded many of his visions and revelations received from the Lord. Within these pages Alf has drawn together a vast range of information sources to provide the reader an explanation and a structure for his conclusions. The cogently written explanations provide compelling reading.

The challenge that is boldly, and in certain places provocatively, asked, "When will the Lord return?" maybe a more profound question to ask us is "When the Lord returns will He find faith?" You may not agree with Alf's conclusions, but do not let your intellectual logic blind you to the fact that Alf has a burning passion for the Lord. His desire is to do God's will, and to stand on that obedience, placing his trust in nothing or no one else. Delight in this godly fervour and feel the warmth of God's breath upon your cheek. The Lord **is** returning and by reading this book you will gain a broader understanding of the background to the whole issue of eschatology.
Even so, Maranatha, Come Lord Jesus.

Nick Thompson.
Former Director of Good News Broadcasting Association

INTRODUCTION

In the light of the evidence of the prophecy contained on page 148 of the first edition of Wake Up!...with regard to the outbreak of an international religious world war, and the oblique references I made to a suicide attack on the Twin Towers and other sensitive targets in America, by Muslim extremists, it has proved necessary for me to offer a reasoned explanation just where Mohammed and the Muslims featured in the Book of Revelation; plus a greater insight into when and how I experienced divine appointments, that focused my attention on what God was revealing to me. Now read on.

It is both necessary and desirable to study the word of God, for Christ is the Word become flesh, that humanity might better understand the person of God and His purposes for mankind's future. The Hebrew sages have said that the study of God's revealed word is the highest form of worship. I would add that the noblest pursuit of Christians is the searching out of the will of God for their lives. Pope John Paul II has said: "***Europe can choose between nihilism and the rediscovery of the Christian faith***". The World Evangelistic Research Centre claims that throughout the world, 156 million non-whites do not accept Western-style Christianity, with its institutional and traditional forms of churchmanship infected with the yeast of ***Romanism*** (Catholicism). Westernised Christianity has replaced revelation with reason, correct standards with expediency and both moral and ethical perception over personal choice with liberal '***humanism***'[1] (a form of ***existentialism***[2]). The reader of this book may be from such a background, or alternatively, may have received as a child an objective understanding of God, from parents or schoolteachers. Every believer having doubts over doctrine must be prepared to have one's expressed views criticised or corrected, in order to mature in one's faith. I am constrained to publish my experiences and conclusions in this book that many non-believers may themselves come to know the Messiah Jesus ***subjectively***. Perhaps my readers will guide others of their family or friends (who find the Church to be hypocritical or too Westernised), back into God's fold;

---

[1] Humanism is the denial of any power or moral value thought to be superior to that of humanity. This is the rejection of all religions in favour of the advancement of humanity by its own efforts, and regards God as an absent Creator, who is no longer interested in His creation, and who should equally be disregarded by man.

[2] Existentialism teaches that each person is responsible only to himself or herself as to how they react to the experiences of life, which determines their behaviour in a seemingly meaningless universe. Existentialists believe that God created mankind to be an extension of God Himself; therefore we should be free to express ourselves in any way to which we may be so inclined. Existentialists consider atrocity and other forms of anti-social behaviour not as evil but as a matter of preference.

if so, the writing of this book will have proven profitable (James Ch 5:19). I believe God commissioned me to write this book as a warning to readers to prepare for Christ's Second Coming through heartfelt repentance and faithful obedience.

I am well aware that my own salvation is solely dependent upon God's mercy. Many 'born again'[3] believers prefer to internalise their faith in Jesus, but being a committed Christian should mean thankfully testifying to others. I believe that 'actions speak louder than words', all believers should be activists, available as open conduits of use to the Holy Spirit. It is vital that my reader understands that at the ***Second Coming***[4] Christ will be dispensing ***judgement***, and not an invitation to join Him in His new kingdom. In the compilation of this book, strewn with prophecies and revelations given to me, I have constantly used the pronoun 'I', for which I apologise. I am equally concerned to expose the false doctrine of '***replacement***' or '***fulfilment***'[5] theology. My opinions and conclusions do not represent the views of the church of which I am a member, nor the group of churches to which it belongs.

Some years ago the Anglican Church lost millions of pounds in stock-exchange dealings, sparking off concern that, in future, the church would be unable to meet its liability to provide the retired clergy their pensions. The maintenance costs of the 10,000 churches (7,000 of which were built before 1300 AD!) are huge and ever increasing; whilst the tithing level of its members in 1997 was estimated to be only 3.2% (per cent) of the 'take home pay' of its followers. Empirically the funding of even current commitments of providing pensions and the repair of buildings is causing concern. Quite apart from the funding, the church's politics and tradition are in need of drastic appraisal. Archbishop George Carey observed at the Assembly of the World Council of Churches (WCC) in December 1998: "***Some sections of***

---

[3] Born not through emerging from a water filled chrysalis some nine months after conception, but supernaturally regenerated, born of the Holy Spirit of God, born of fire and filled with the Spirit of God on recognising Jesus Christ as the living Lord and saviour of souls, on repenting of one's sins, willingly submit their free will into bondage to the Holy Spirit. Wherever in this book I use the term '***Christian***' or '***believer***', I am writing of '***born again***' disciples of Christ, and not 'nominal' Christians.

[4] The Second Coming of Jesus Christ to rule throughout the Earth as Messiah. The events that must be fulfilled prior to Christ's Second Coming, are sandwiched between His declaration in Matthew Ch 23:39, where Jesus plainly said that He would only return when the Jews prayed fervently for His Second Coming, and in Matthew Ch 24:34, where Jesus said: "***This generation will not pass away until all these things have taken place.***"

[5] Replacement theology (or supersessionism) is the belief that God has chosen the Church in place of the rejected nation of Israel.

the Western Church are bleeding to death." Three months later, whilst addressing an Anglican Conference of Bishops, missionaries and the priesthood, he spoke more specifically of declining membership of the Anglican Church by stating: "***The Church is one generation away from extinction***." Figures extrapolated on current trends (contained in the 1998 English Church Attendance Survey), suggest starkly that if the trend is not halted, by 2016 church attendance in Britain will have fallen by one-third across all persuasions of churchmanship. Perhaps the greatest concern is the problem of attracting teenagers, whose disaffected parents consider the established Church an irrelevance by today's society. Since 1994 e***ach week*** in Britain, 2,200 people have ceased attending church. Six churches have closed their doors, whilst four (in the main non-denominational fellowships) groups, have planted churches in schools and other public multi-purpose buildings. Many disaffected believers from the established denominations have joined such congregations, despite the inconvenience of setting up the assembly room for Sunday worship, each week, and then restoring the rooms used to their normal function, whilst finding a secure place to lock in the items needed for the next service. Members often become frustrated by such arrangements and may 'split' or break-away into smaller groups[6] in their homes.

As a watchman I take very seriously the injunction contained in Ezekiel Ch 3:17-21 and the exhortation from James Ch 5:20 to argue convincingly and logically to those whom I believe to be in need of correction or guidance. I have quoted many Bible passages that the reader should double-check for accuracy (as commanded in 1 Thessalonians Ch 5:19-21 and 1 John Ch 4:1-3), and not blindly accept tradition or the doctrine of any particular denomination. The Bereans studied their Scriptures to confirm St Paul's claims (Acts Ch 17:10-15); surely we should all do likewise? If you were given permission to offer to your loved ones, invitations to the wedding of Christ at His return, would you be able to convince them of their need to attend? Many Christians are superstitious of spending time in meditation over the circumstances and date of Christ's Second Coming, believing that such idle speculation is harmful to one's salvation. I would point out from Daniel Ch 12:4 that Daniel was shown the scroll of history, and was told to close and seal it ***until*** the end times (***eschatology***), when presumably the seals will be opened once

---

[6] One in four new churches fail in the first two years, and as 50% of all Protestants attend just 15% of the churches; the conclusion must be drawn that small congregations have little modern appeal.

more, and the prophecy contained in Joel Ch 2:28 will be fulfilled. The Holy Spirit will then be poured out in greater measure than at the first Pentecost; clarifying that Isaiah Ch 29:18 was prophesying of a time when the incontestable truth of Jesus' ***Immaculate Conception***, His ***atoning sacrifice*** and ***resurrection***, hidden throughout history from the faithless and the doubter, will be revealed (Daniel Ch 12:10 states that those who are spiritually wise will understand the Scriptures pertaining to the 'end times', whilst those who are not will have to wait until events unfold).

I have not used the term AD (***anno Domini***-after Christ) when quoting 19th and 20th century dates, except where I consider that usage helps the flow of my thoughts. Where I have referred to dates in earlier centuries I have used the terms AD or BC (before Christ) as necessary, rather than using the terms CE or BCE (to indicate Common Era or Before Common Era, which are not used in common parlance). Where I have used the term '**paraphrased**', the summary represents my understanding of the passage.

Chapter 1

OUR CREATOR GOD

Many geologists have concluded from the radiometric dating[7] of rock (granite), under laboratory conditions, that planet Earth is at least 4.5 billion years of age. The belief (that this world, and indeed this and many other universes are very '***old***') is supported by Professor Martin Rees, whose research emphatically stresses that planet Earth is 'old', with other galaxies having been formed ***before*** our own galaxy came into being. His book entitled ***Just Six Numbers***, explains his reason ***mathematically***. Two of the numbers relate to the size and 'texture' of every galaxy, two relate to the basic forces of natural law, and two determine the properties of space. Unfortunately the 'old' Earth hypothesis leads to the acceptance of the unproven theory of evolution. In His infinite wisdom, God has chosen not to reveal every detail of Creation to mankind, but this has opened the door for doubt, that the biblical Creation narrative is incorrect. The great age attributed to rock samples was challenged by American scientist, Dr Robert Gentry, who had taken more than 200,000 core samples around the world of granite at various depths of drilling. Every sample he examined contained halos of black flakes known as mica, scored into the varying laminations of granite, confirming that radioactivity had been present at the time of the crystallising of the granite. Each sample had traces of polonium 210, 218 or 214; the half-life of these three materials respectively is 22 days, 3 minutes, or just 164 milliseconds, suggesting that granite was formed in ***less than a day***.

Many Christian scientists and scholars accept as incontrovertible fact, that planet Earth is a very old creation despite the alternative conclusions of equally renowned scholarship, that the Earth is a relatively new creation. In 1835 Carl Friedrich Gauss calculated that the strength of the Earth's magnetic field halves in intensity every 1,400 years as the planet cools. Calculating backwards empirically

---

[7]Radiometric dating is assessed from the amount of decay of naturally occurring long-lived isotopes, such as potassium-40 dating up to 10 million years of age, rubidium 87 dating up to 20 million years, thorium-232 and uranium-238 dating is suitable for rocks formed more than 20 million years ago, traces are present in all rocks. The Hebrew cabbalist Nechunya ben HaKanah believed that God was mysteriously active before Creation, during a period he named as '***a concept in the mind of God***'. He believed that our universe came into existence 15.3 million years ago. Nechunya reasoned that the 42 lettered name of God, encoded into the first 42 letters of Genesis, represent 42,000 ***divine years***, each of 365.25 years in length (42,000 x 365.25 years = 15.3 million years).

from 2000 AD, in 600 AD the magnetic field had been twice as strong as it currently is, whilst in 800 BC it was four times stronger. In 2200 BC, the force of magnetism would have been eight times stronger, and in 3600 BC 16 times stronger than today's magnetic force. In 10000 BC planet Earth would have had a magnetic strength of a star, and the surface temperature would have been far too hot to support life.

Australian scientist, Barry Setterfield, extrapolated that the speed of light approached infinity approximately 6,000 years[8] ago, empirically calculating that the decrease in the power of radiation is proportional to the slowing speed of light, which provides a measurable effect of the universes expanding, a phenomenon known as '*Red Shift*'. A specialist in the theory of quantum mechanics[9], Russian scientist, Dr David Otway-Wray, subjected the Book of Genesis to particle and solid-state physics, and algebraic formula, concluding that this universe (not only planet Earth) could not be any older than between

---

[8] Mankind's task was to procreate and fill the earth as commanded throughout the 6,000 years leading to the day of rest (***eternity outside of time***). This must mean that this generation could be the last before the Second Coming of Christ. I have come to believe that when God said that man would not live beyond 120 years, Genesis Ch 6:3-5), He was in effect saying that ***mankind*** would not live beyond 120 jubilees of 50 years duration. This is the sum total of years, before the seventh day of the millennium of Christ's reign on Earth commences. There will be 6,000 years between the birth of the first Adam and the Second Coming of the second Adam (Christ). Adam died at 930 years of age, whilst the son of the prophet Enoch, Methuselah (which means '***when he dies, the waters will come***'), lived for 962 years. Therefore God had obviously decided to eradicate most of mankind before He told Noah of His intentions. Post-flood longevity of individuals was generally restricted to 70 years. It is stated in Psalm 90:10 that man shall live three score years and ten, or if strong and healthy, perhaps reaching 80 years. This shortened period of longevity was in effect a curse on mankind, owing to his rebellious nature. God decreed in Leviticus Ch 25:1-12 that each seventh year was a ***holy Shabbat year*** (the ***schmitta***, or ***sacred*** year), and on the completion of 'seven' being '***squared***', $7^2 = 49$ years (the squaring of any number by itself with no remainder is God's signature of completion), the diamond year of jubilee would follow, when again the land was to lie fallow, as it had during the *schmitta* years. I believe that God counts the cycles of time in 50-year groupings. The sages believed that God calculated the seventh year of *Shabbat* from the first day of Creation, 5,761 years ago, as they have determined. This is why the *schmitta* year that commenced on the 29th of September 2000 is known in the Hebrew Calendar as year 5761 (that is 3,761 years + 2,000 years of the Gregorian Calendar since Christ's birth).

[9] Quantum (or wave mechanics), in physics is the theory that atomic and nuclear particles produce a discontinuous range of values of energy. Energy is absorbed or radiated discontinuously in multiples of definite, indivisible units called quanta, and move in waves, like electrical, light and sound waves. All these moving bodies possess kinetic energy, which can be converted from one form of energy to another, but the total quantity stays the same, (in accordance with the conservation of energy principle).

6,000 - 10,000[10] years of age. As a child and into adulthood, I read stories and watched spine-chilling films of witches, zombies, devil worshippers, spirit guides etc. I believed the sensational stories featured by the popular press that planet Earth was visited by aliens in spaceships from other planets; whose crew collected random samples of life forms. Stories often featured psychic encounters[11], of people being taken away as prisoners. These 'specimens' prisoners were sometimes returned to planet Earth after their various behavioural traits were documented and following laboratory experiments on them had been completed. Some of these returned 'specimens' sold their story to the world's press, and with the many corroborated independent eyewitness reports and photographs, of 'unidentified flying objects' (UFO's) the stories gained credulity. At that time I believed these stories disproved the biblical Creation narrative.

Before I was 'born again', I believed that Adam and Eve were just random examples of humanity, used as examples by the sages of old, to demonstrate how the world became populated on mankind evolving from pre-historic times. The Garden of Eden was the fairy-tale homeland of Adam and Eve, who were a microcosm of a greater number of ancient civilisations, which was why so many people groups included the story of a ***universal flood*** in their folklore. This is what my schoolteachers taught, based on the findings of cosmologists, geologists and anthropologists, and secular scientists in other fields of expertise. I reasoned that Christianity was just a sophisticated superstition no less believable than any other religion practiced by other cultures, designed to encourage good community law-abiding life. I knew the theology of a tripartite supernatural God, but Jesus was nothing more than a legend to my mind, no more or less believable than Robin Hood or Dick Turpin. In my mid-teens, I became interested

---

[10] The amount of helium present in the Earth's atmosphere indicates an approximate age of 10,000 years. The scientists from the National Aeronautics and Space Administration (NASA) concluded from the first Viking Moon landing in 1976 that the planets of the Milky Way draw helium (a colourless, odourless, light inert gaseous element, produced by the action of cosmic rays on the atmosphere), from our Sun continuously. Gene Faulstich (of whom I write in Chapter 2) believes that the Earth was created at 6:00[PM], on the 18th March 4001 BC, at the commencement of, what he perceives to be, the first Spring Equinox. Using a computer, Faulstich has been able to determine that the Moon and the planets, Mercury, Venus, Mars and Pluto were within one degree of geometric alignment with each other and Earth at 343° (degrees) on the day preceding the rising of the new moon over planet Earth on 21st March 4001 BC (day four). The scientists of the Center for Astrophysics at Harvard University in the United States of America (USA) agreed with the accuracy of Faulstich's calculations, but hold to the view that an alignment of the planets could have occurred aeons earlier.

[11] These reports included stories of people recalling incidents supposedly occurring during previous lifetimes, supporting a belief in reincarnation.

in ***Spiritualism***[12], taking part in séances and dabbling in spiritual manifestations with notable results. Spiritualists believe that perfection as human beings is reached after several quality lifetimes on Earth have been completed.

Most people have puzzled over the meaning to their life, not accepting the evolutionists' premise that one's existence is an accident of birth, originating from an ignition of chemicals. I cannot accept the evolutionist's theory that planet Earth was created through a single or series of chance explosions (the '***big bang***' theory). A theory that dissimilar inflammable chemical compounds collided in space with sufficient force to split into new molecules that evolved into chromosomes which developed into genes[13], that through mutation with dissimilar non-life forms, perhaps over many years, became capable of sustaining both plant and animal life asexually.

Many 'Christian' evolutionists theorise that some of these genes (of unconvincing origin) evolved into an early primate (a humanoid, which was given the name 'Neanderthal man'), who later developed into ***Homo sapiens***, whilst other genes developed into vegetation or animal life. Because no 'missing links' have been found, some scientists hold to a theory that there must have been many components in a primordial soup, which may have formed into various life forms, through being struck by a bolt of lightening. Pope

---

[12] The most modern feature of Spiritualism is 'Channelling,' a modern name for contacting and dialoguing with the spirit world, expressly forbidden in Scripture (Deuteronomy Ch 18:10-12). '*Channelling*' has been popularised by film star Shirley MacLaine, the self-proclaimed high priestess of the New Age movement. Biblical teaching is clear "***Do not turn to mediums or wizards. Do not seek them out to be defiled by them***" (Leviticus Ch 19:31). Believers are warned against practicing divination or sorcery in Deuteronomy Ch 18:10 "*Whoever does these things is an abomination to the Lord*". The consequences are made clear in Leviticus Ch 20:6: "***As for the person who turns to mediums and to spiritists, to play the harlot after them, I will also set My face against that person and will cut him off from among his people***". To those who seek guidance from astrology, God says in Isaiah Ch 47:13-14: "***Let your astrologists come forward, those star-gazers who make predictions month by month, let them save you from what is coming upon you. Surely they are like stubble; the fire will burn them up***". The cursing is unmistakable in Micah Ch 5:12: "***I will destroy your witchcraft***".

[13] Genetic 'instructions' are written (just as the 26 letters of the English alphabet that sentences are ordered) from the four chemical building blocks of DNA, which is an *independent cell* (named the mitochondria) created by the mixture of sperm at conception. The cells amalgamate in the formation of the chromosomes, and contain genetic material, which (in previous generations) could only be passed to succeeding generations ***through the egg of the mother***. An individual gene is a specific tract of DNA which is itself part of a much longer DNA molecule. A string of genes complete a chromosome. Since the turn of the 21st century, microbiologists have been able to fully interpret the genetic code, proving beyond doubt that it is ***impossible to create genes through isolation, selection, mutation or breeding***.

John Paul II has pontificated '***ex cathedra***' (Latin, meaning 'from the throne') that God may have placed a living soul into a creature that evolved into a humanoid, which He found acceptable to be changed into His image. This theory is definitely not inspiration from the heart of God. It is clearly written in Genesis Ch 2:7 that mankind was a new species of creature, formed in the image of God, from dust; this statement should be incontestable. I realise that belief in a '***young***' Earth is difficult to accept, but belief that Christ is the second Adam, means accepting that Adam was the first person fashioned of mankind, who has infected the remainder of mankind with '***original sin***'.

All birth is miraculous, a product of design. It is illogical and irrational to believe that the gills of a fish and the lungs of a porpoise, the antennae of a moth and the radar of a bat, occurred 'by chance'. It is much more believable to reason that a master creator developed all the magnificent variations of nature 'after their kind'. I find difficulty believing that Adam named the dinosaurs and the pterodactyls, but perhaps these extinct animals may have been formed from the genus of the Leviathan and the behemoth? I have developed my own 'Droy mythology'[14], because I doubt that the mastodon and the sabre-toothed tiger were docile animals, even whilst living in the Garden of Eden (paradise)! Whether prehistoric animals and anthropoids ever existed prior to the creation of mankind is irrelevant to the belief in a personal saviour of each human soul. It is absurd to consider vast periods of 'time', as developing life-giving properties. Time is inert offering nothing to civilisation except history. The complexity and the uncertainty of a full lifespan for all creatures, is meant to reveal to mankind that an omniscient and omnipotent creator grants life. If science has convinced some Christians that the biblical Creation story is a myth, or is in error, then such believers have an ***uncertain faith***.

---

[14] Lucifer, the chief of angels was cast out of heaven down to the Abyss, together with the fallen angels that were chained (four at the Euphrates River, see Revelation Ch 9;14). He was allowed to form a creation, during which time he created prehistoric man, and the prehistoric animals. (The co-existence of the two species cannot be denied, for skeletal remains and footprints of both species have been found in the same layer of sedimentation, at many places around the world). God saw Satan's attempt at creation as an unholy chaos, and destroyed it. At the same time God allowed Lucifer to be 'Prince of the Air' (see Ephesians Ch 2:2, where Satan is spoken of as the ruler of the kingdom of the air). God did not ***make*** anything on Earth, other than light, during the first two days; He just separated the dark from the light and the two areas of water, which produced the ***realm of the air***. It can be seen that God did not bless day two of Creation as 'good', which may have been the day of Satan's appointment. Since that time, Satan has tried to wrest all authority for himself.

The hypothesis of growth on an evolutionary tree, which has its roots firmly embedded in non-living granite, is not acceptable to entomologists, who can provide a great deal of evidence of co-dependency of dissimilar species. For example there is one particular type of fig tree that cannot produce fruit without the co-operation of the fig wasp. Both tree and wasp had to have been created within the same week, for neither species could have survived without the other. Inside the fig are closed male (and female) flowers, out of which a male wasp emerges. The wasp fertilises every unopened female flower and then eats its way out of the growing fig (to form a tunnel), the wasp then returns to its 'chrysalis' and dies. The female wasp hatches some time later, at which time she visits all the other flowers, covering herself with pollen in the process, pollinating the 'anthers' of every flower. She deposits her eggs onto the female flowers, and then she dies. The blossoming of the fig tree in season is repeated annually.

Nuclear scientist Robert W Faid writes in his book, ***A Scientific Approach to Christianity*** of the interdependence of the Pronuba moth with the yucca plant, and of many other instances of dissimilar co-dependent species flourishing. The evidence of co-dependency does not support the random mutation theory of evolution. These conflicting controversial theories have beset the scholarly world since 19th century Darwinism[15]. Anthropologist Allan Wilson, extracted deoxyribonucleic acid (DNA) from the calcified skeletal remains of a human being subjecting them to radiocarbon dating[16]. Wilson concluded that the final development of *Homo sapiens* occurred *c*100,000 -140,000 years ago, within a tribe of cavemen living in Africa. However in 2001 archaeologists in Australia excavated the fossilised bones of a human, that were calibrated as being *c*1½ million years of age; even older are the fossilised bones of an excavated female humanoid 42 inches in height that walked upright, which was calculated as being 3½ million years of age. These discoveries do not ***confirm*** the theory of an evolving

---

[15] Darwinism is the theory that animals and plants evolved through a process of natural selection.

[16] Radiocarbon (or carbon dating) of organic materials was first developed in 1949 by American chemist Willard Libby. The carbon dioxide gas in all organic materials is absorbed into the body through eating plants. The dead tissue loses half of its isotope value over a 5,730-year period. The tissue decays exponentially, over the second 5,730 years a further 25% is lost ad infinitum, except that this method is only reliable over 50,000 years. For lengthier periods of fossilisation, beta particles are counted using specialist equipment, and uranium/thorium dates obtained from coral. A more recent advance is the accelerator mass spectrometry, requiring only minute samples of carbon 14 for calibration, regardless of age.

amphibious crawling creature that then evolved into a tree-climbing ape; that, although they do support the old Creation hypothesis, convincing many of evolution, but surely, if this were so, all other monkeys would now be humans! This conjecture denies that Adam was the first human, who God formed from dust. Disbelief that Adam and Eve were the first created male and female humans, is a denial that Adam was the progenitor of the sinful nature inherited through the birthmark of original sin, which stained humanity; caused by Adam believing Satan's lying promise from Genesis Ch 4:4:

> *"You will not surely die, and you will be as wise as God, knowing good from evil."* (paraphrased)

Adam was a mortal; he did not lose his immortality through original sin. Adam needed his mind, imagination and his ego, as well as his body being ***sanctified***[17] (purified, or made holy), from its sinful nature; he was as much in need of a saviour redeemer as his progeny. Following the '***fall***' into '***original sin***', God posed the question of Adam's nakedness in the way that He did, to point to Adam's interest on 'self' and away from God, which ultimately results in Narcissism[18]. I believe that God planted a supernatural (unregenerate) soul into mankind, developing on '**trust**' and '**free will**', but not of '**faith**', for this would invalidate the need of a saviour. God foreknew that the ***trust*** that Adam and Eve had been invested with would fail, and like the fallen angels, they would eventually succumb to their fleshly desires resulting in their banishment. God's response to Adam's rebellion was (a) "*who convinced you to doubt My word*?" and (b) "*What have you done*?" God showed clearly that it was Satan who countermanded God's decree, and God asks the question, "Who was morally responsible for Adam's sin?" Adam's excuses were indefensible before God. ***Mankind, corrupted by original sin, became an unregenerate beast of burden, henceforth governing the Earth not benignly but by subjugation equivalent in stature to a***

---

17 Sanctification is the setting apart for service to God. On conversion, a person's body and spirit become sanctified and sensitised, and through submission, offers control of the individual will to the Holy Spirit, resulting in holiness (Romans Ch 8:6). Confession does not bring absolution but exoneration.

18 Narcissism is the exceptional interest or admiration paid to oneself.

donkey[19] (an animal that was supernaturally used by God to speak His word to the prophet Balaam).

It is certain that the angels were created earlier than the planets, for it is written in Job Ch 38:7:

> *"The creation of planet Earth was watched by the angels, who shouted for joy at God's bountiful and consistent mercies."*

God said in Job Ch 38:31-33:

> *"Can you bind the chains of Plaides, or loosen the cords of Orion? Can you lead the constellations in their seasons, and guide the Bear with her satellites in their seasons? Have you fixed the proximity of the planets to each other, to answer your every command?"*

God was rhetorically saying that He ordered these events.

Many non-Christian scientists, known as '***theistic evolutionists***' have a belief in a master Creator, who may have been involved at the birthing of planet Earth *c*3,000-4,600 million years ago, and in creating every other galaxy, but acting only as a watchmaker might (by taking no further part in future developments). Those people who do not accept the Genesis Ch 1-Ch 4:16 seven-day account of Creation, but believe that many millions of years could have occurred between Genesis Ch 1:1-2 and verse 3, or who argue that there can be no sure way of knowing if the first three days were of equal length as the remainder of 'Earth-length' days which followed (for the Sun and the Moon, which regulated the seasons, were not put in place until day four (Genesis Ch 1:14-20), are known as ***progressive*** *(or '**step**')*

---

[19] In Exodus Ch 34:20 Moses was told to offer a lamb for the redemption of sin for the life of the first-born donkey of every family. If redemption was not paid, that donkey was to have been destroyed. From Genesis Ch 16:12 - Ch 17:20 we read that Ishmael is a wild donkey, who although enjoying God's blessing, was not the child of the covenant (the promise) that established the royal line of inheritance. It is no coincidence that when Jesus entered Jerusalem for the final time, He demonstrated by untethering and riding the foal of a donkey, that He wanted to take the reins and guide this submissive donkey. I believe Jesus' action was analogous to His ultimate goal to reign over the crowd lining the route that recognised (from Zechariah Ch 9:9) His sovereign authority. The donkey is the only creature of which Jesus said He had need (Matthew Ch 21:3). Genesis Ch 49:11 prophesied that the Messianic king to come would one day tether His donkey to the chosen branch in His vineyard. I believe that these Scriptures concerning the donkey confirm that although God placed cherubim on the east side of the Garden of Eden to prevent illegal entry (by a short cut). One day redeemed man will 'spiritually' have circumnavigated the Earth from the west, and, after the Rapture, will be allowed entry and permitted to eat from the Tree of Life (Revelation Ch 2:7). The redeemed turn about and travel westward on the day they accept Christ; always looking towards their final home.

creationists[20]. Belief in '***time seemingly standing still***' is much more acceptable to me than '***built-in obsolescence***'. If you the reader accept that God is able to 'operate' outside of time (as detailed in footnote 20), then you share my assurance that nothing has occurred on Earth that God did not ordain.

One needs to reason ***individually*** for oneself, that Christ's claims to be ***"the way, the truth and the life***" (John Ch14:6) are true, in order to accept Christ's atoning sacrifice. The philosophy of the ***relativist***[21] is that there is no absolute all-encompassing truth, and that every theory is 'relative' to every other theory; the acceptance or denial of which is personal, and not open to argument. Truth is the very embodiment of Christ suffusing one's existence totally as one sacrifices one's will to the spirit of God; a process known as being '***born again***'. Only the spirit of God can 'prove' to atheists, or to believers of other faiths, that Jesus is God and that only through belief and obedience in Him lays salvation and resurrection to eternal life. I have shone the light of revelation to non-believers, some of whom have repented of their former life and accepted Jesus as Lord and Saviour. Many others I have discussed these matters with are totally indifferent to salvation, caring only to make the best of their life, which

---

[20] Step creationists believe that God created this world and the galaxies, ***suddenly but progressively***, over a series of steps (the 'gap' or 'step' theory), creating the main groups of animals and plants at varying intervals of time. The theory does not mean that the creation account of Adam and Eve is untrue, only that they think this first couple were created much earlier than the bald statements in the Bible. However a more likely explanation is the ***time distortion***, caused on days one to four, through God creating a static mass in an empty expanse in a Time/Space continuum. I believe that, having created planet Earth, God did not set the planet rotating until day four. I believe that the separation of darkness (night) from light (day) of Genesis Ch I:4 was artificial but of course supernatural. It may be assumed that an infinite amount of time passed ***before*** God set the planet rotating on ***day four, on the remainder of the galaxy being formed and magnetised, when each planet was put in its correct place and sent spinning at the necessary speeds***. I imagine that the other galaxies of the universe started expanding from that time. From that moment on, God measures time on Earth according to its daily rotations. It is the rotation of the Earth that governs '***time***'. Another explanation could be that because light travels at ***186,000 miles per second***; and God, being the source of '***light***', and outside of '***time***', He could travel so fast that '***time***' apparently stood still. God could have carried out all manner of tasks at ***infinite speed***. Mankind has not understood God's magisterial activities, believing that God confined Himself to '**normal length**' days, and needful of a rest from His labours on the seventh day! In the same way that a ***thousand*** years is as a single day to an eternal God, so possibly is a ***million*** years. Perhaps millions of years could have passed, before Adam and Eve were banished from the Garden.

[21] ***Relativism*** is the philosophical position that denies the possibility of objective truth independent of some specific social or historical context or conceptual framework. These ***philosophical shades of the meaning*** of 'truth' were taught by the ***Hellenists*** (imported Greek, or 'Westernised' culture), and opened the door to modern day ***obscurantism***.

they believe they have received through '***chance***', as if some giant wheel of fortune or lottery decides life and death by fate. Countering the error of the belief of those who hold to a different 'philosophy of faith' is difficult, but their arguments should not pass by unanswered. The Bible does not answer every question; there are many truths that are hidden from man; which I hold as being God's method of increasing our dependence through faith on His word. God makes it clear in Job Ch's 38-40, that His wisdom is beyond the capability of mankind's understanding. We are exhorted (in Proverbs Ch 3:5) to ' '***Lean not on our own understanding***' (which includes not being able to comprehend how and when God developed the foundations of His creation). My hypothesis of how mankind could have populated the world very rapidly offers an explanation, but exactly what method God chose, is not known. The Hebraic mindset advocates that 'truth' is far deeper than observable confirmation, an experience of the supernatural, or scientific corroboration. In Job Ch 12, God says that even the animals are aware of His '***hands on'*** involvement in every aspect of Creation. Humans have a brain that discriminates between instinct and logic. Self-survival is an instinct humans share with animals. We should be able to reason through problems a little better than animals! I write in this book of some scientific theories on some aspects of God's Creation proposed by experts, and offer some conclusions of my own.

From the Viking space missions, the scientists of the National Aeronautics and Space Administration (NASA) established that a 10-centimetre (cm) layer of cosmic dust particles[22] covered the surface of the Moon (as was later found on Mars), and concluded that the planets of this galaxy were formed at the same instant of time. This contention supports the theory developed by the scientists of the University of California in Los Angeles (UCLA) of 'sono-luminescence'. They theorise that on God speaking out His initial command for light to appear, reverberating sound waves would have produced radiant energy. The admixture beneath the surface of the waters may have solidified and splintered into inert granite masses, which were exploded into space instantaneously by chemical reaction. These masses formed the stars and planets of our galaxy. The scientists reached their conclusions from simulated laboratory

---

[22] Nickel, uranium and silicon are all formed from cosmic dust. If the oceans were 4.5 billion years of age, there should be approximately 950 lbs of these deposits per square foot of ocean floor; however the actual deposits indicate that the oceans are approximately 10,000 years of age. Cosmic dust enters the atmosphere at the rate of 14.3 million tons per annum. If the Earth were 4.5 billion years of age, there would be a dust blanket in excess of 30meters (m) in depth!

conditions, where it was discovered that oxygen and hydrogen bubbles form systematically, collapsing and exploding under the intensity of pressure exerted by sound waves (this theory supports my own understanding, which I outlined in footnote 20). The UCLA scientists theorised that the atmospheric pressure at sea level prior to the Great Flood was probably double that of today (14.7 pounds per square inch (lbs psi), which may have caused the temperature of Earth's highly energised water to rise to 700,000° Fahrenheit. Dr Kie Mori[23] suggests that the pressure would have been closer to 30 lbs psi. Other scientists have suggested that as a cooling star would have had a pressure of 970 lbs psi, the pressure would have been too great to sustain life. Neither the enzymes of functioning cells nor any atom could have sustained life if subjected to such intense pressure, and temperature. Gauss maintains that planet Earth could not have been created from a cooling star, and the magnetic field must have been created ***less than 10,000 years previously***, when atmospheric pressure must have been introduced. God delineated the boundaries of the solar systems of every galaxy, in an identical way that He commanded the waters on Earth to recede. He ordered the magnetising of the planets, the satellites and comets etc, in their orbits around the Sun, to ensure that none would collide (unless sanctioned otherwise).

---

[23] Scientist Dr Kei Mori of Kao University, Tokyo, Japan, carried out controlled laboratory experiments on a cherry tomato plant, which could be expected to grow to a height of 1m. Dr Mori subjected the roots of the plant to a heated and moistened earth, whilst the stem and its branches were encased in a fibre optic membrane, at an atmospheric pressure of 30 lbs psi (which was thought to be the pressure exerted at ground level prior to the Flood). After two years the plant had grown in height to 4 ms producing 900 tomatoes the size of tennis balls. Some 12 years later the tomato plant was 12m in height and had 15,000 huge tomatoes growing on its branches. Surely this experiment confirms the installation of a cryogenic ice-canopy encasing this planet?

Earthquakes[24] may be caused by impact with even the smallest of asteroids. Scientists in modern times have located in our solar system 1,700 asteroids approximately 1 kilometre (km) wide, which are capable of totally destroying Earth. There are more than a million asteroids approximately 90m wide travelling through space at 100,000 miles per hour (mph), each one capable of destroying a large city on impact. Cosmologists believe they have discovered evidence of a 'black hole'[25] in our galaxy, if they are right, there may be others as yet undetected. Perhaps it may be difficult to believe a loving Father God would create such a chaotic unpredictable solar system. A newly prepared planet, (the Holy City, called the '***New Jerusalem***'), will replace planet Earth on its destruction by fire; Isaiah Ch 65:20-25 supports this contention.

In 1930 Austrian physicist Wolfgang Pauli was ruminating over the mysterious loss of energy in certain nuclear reactions. He was familiar with Einstein's 'special theory of relativity' (that any moving particle or mass, emitted by the sun, embodies kinetic energy, and is capable of conversion into dissimilar atomic or nuclear particles). Pauli came to the conclusion that there had to be, at that time, an undiscovered subatomic particle which carried no electrical charge, so small and light, yet having a force-field or a magnetic repulse reaction to invasion, that would allow it to pass between other particles of matter (atoms), rarely colliding. He named this undetected particle, the ***neutrino*** (which means 'little neutral one'). Pauli's theory was proven correct in 1956 when two undetected particles collided resulting in a nuclear explosion, which was monitored by two physicists,

---

[24] Scientists have monitored since 1981 that planet Earth has been 'wobbling' violently on its axis, which it is feared could cause a reversal of the roles of the magnetic poles. There has been a huge rise in the number of earthquakes since that time, and in May 2000, six planets; Mercury, Mars, Pluto, Saturn, Jupiter and Venus came into alignment with planet Earth. Astronomers have observed that there has not been a conjunction of this many planets for 6,000 years! It was suggested that the spontaneous reaction caused by this strong magnetic conjunction could initiate earthquakes of greater severity; unpredictable freak weather conditions might result in mile-high waves, whilst there could be an increase in the number and intensity of hurricane force winds, and volcanic eruptions. Many scientists believe that originally Earth was only one landmass (Pangaea), which split into two 200 million years ago, due to a satellite smashing into Earth. Asteroids are rocky metallic pieces that have broken off from planets that continue to orbit around the Sun, becoming a potential threat to mankind through occasionally crashing into Earth. The International Astronomical Union set up 'Project Spacewatch' in 1981, to keep watch for any likely bombardment by asteroids, meteorites or comets.

[25] A black hole is thought to be the end-product of a total gravitational collapse of a massive star into itself following the exhaustion of its nuclear fuel: the matter inside is crushed to unimaginably high density. It acts as a centre of gravitational attraction: matter is drawn towards it, and once drawn inside nothing can escape, not even light.

Frederick Reines and Clyde Cowan, at the Los Alamos National Laboratory in New Mexico, confirming the neutrino's existence. Three types (or flavours) of neutrinos have been identified, which can oscillate into one of the other types, whilst moving almost at the speed of light. It has proven possible to accurately calculate how many neutrinos result from the fusion of a given mass of hydrogen. It is now believed that much of the mass in the universe is in the form of neutrinos.

Recently scientists from the Harvard-Smithsonian National Center for Atmospheric Research have calculated that our Sun contracts about 1.5m in diameter ***each hour***, that amounts to 13.15 km ***every year***! The joint Soviet-American, Gallium-Experiment (SAGE) is monitored from Russia. Since 1987 detection equipment has been installed around the world to monitor the consistency of emission of the sun's subatomic particles. It has been calculated empirically that only 20% of the originally emitted neutrinos bombarding Earth are produced today, suggesting that the Sun's strength is diminishing. It would seem that God is shutting down the Sun; which one-day could explode or alternatively implode[26]. Therefore, by extrapolation it may be visualised that the days of this planet are finite, as is the body our own soul inhabits. If the Sun's solar furnace expires, it would collapse inwards, starting a nuclear reaction of incalculable ferocity that would totally destroy our Universe. 2 Peter Ch 3:10 states:

> *"The heavens will disappear with a roar, and the elements of the Earth will be destroyed by fire."*

This claim is supported by Revelation Ch 21:1-2:

> *"Then I saw a new heaven and a new Earth, for the first heaven and the first Earth had disappeared."*

In a recent paper entitled ***The Anthropic Principle and the Structure of the Universe,*** the two authors, physicists, B J Rees and M J Carr, explained that the geometric mean size (average mass of the human body), of every micro and macrocosm contained in the universe, including the tiniest of protons and the largest of planets, is directly proportionate to the mass of planet Earth (which is in direct mean proportion to the universe). Every component of a cell is interdependent and co-dependent, each proton responding to its specific function. Haemoglobin could not fulfil its function if the iron atoms, surrounded by other atoms, did not receive sufficient current to transfer the oxygen into the human body. Without the

[26] The hydrogen of a star is gradually heated before finally vaporising and becoming helium. Once a star's atmosphere becomes 40% helium it explodes. Our Sun's core is already 50% helium, and scientists cannot explain why it has not already exploded!

automatic spin (or mass) of the proton, life-producing blood could not circulate and be sustained. Mankind thrives in a perfectly orchestrated, ecologically balanced environment, in which Earth and creation are sustained in harmony, seemingly the only planet supporting life. I therefore accept that God's intention for humanity is loving and benevolent, even though the laws of nature that God has imposed on His creation, might result in catastrophic natural disasters, brought about by mans' exploitation of that which God created and declared as good.

It seems unlikely to me that God did not open Eve's womb until Cain and Abel were conceived (as twins), and then only once more (on Seth's birth 130 years after Creation, after all, God's injunction to procreate was not only for animals to obey! Possibly, every female experienced painless ***multiple*** births (similar to the animals) ***before*** Adam and Eve were banished from the Garden. From God's curse of Genesis Ch 3:16-17 it can be deduced that as the unnamed woman was called the *wife of Adam*; that she had a different relationship with Adam than any other female that existed. Henceforth every woman was to suffer an increase in pain through childbirth, which leads me to believe that Eve ***and any other women alive*** may have earlier produced '***pain-free litters***'. How else would Eve have been able to recognise the difference in the level of pain during labour, if she and her daughters and granddaughters had not already experienced pain-free deliveries? If my hypothesis is correct, any children not born of Eve, but by one of her daughters, would have been conceived through intercourse with one of her brothers or half-brothers, and in later years through cousins, but it was unnecessary to record any other birth in the Book of Genesis as any such children were outside of the parameters necessary to establish the ***royal line*** of succession.

P J Wiseman's developed the theme in his book ***Ancient Records and the Structure of Genesis***, that language must have been bequeathed and not learned, for Adam and Eve could communicate with each other and with God. Wiseman deduced that colophons (clay tablets[27]) were an historical record of biblical events that occurred during the lifetime of the royal lineage of patriarchs, initially composed by God to His 'scribe' *verbatim*. Wiseman reasoned that the first colophon was the dictated Creation narrative of Genesis Ch 1:1-Ch 2:3[28]. If Wiseman is correct, then it is certain that it was Adam who invented the pictorial method of communication, known as hieroglyphics[29]. I believe that Adam would have taught his progeny of God's injunction to "***Be fruitful and multiply throughout the Earth***" Adam developed the skills in animal husbandry, to tend his various 'flocks' and imparted those skills to every child born in the Garden of

[27] The tablets are formed through pouring liquid clay into a frame, and allowing the mixture to harden slowly in the sun. Once the clay slate had hardened sufficiently to be cut into with a pointed wedge, illustrations were inscribed and on completion the whole sheet was baked hard in an oven to preserve the information. If Adam had manufactured the colophons, it would suggest that Adam was endowed with an ability to communicate with his family other than with signs and gestures. It seems that Adam would have been able to draw pictures as well as write legibly; a science he would have taught his progeny. Colophons have been unearthed from later periods of history, depicted in a pictographic line picture form of hieroglyphics that later developed into cuneiform. The word cuneiform is derived from the Latin word '***cuneius***' meaning 'wedge'. The Sumerian king list, unearthed at Nineveh, is the earliest tablet to be found, and is preserved at the Ashmolean Museum in Oxford. It is the earliest example of a written tradition, transcribed from cuneiform into written form c2340 BC. I guess that it could have been written pre-Flood (*c*2346 BC), and the confusion of tongues at Babel may have been *c*2146 BC. To put the antiquity of the king list in perspective, Moses was born in 1546 BC, several hundred years later.

[28] The Hebrew sages believed that Cain and Abel were twins (Cain became synonymous with the overlooked elder brother, whose sacrifice was rejected). We Christian Gentiles are our older brother's keeper, for his blood cries out from the ground against injustice perpetrated against the Jew. Ishmael the firstborn son of Abraham, was not the '***child of the promise***', that privilege being reserved for the younger son Isaac, Sarah's only child (although Ishmael did have blessings spoken over him by God). I believe Ishmael follows in the line of the second placed, but firstborn son. It can be seen from Genesis Ch 48:14 that again the younger was chosen to receive the prime blessings. The birth of the next pair of twin brothers is recorded in Genesis Ch 25:21-23, and represented the birth of two nations. God told the mother, Rebecca, that the older brother (Esau) would serve the younger (Jacob). In Genesis Ch 38:27-30, we read of the twins Perez and Zerah, fighting to be firstborn. Again the older serves the younger, as Perez became the head of the tribe of Judah in direct line of ascendancy to King David and Messiah Jesus, whilst Zerah is seemingly not given recognition. I believe that the history of these male twins are apocalyptic and refer to a situation that will be righted during the millennial reign. I believe that Zerah (which means '***scarlet***') is pointing to the priesthood of all believers, whilst Perez (which means '**breaking out**') is pointing to the end time Rapture, and the releasing of imprisoned souls from their graves or their fleshly bodies.

[29] Archaeologist S F Hood found a series of 241 geometric symbols scratched prominently on rock surfaces throughout most Continents of the world. He concluded from his research that a geometric series of symbols had been systemised ***following*** the Great Flood, to give information that would enable earlier pioneers to communicate with those who followed in their footsteps. Perhaps Hood was wrong over just when and who had drawn these symbols.

Eden. Adam would have taught his pioneering progenies the importance of transmitting pictorial messages, to inform those who followed in their footsteps any details of importance of earlier exploration. The earliest explorers probably planted areas with crops that would sustain later explorers, as the circle of exploration widened. Also seeds may have been carried by the wind, or dropped from the beaks of birds, which would have produced crops.

Wiseman believed that the second of the ten colophons was started by Adam but completed by Seth at Genesis Ch 5:1-2, and that the third colophon, constructed from Genesis Ch 5:3, was opened by Seth but completed in Genesis Ch 6:9 by Noah. Noah preached that the ***royal seed*** of righteousness and faith had been passed on to Seth, and had not been lost at Abel's murder. Shem completed the second part of the fourth colophon, and manufactured the fifth colophon from Genesis Ch 10:1. The complete history of the family of God prior to the Israelites becoming a nation[30] was written into these colophons, and provided the bedrock that led to the oral tradition. After Noah's death, Shem was entrusted with the colophon tablets, which were passed down to Terah and then the ***family*** patriarch Abraham. On the death of Eber, Isaac became the tribal patriarch[31]. Jacob who took the colophons to Egypt, where, perhaps they were entombed with him at his death, succeeded Isaac. Archaeologist David Rohl obviously agrees with Wiseman, and suggests that Abraham may have entrusted the colophons to Midian, Abraham's son by his second concubine, Keturah. Jethro, the Midian priest inherited the tablets, and may have instructed Moses, his son-in-law, over their contents, which would have given Moses a recorded interpretation of pre-Flood history. None of the colophons (or the tablets of stone on which were written the Ten Commandments) have been excavated to date, which means that Wiseman's theory is unproven, but complimentary to my own theories of the population explosion.

The Hebrew sages and Rabbinical Judaism insists that the first five Books of Scripture known as the *Torah* in Hebrew, (the *Pentateuch* in Greek) was an oral tradition, passed down through the generations, until God gave to Moses a continuous cryptographic string, letter by letter, without any spaces between the letters, which formed the *Torah* a belief accepted by most biblical scholars. The biblical critical scholarship of the 19th century believes that the *Torah* was compiled

---

[30] The Israelites were named Hebrews after Eber (or Heber, meaning 'the one who emigrates', or *hábiru* which means 'wanderer'), who was the ***tribal*** patriarch at the time of Abraham.

[31] The final two patriarchs were Judah and Jesus Christ.

through the writings of a number of authors. The *Avot* (or *Halacha*, a collection of the cherished sayings of more than 60 illustrious sages) teaches that there has been an unbroken oral chain passed on through the generations until the compilation of the *Mishnah* (oral law) by Rabbi Yehudah Ha Nasi around 200 AD. The subject matter of the *Mishnah* is primarily a legal document; the *Avot* is devotional in nature, dealing almost wholly with moral behaviour.

An omniscient God is far more precise in design than any manufactured precision instruments. Swiss astronomer M de Cheseaux discovered that the timing of the completion of the orbits of both the Sun and the Moon, when the planets return to where they were initially installed, is exactly 1,260 years. Previously the Calippus' Metonic cycle had been employed, which calculated orbits over a 19-year cycle, which proved to be ten times less accurate. de Cheseaux quickly realised that 315 years was one fourth of the 1,260-year cycle of God's chosen timepiece, and twice 1,260 years was the amount of years of sentence of the Israelites. These figures corresponded with the 2,520 years of grace in which the Gentiles would be given the light of the Gospel through the experience and witness of Hebrew history. On the 23rd of July 1995, two astronomers using powerful telescopes discovered the existence of the same previously undiscovered comet, *c*120 million miles from Earth. One of the astronomers (Alan Hale) observed the comet from New Mexico, the other (Thomas Bopp) from Arizona. It was calculated that, almost two years into the future, the Hale-Bopp comet, would be at its closest to Earth, on the 23rd of March 1997, and visible to the naked eye! The two scientists independently calculated the comet's size and speed; their findings agreed that the comet took 2,380 solar years to complete its orbit. All world events are cyclical, and pictures or 'mirror images' of previous historical events. It is written in Ecclesiastes Ch 1:9:

> *"What has been will be again; there is nothing new under the sun."*

<u>The Six Days Of Creation.</u>

The Hebrew sages believed that Creation occurred over a cosmic six days, each day mirroring 1,000 years of human history, with the seventh day mirroring eternity. They believe that on day one, at the instant God commanded light to appear, planet Earth was sent spinning on its axis, at the same controlled rate of 1,100 mph which has been maintained ever since (apart from any time that God may have seemingly put the world into a state of suspended animation by fulfilling His purposes outside of time). This precision timing and the

23°[32] tilt from upright being essential in order for the length of a 24-hour day, consisting of an evening and a morning, to be established into eternity. This is not a universally accepted view.

My own belief is as stated in footnote 20. On day two of Creation, God separated the waters of the sea by inserting a cushion of air between the sea and the waters above, which condensed on cooling. I believe that the firmament was cryogenically frozen (forming an ice-canopy, which supernaturally enforced growth and decay[33]). Scientists from the Lawrence Livermore National Laboratories of the USA discovered that, when oxygen and nitrogen are separated out by compression, oxygen turns blue in colour, whilst hydrogen turns pink (magenta). When subject to cryogenic freezing, hydrogen solidifies into a transparent crystalline metallic lattice-work, later becoming opaque, but transparent veins interlace an otherwise solid ice-canopy, allowed filtered light and energy to pass through its intricate web. It was this finished ice-canopy that separated the waters, both covering and encircling the Earth, filtering out harmful rays, whilst attracting short-wave energy from outer space to nourish and sustain the life systems created on Earth. The encircling ice-canopy was engineered to act as a giant fibre optic, throughout the 24-hour day; bestowing the suffused beneficial pink coloured rays at dusk and throughout the twilight hours, when the direct rays of the sun were hidden, owing to the rotation of the Earth.

On day three, God separated the seawater from the land, delineating the boundaries of the sea. The sodden land presumably dried through the effects of a supernatural wind, in a similar way to the earth drying following the abatement of the Great Flood of Genesis

[32] Some Christian research scientists believe that the initial tilt was much less, but was increased at the time of the Great Flood. Professor Alexander Tollman, of the Institute of Geology in Vienna believes that at this time, a large asteroid entered our stratosphere, crashing with huge impact on Earth. I personally believe that there may have been an asteroid 'invasion', at the time of the Great Flood, and was possibly the method used to destroy the ice-canopy. Many Christian geologists believe this was a possibility; certainly there are many references in the Bible to extra terrestrial activity affecting this planet (Isaiah Ch 24:17-20, Luke Ch 17:24-27, Ch 21:11, 25-26, Revelation Ch 6:13, Ch 16:17-20). The intrusion of an asteroid could have caused the floodgates of the heavens to open, before breaking the crust of the Earth, causing the fountains of the deep and the tectonic plates to be released. There is in Arizona a deep 200m crater, and a further 150 craters around the world, that may have been caused by asteroid impact. It is impossible to determine how and when these craters were formed.

[33] I support my contention by reference to the Creation miracle of God, mirrored by Jesus' first miracle at Cana. Using miraculous power, Jesus expedited a process that in the natural course of events would have taken a whole summer season for the grapes of a vineyard to ripen. For the wine to be of superior quality it would have needed to mature perhaps over a number of years, and yet Jesus' first miracle took only an instant of time.

Ch 8:1[34]. There is geological evidence to suggest that no mountain would have been of greater height than12,500 feet above sea level (asl) in the time period preceding the Flood. Geologists have theorised that 75% of all rock prior to the Flood was pressured into sedimentary rock, whilst covered by a depth of at least 300m of seawater for an unknown period of time. The emerging land beyond the shorelines were presumably already covered the enriched with soil, into which plants were easily rooted. On day four God set the planets of this galaxy spinning in their magnetic orbits, and on day five the vegetation was created in full flower or fruit for the animals and birds, also created on this day, to feed from. On day six, God created humanity but rested on the seventh day. There was no mention of evening and morning or of the seventh day being 'good', for this day remains to be completed.

The Age of Human Government

At the end of the 19th century, whilst boring core samples from the ocean floor from a ship moored in the bay of Naples, German geologist Johannes Vulta discovered that the banks of strata on the sea bed in the deeper waters of the bay were formed vertically and sideways, in exactly the same sequence as the banks at the coast. Vulta realised he had found the explanation why fossilised trees, at several excavations throughout the world, were found in a vertical position through several layers of sedimentation, supposedly laid over several centuries. Acceptance of the earlier hypothesis of stratification, that each layer was formed horizontally on top of the previous layer, was nonsensical for no tree deprived of air, water and light, could continue to grow for several more centuries. Vulta's thesis was reinforced by the scientific investigations carried out in the 1970's and 1980's, in the Pacific Ocean, from the Gloma Challenger vessel. All loose submerged rock pounded to fine ash by forces of great violence, and most if not every sea creature died through ingesting minute particles of sediment through their gills, whilst land creatures were drowned in the rising waters[35]. In the absence of a literal

---

[34] I would remind my reader that God sent a strong wind to part the waters of the Red Sea, causing the waters to stack up and congeal, that must mean that the waters turned into ice (Exodus Ch 15:8).

[35] The heavier deposits of sediment carried (by the flow of rivers at times of flood, or through the movement of wind into the sea), do settle earlier than lighter particles, but not entirely, as some micro-sediment settles between the interstices of the larger particles, but it is the force of the ***flow*** of water carrying the deposits and the slurry that determines where and how these vertical banks are formed. It logically follows that the earliest fossils encased in sedimentary rock were of species that died during the violent upheaval of the Flood. In recent times, some samples of 'living fossils' in fish and plant life have been discovered, which means that some species of fish survived or were put into a state of suspended animation.

transcript of events, it seems reasonable to assume that no sea creatures were taken into the Ark, and that God restocked the seas, at the receding of the floodwaters. The fossils lay at the level at which the species had lived and subsequently died, and became part of that particular (sideways formed) bank. Vulta's discovery disproves the theory that fossils of arthropods encased at ***deeper*** levels had existed many centuries earlier.

In 1965, researchers exploring off the coast of Peru at depths of 1,000 fathoms made a startling discovery on the ocean floor. A powerful underwater camera filmed statues on stone pedestals, enormous stone pillars, and massive areas of broken walls. The photographs confirmed the presence of a city that had been inundated in ancient days, remaining submerged even today. The saline Lake Titicaca is located high in the Andes, some 3962m asl, having seashells galore scattered around its shoreline. Agricultural terraces are easily discernible from ground level, steeply rising to 1524m asl and disappearing into the snowy heights above. A short distance away, is the huge abandoned former dockland city of Tiahuanaco, where evidence, of provisions for docking ocean-going vessels from centuries earlier have been discovered.

A satellite storm striking the Earth may have caused the release of the tectonic plates, which repeatedly collided because of the terrific upheaval, pulverising the satellite material to pieces. Normally the plates slide by each other, and more severely but less frequently pass one beneath another (subduction), either way there can be massive upheaval of the land, when just two plates collide. The effects must have been devastating in ferocity, scoring huge ravines (gorges) 1,000 fathoms deep plunging one city into a deep ravine, yet powerfully forcing another city from the ***same land mass*** 5486m high into a newly developed range of mountains, the highest of which were covered by water to a depth of 7m totally changing the topography! Geologists have found evidence from the examination of magnetite specimens of hardened lava, that as many as ten variations at the Earth's magnetic poles during this same cataclysmic violent disturbance.

The Age of Conscience

Noah preached to his fellow men over their sinful condition, which may have included their sexual proclivities and any experimenting with genetic engineering[36] and cloning, in which their 'pre-Flood illuminated' minds might have indulged. Professor M E Clarke of the University of

[36] A simple bacterial cell can read the 'language' of a mammalian or a plant gene; were this not so, then genetic engineering would not be possible.

Illinois lectures widely on the human vascular system. He believes that pre-Flood man would have ingested supercharged air, with nutrients feeding the brain with fully-oxygenated blood, allowing a greater generic capacity. The people would have been very learned by today's standards explaining the miracles of construction that archaeologists have discovered from a bygone age. But that is not to say that mankind was totally evil (Genesis Ch 6:5). Many believe that the ***'sons of God'***, were fallen angels that had 'fathered' children through sexual intercourse with humans, and may have produced the Nephilim of abnormal proportions (Genesis Ch 6:4). A discovery was made in Morocco of a hoard of 500 double-edged axes, each weighing 8.5 kilograms (kg), 20 times heavier than a man of today's average height could wield. Anthropologists have calculated that, in order to use the axes as a working tool, a giant of even proportions, would have to have been 4m tall, and weighed approximately 250kg. In Australia, a similar cache was unearthed consisting of adzes, hand axes, chisels, and knives of extraordinary weight and size. Kangaroos (having skulls 1 m long) as large as hippopotami, koalas and wombats as large as rhinoceros suggest a tampering with genetics.

Nimrod's parentage is not clear; he was raised, maybe adopted, by the Cush[37] family. Bacchus (Bar-Cush, or son of Cush, alias Nimrod) was ***begat***. He is not listed with the other sons of Cush in Genesis Ch 10:7-8 of the New King James (NKJ) version of the Bible. Nimrod travelled with his entourage and their flocks along the River Euphrates until they came to the Plain of Shinar (Babylonia), at the foot of a snow-covered mountain range, where they settled. The legend was perpetuated of the winged-god who wore the tunic made from the coat of a ***spotted beast*** (a fawn, leopard or jaguar). This mythological god had been torn to pieces in suffering death, before entering heaven or Nirvana, Valhalla, Paradise, or wherever purity was popularly thought by a culture to exist. Mythological Orion was a mighty hunter, who was deified after his legendary violent death. His followers believed that he was laid to rest by the gods amongst the stars in the heavens. The historians, Herodotus and Diodorus Siculus, recognised the legends of Osiris and Bacchus as being culturally interchangeable. These false gods or 'mighty ones' of Greek, Egyptian and Babylonian mythology were thought to live on Earth at the time of Nimrod's reign. Nimrod had established his prowess, and, as evidence of his skill as a

[37] Cush was known to pagan antiquity under the character of Bel the 'confounder' (the god of confusion). Chaos is a form of the name Cush in Chaldaic pronunciation.

hunter clothed himself in the skin of a leopard[38]. Nimrod's priests wore leopard-skin robes and a headdress of horned animals to associate their priestly role with divine authority[39]. Followers prayed to a ***territorial god*** for plentiful harvests, and to a ***mother-god of fertility,*** for the birth of strong children capable of surviving the rigours of the harsh weather conditions[40].

Archaeologists have unearthed tablets bearing the inscription that Nimrod married Semiramis, the most exquisite female ever formed. Her parents had been of humble peasant stock, and she was raised in impoverished circumstances. Perhaps it was her feminine wiles, or her impoverished upbringing, that caused Semiramis to desire immortal status through her revered husband. Semiramis claimed to have received a visitation from an angelic being, which informed her that her late husband Nimrod, who had died during her pregnancy, would be reincarnated as her son. On the 25th December, she subsequently

---

[38] Wild carnivorous cats proliferated in the area, because the land had been previously uninhabited. Much of the big cat's prey was too shy of mankind and left the area, which meant that the big cats, out of hunger, attacked the domestic flocks. The cats were hunted to drive them away, partly to protect both the flocks and herds, but mostly through a need for personal protection.

[39] In December 2000 Egyptologist Dr Toby Wilkinson of Christ College Cambridge found 30 previously undiscovered sites in the deserts of Egypt, which in 2700 BC had been 'wadis' (old river beds), at which carvings had been illustrated on rock, depicting humans prostrating themselves in obeisance before gods. The Great Pyramid of Giza in Egypt, and the Great Circle at Stonehenge in England, constructed *c*2700 BC confirms to me that humanity had not only rejected God, but were worshipping other gods long before the Flood.

[40] A recently excavated cave in Catal Hüyük, in Turkey, displays a painting on a wall, portraying a community being threatened by an active volcano throwing out molten magma. In the same cave was found a statuette of a seated naked mother-goddess. The statuette was made from a dark, vitreous, solidified lava named '***obsidian***' (which is more familiarly known as '***bottle glass***'). Interestingly all obsidian specimens can be traced back to the volcano of their origination. The volcano at Nemrut Dag nearer to Mount Ararat did not become active until some years after the Catal Hüyük volcano became inactive. Interestingly specimens recovered of ornaments and vessels from this excavation; do not include idols, possibly indicating that some of Noah's descendants, who settled in Mesopotamia, remained faithful to God. The most important information to be derived from the 20th century archaeological digs in the Turkey/Babel area, is that the obsidian pieces found have been classified as '***Palaeolithic***' or '***stone age***' whilst another site 30km distant, the artefacts found are labelled as '***Neolithic***' and classed as being from later civilisations. Other archaeologists argue that what separated the communities was not '***time***', but the practical skills of the artisans whose language group may not have included any skilled potters, weavers or mechanics amongst their family members, but who may have developed outdoor skills such as agricultural harvesting, animal husbandry or hunting, or scientific skills such as astronomy or medicine.

bore her child and named him as Tammuz[41] (the derivation of which means the 'lamented one'), and the cult of worshipping *a **'blessed mother and her son**'* commenced. Noah had taught that Eve was a revered woman, knowing good from evil, and that one of her descendants would bruise the heel of the '***evil one***', and the passage was misinterpreted as referring to their beloved leader as the '***Great Deliverer***' (of salvation) of Genesis Ch 3:15. Nimrod's followers believed that Semiramis and Tammuz fulfilled this teaching. Semiramis was immortalised as the Queen of Heaven (Jeremiah Ch 7:18, Ch 44:17-19), with the introduction of an annual festival of remembrance to the mother goddess of mankind, of which early historians, Athenagoras and Lucian both wrote. She and her son were worshipped as divine mediators between bad luck and good fortune, and so the fable was perpetuated. Semiramis was associated with Venus and was worshipped as Rhea (mother of many gods). From the time of Semiramis, gods were often thought of as female.

Nimrod in Assyrian folklore was thought to be a Sumerian shepherd, who was married to the Syrian goddess Ishtar. The name Ishtar or Astarte has metamorphosed into Easter, and is a pagan name given to a pagan festival[42]. Later generations of Nimrod's followers migrated into Mesopotamia. Abram's father was one of the tribe that settled in the land, and that is the path through which the Scriptures thread its way. The historian Eusebius wrote that Abram was born eight years before the death of King Ninus of Ur[43]. His subjects accepted Ninus as a reincarnation of Nimrod (alias Tammuz, or Bacchus), although many years elapsed between their lifetimes. Tammuz the Great Deliverer, alternatively known as Zoroastra or Zero Ashta (meaning *the* '***seed***'), or Zoroastes (meaning the '***seed of the woman***'), was venerated as the high priest, whose soul was transferred in some illusory way to his successor.

Noah probably told those of his extended family who yearned to emigrate to a more amenable environment, that they should follow the path the animals had taken. Many of the migrating animals on travelling to and on leaving the Ark had travelled along the Sundra

[41]The only reference in the Scriptures to the man/god Tammuz is in Ezekiel Ch 8:13-14. During, and since the Babylonian Exile, many from the House of Judah worshipped Tammuz as both father and son.

[42] This festival of celebration was to the Queen of Heaven to whom baked cakes were offered as a sacrifice. More latterly in the Western nations, the Easter egg (and Easter bunny) is a reminder that it was fertility rites that were originally celebrated.

[43] Ninus is a derivation of Nin-neveh, meaning 'the habitation of Ninus'.

Shelf[44]. Peleg, the second son of Eber, was so named to mark the time in history in which the division into continents, as the coastlines of every land mass was formed, separated by huge oceans, took place. Peleg was born 100 years after the Flood, and, if has been calculated, the Flood took place c2346 BC, and as Peleg lived for 239 years; it follows that the continents were formed by 2007 BC.

I had been fasting for three weeks in order to seek the Lord's answers to my prayers, and was heartened on Sunday the 1st of March 1998, to experience a trance[45].

> I was sitting on a stone amongst a large number of people from a bygone age, some dressed in animal skins and others in cloth. I was one of a number of the men living in a fishing village. We were listening to a man whom I knew to be Noah, speaking of the error of following a false god in order to receive short term benefits at the expense of a later but greater reward.

I retired to bed that night, pondering over the trance, and was rewarded with a *'revelatory dream'*. I awoke having a deeper understanding of a dream that had often been repeated to me since 1983, but for which I had never previously received any enlightenment.

---

[44] Oceanographers have calculated that after the Flood subsided, the sea level was 304m lower than it is currently. The formation and growth of coral reefs around the world was only possible whilst covered by the shallower sea, at which time the sun's rays were able to penetrate the clearer waters, thereby cultivating the coral. I am certain that God allowed the growth of reefs in order to confirm to the sceptic that, in earlier times, the seas covering the earth were not as deep as they are today. This process was enhanced by the surface of the Earth becoming one-third ice-capped, with more land being forced upwards forming towering mountain ranges; whilst lowering the ocean floor, on which mountains formed that later erupted, spilling out their lava, and forming islands between the Continents. Oceanographers believe the Sundra Shelf connected together every landmass following the convulsions, owing to the sea level lowering dramatically. Voluminous amounts of rock and ice, were homogenised, and formed into mountain ranges. As the waters subsided, huge land-locked glacial reservoirs were trapped in the mountains, which on melting over the centuries became inland seas and lakes. The sun's rays heated and eventually melted the hardened icy crust. The base of every mountain receives heat from the fierce heat generated by the central core of the Earth. The combination produced earthquakes and after-tremors, leading to increased volcanic activity. Seismic activity allowed the trapped reservoirs of water from the melt-water lakes, to eventually cascade into the oceans, finally engulfing the Sundra Shelf. As the 21st century commenced, 90% of the earth's volcanic mountains are surrounded by sea, and seismic activity is therefore increasing.

[45] A trance is a vision received whilst awake. Both St Peter and St Paul experienced trances having met with Jesus and although the term 'trance' has become synonymous with the occult, transcendental meditation, or hallucinatory drugs, I will not be chary of using this biblical term.

Again I was sitting with others listening to Noah. Noah emphasised that salvation lay in believing that only the God of all creation held power over each person's soul. Many of Noah's extended family, which had loyally followed his teachings, were experiencing difficult trials, of which volcanic activity including earthquakes accompanied by the other twin terrors of after-tremors and widespread flooding, caused by glaciers being breached. Noah had travelled to this fishing village to advise his fellow clansmen of their need to believe only in this one true God, now that their earthly lives were threatened by the consequences of the coming calamity. The eruption of volcanoes, together with the effects of the hot sun on the frozen surfaces of mountainous glaciers, had caused these huge creeping bulks to slowly slide, or swiftly develop avalanches, engulfing whole communities that had settled in the plains between the mountain ranges. I became convinced that Noah's words were true and I had retired to bed, confident that a watchman would call me if the conditions became critical. As daylight dawned, a group of men knocked and shouted loudly outside my home, encouraging me to join them in escaping in one of several large trading ships that had anchored in the harbour overnight. As we made our way down the steep slope to the quayside, I could clearly see the mariners and the fishermen from the village assisting the passengers from the rowing boats on to the deck of the larger boats. Hastily but orderly, the rescuers rowed their empty boats back to the quayside steps, where families and individuals queued to board. The field on my right was illuminated by the multi-coloured phosphorous globules of flaming molten lava, that rained down from the sky, hissing on impact with the sodden ground, creating a low mist as the moisture on the damp surface turned to steam. The field on my left was strangely dark and quiet. Lightning flashes and thunderclaps added to the dramatic vision. The cliff road ahead was now impassable, having been previously engulfed by avalanches; the valley road and the harbour were both similarly threatened.

Without warning, but not unexpectedly, the massive wall of ice tumbled into the road and on to the quayside. The villagers in the boats screamed in terror as they were knocked overboard by the boulders of ice that rained down, holing the boats. Frightened people were wildly splashing about in the icy sea

> in their panic. I could see that the rescue ships were raising their anchors, and moving out of the harbour for safety. I placed my hands over my ears to drown out the terrified screams, closing my eyes to block out the vision of the disaster that I was witnessing. I turned swiftly and clambered over a secured five-barred wooden-gate into a field, and sought shelter from the strong wind, in a shallow hollow. Snowflakes rapidly blanketed the grass around my feet, as the wind banked the drifting snow around me, filling the hollow in which I stood. I prayed to God and committed myself to Him. My numbed body felt no pain as I physically died.

I knew that I was eternally saved in my own unusual baptism into Christ.

Chapter 2

FROM ABRAHAM TO CHRIST

During Lent 1983 I lay in my bed indulging in reverie, as I sought to focus my mind on the priorities for the day ahead. My thoughts were persistently arrested and brought back to reviewing how inconsequential and insular my life to date had been, having little impact on the world. I thought of the hurting people, with whom I had formed relationships, through whom I had sought personal advantage and control of the circumstances surrounding each situation that motivated me, often at the expense of friends and relatives I had increasingly enjoyed the creature comforts that money and success attracted. My conscience was strangely disquieted this day, as memories of my selfish motives and the manipulation of people and events behind every decision I had taken were paraded in front of my mind's eye. My greatly loved father had achieved very little in his life, and I realised pragmatically that, after my death, the impact of my life on earth would be equally soon forgotten. Would I have to answer to a heavenly court for the talents given to me that I had squandered? I thought of the servant in the parable of Matthew Ch 25, who was recognised by his master as being both wicked and fearful, surely I was even more wicked? I had attended a church twice each Sunday for over two years, but nothing had perceptibly changed in my lifestyle. I was not convinced of Christ's deified immortality, or that I could enter into a personal relationship with Him. I had read passages from the Bible only as an interesting storybook, but regretfully not as a manual on how to live my own life. I knew of Jesus '***objectively***', but only in the way that I knew of other biblical and historical characters.

Without warning I experienced a totally new sensation, a dull ringing in my ears deadening all extraneous noises accompanied by a '***heaviness of presence***', imposed upon every inch of my body. This symptomatic weightiness impressed upon me that I was being spoken to from within my psyche:

> ***"Alf Droy, I know every thought you have ever had, and I am aware of all your deeds. You believe that with your quick wits and your silver tongue, you can persuade your entry into eternal life by charm. You have never acknowledged that you are responsible for your life's outworking only to Me, as Lord of your life. If you surrender your life over to Me and repent of your sinfulness and accept My forgiveness, offered by grace***

> ***and not performance, and declare your dishonesty publicly and make restitution, I will grant you a place in heaven beside Me, your Lord Jesus Christ. "***

In my amazement of having been spoken to by Jesus Christ, I hurriedly dressed and breakfasted, and, ignoring the protocol of making an appointment, I visited the offices of the Inland Revenue in Cambridge. On being ushered into the office of the Chief Inspector of Taxes, I furnished him with previously undisclosed bank statements from a hitherto secret bank account into which I had placed deposits from the various businesses that I owned, and had embezzled from, but that is another story[46]! My scepticism over Jesus' claim to be the Son of God immediately turned to ashes. I now knew Jesus '***subjectively***'; He is alive today and had died for my salvation. I repented of my sin-filled life, resolving to follow and emulate Christ's ministry, telling others wherever and whenever I could, of my understanding of biblical truth, and the urgency of the times in which we live. Hebrews Ch 9:27-28 states:

> *"Just as man is destined to die once, and after that to face judgement, so Christ was sacrificed once to take away the sins of many people; and He will appear a second time, not*

[46]I have written fully, of the circumstances surrounding my life prior to and since conversion, and of my experience of the supernatural gifts of the Holy Spirit in my everyday walk with Christ Jesus (in my autobiography, The Lord is My Shepherd). I had been taught that the supernatural gifts of the Holy Spirit had been withdrawn with the death of the apostles. I regularly see in my mind's eye pictures, as camera shots but mostly as moving cameos, which are sometimes extended into 'trances', in which I am a participant (at such times I might receive 'words of knowledge' or 'wisdom', giving revelation, or suggesting that I take a particular course of action). '***Revelatory visions, trances*** **and** ***dreams***', are not unique to me, and are certainly not earned! Increasingly, one reads of supernatural appearances of the Lord or His angels to quite ordinary folk (usually former unbelievers), and of the supernatural gift of '***tongues***' and '***translation***' or '***healing power***' being bestowed on believers who pray earnestly for Holy Spirit anointing. There has not been one specific method used by the Lord to arrest my attention. I have received revelations whilst sleeping but just as often whilst awake. Sometimes I receive a persistent ringing in my ears as loud and intrusive as an incoming telephone call. At other times I experience a numbing silence in my eardrums, similar to the pressure experienced when diving deeply into the sea. Sometimes I experience a *'heaviness of presence*' during which time I cannot move a muscle, and at other times I am quickened by a deep conviction of what action I should take. Quite often I receive revelation overnight, having meditated on a Bible passage during the previous day. Many biblical figures experienced supernatural activity, and from the prophecy of Joel Ch 2:28, mankind can expect God, throughout the ***Great Tribulation*** (which is the final period of seven years, preceding Christ's sudden cataclysmic Second Coming affecting Jew and Gentile, both Christian and pagan), to universally pour out His Holy Spirit, on all flesh, on both believers and pagans: "***Your sons and daughters will prophesy, your old men will dream dreams, your young men will see visions***."

> *to bear sin, but to bring salvation to those who are waiting for Him."*

I knew unequivocally that reincarnation was a myth, there is only one lifetime allocated for each person to accept and follow Jesus.

During the night following my visit to the tax inspector, I received the first of an incredible series of supernatural revelatory dreams and visions:

> I saw a gigantic representation of Jesus' naked body, half submerged in the River of Life, which represented God's main artery flowing through every galaxy and back to God's heart. The temperature and the flow of this 'divine' river were controlled by Christ's contact with it. I watched a cameo of a continuous column of Jews, in groups and singly, crossing over a river (from death to life) walking across on Christ's outstretched arms, which rested on opposite banks, reminding me of the crucifixion. I was told from the passage in Ezekiel Ch 37 that God was the living temple, from which the River of Life flowed. From Revelation Ch 21 and 22, it can be understood that during the millennium reign of Christ, the shed leaves of the trees of life growing on either side of the river, will provide healing to the nations (Ezekiel Ch 47:12). Once the 'Being' that was my companion, who I knew to be an angel, was satisfied with my response, the luminescence faded and I resumed my usual sleep pattern.

The following morning, whilst walking through from the lounge into the kitchen, I received a vision in the form of a trance:

> A dead leaf fluttering to the ground in front of my eyes, startling me, causing me to stop and blink. The leaf blown by a wind skittered across the floor, into a stream, slowly sinking to the riverbed, where it would finally decompose. I understood that this autumn leaf represented a Christian who had died and become part of the River of Life, that flowed from the sanctuary of the yet to be created Temple of God. I became aware that my whole being, spirit, mind and body had been touched and changed by God's supernatural blessings. During the following night I was reminded of the two earlier revelations before my attention was drawn to a mature oak tree growing on the bank of the River of Life. I heard an authoritative voice ring out: "Saw down the tree and lop off all the branches. Bind the stump with bands of iron and bronze." Stripped of all its splendour, the lopped oak tree bridged the river. I watched as a succession of Gentile

families (who had accepted Christ as Lord and Saviour) crossed over from death to life. My attention was then drawn to the stump of the tree, with its roots firmly fixed in the ground. Metal bands had been tightened around the circumference of the tree-stump, to prevent fraying. "What do you see Alf?" asked the unseen angel who had visited me the previous night. Once the angel was satisfied that I had absorbed everything of importance, the vision continued: A cross-shaped pattern at the centre of the stump, imposed over the inner rings, showed this tree to be sacred, it indeed is the stump, the Holy Seed (Isaiah Ch 6:13, and Ch 11:1), where it is written:
"There shall come forth a shoot from the stump of Jesse", (***and the Church shall be spliced into the branches*** - my interpretation).
I was told that the tree represented the statue of King Nebuchadnezzar, but it also represented the archetype of every emperor throughout history, who, sometime in the future would lie prostrate before the King of Kings. Written in numerals at the circumference of the tree-stump, were the four digits 2,0,0,0, which represented 2000 AD. Again the angel asked me what I had seen, and on my satisfactory reply, the metal bands were struck with the back of a long-handled axe, producing the sound of a gong being struck. The wood graining shimmered into eddying ripples of sluggishly circling oozing, liquid, a viscous mixture of blood and noxious fluids. Gaseous, sulphuric bubbles coloured predominantly yellow, silver and black, rose to the surface. The bands coalesced becoming an iron cooking pot, which was struck once again by the axe to inform me that the vision was about to change. The liquid at the outer edge of the cooking pot began circling, slowly at first, but increasing in speed towards the centre, producing an effect similar to a whirlpool. Suddenly the sun appeared from behind a cloud, the bright rays glinted on the nauseating concoction, suffusing the dully-coloured contents into bright metallic colours of silver, gold and ruby red. The circling liquid slowly ceased spinning as the molten mixture thickened and solidified. The materials of metal and wood altered in nature, transforming into a chalice, a priceless communion cup not formed by human hands. In reverential silence I watched the cupped hands of Jesus Christ the Messiah, placing the

chalice on a glass-topped table (which reflected His actions). I was told that the liquid in the pot represented the nations of world, throughout which the Jews had been dispersed. God will separate His precious people from the nations at the appropriate time, in order to acclaim them to the Gentiles. Christ's hands had directed and sanctioned every event of world history since Creation. I understood that the length of the base of this chalice, including its stem, represented the 4,000 years of biblical history from the forming of Adam in the Garden of Eden, to the immaculate conception of Christ (the years of pre-Christian history, being two-thirds in length of the whole chalice). The depth of the cup represented one-third of the length of time of *c*2,000 years from the Cross of Christ until His Second Coming. The whole chalice illustrated 6,000 years in total, the whole of pre-salvation existence. The angel told me that I had interpreted correctly the course of action, which He would engineer in my lifetime. A gong sounded, and the luminescence faded away.

Whilst still experiencing this dream I received this prophecy:

> ***"Fear not that you (believers) have not completed the commission I gave you as an undertaking. The harvest is even now being gathered in. Very soon we will be drinking the new wine in heaven together."***

The cameo could best be likened to observing the formation of history from opposite ends of a telescope. The ***detail*** of the object focused upon does not vary, but the ***distance*** from where one observes the object does alter, perhaps changing one's perception of what is seen[47]. Both time and memory are illusory, but I trust that my explanation is helpful. The two periods of salvation history (recognised by the terms BC and AD) are intrinsically linked, and God has decreed the time-span until final judgement. I recalled the passage in Zechariah Ch 13:7:

> *"I will strike the shepherd and the sheep will be scattered."*

Together with the passage from Jeremiah Ch 31:10:

> *"He who scattered Israel will gather her* (to the Promised Land, leased by God to the Israelite nation in perpetuity), *and will shepherd her."*

I am very grateful to have been so blessed by the availability of God's gifts and their use in my redeemed life. I know many people

[47] A kaleidoscope produces a similar effect on turning; the coloured pieces offer patterns, which might be likened to more attractive alternatives. Information is like beauty is in the eye of the beholder; it is either accepted or rejected.

who receive pictures, who have never received a trance or a prophecy, but that does not mean that in any way do I think of myself as superior, for God bequeaths His gifts as He chooses. It was much later that I realised that the visions and prophecies, received by me over many days, mirrored Zechariah's experience of successive visions, although Zechariah received his revelations over one night. Each night I was taken back to the earlier revelations, which continued once the angel was satisfied that I understood what I had seen. Over the course of the following weeks, I became an *eager* evangelist, as I sought to be obedient to the ***Great Commission***[48] of Matthew Ch 28:19. Billy Graham once said that evangelism devoid of eschatology would get the preacher nowhere fast. I am of the same opinion, which is why I always seek to prove the urgency of the hour to everyone who will listen. I was given a supernatural love and respect for the Jewish race, a love born out of gratitude together with a supernatural generosity of spirit in offering heartfelt prayers to God for the circumstances and earthly comfort and relief of all Jews wherever they live, which has never diminished[49]. I understand my affection to have been as sincere as that exhibited by the Egyptians towards the tribal patriarch Joseph and his family, in their gratitude for the wisdom he had demonstrated as Prime Minister (PM). In a similar way that the Egyptians at the Exodus willingly gave the Israelites of their silver and gold (Exodus Ch 3:22), I was to give sacrificially in my efforts to secure the prosperity of the Jews, by offering both prayers and finance in helping them '***make aliyah***'[50] to Israel. On the fourth night of revelations:

I was transported to a railway station where I was placed so close to the platform clock that it filled my whole vision. The hands of the clock informed me that the time was one minute to midnight. I was then transported to a position from which I could see the whole platform. The last train of the day was building up steam prior to leaving the terminus. I knew it was not the clock but myself being

[48] The Great Commission is the instruction to preach the 'Good News of the Gospel of '***grace***' throughout the Earth.

[49] I have deduced from Zechariah Ch 9:13 and Isaiah Ch 66:20-22, that believing Gentiles, who, during the final jubilee and the Great Tribulation, have supported the Jews in both prayer and action, will be God's weapon (the arrow in the drawn bow) against the ***unholy trinity*** of ***Satan and the two beasts*** of Revelation Ch 13. God was not speaking of converts to Judaism through these passages, but to those Gentile believers who assist the Jew in every way. If these Gentiles have helped in the regathering of the Jews to the Promised Land, they may be raised up as Levites, and serve in the kingdom of God as priests with those of Aaron or Levi's lineage.

[50] Departing from the country in which they were living, to reside in the Promised Land the spiritual homeland of their race.

closely examined under a microscope. A disembodied hand tore the clock from its fixings (in the same manner that I might pluck a petal from a flowering rose) and threw it under my feet. I understood that, at the appropriate time, God was going to reveal to me the sequence of events surrounding the end of history. The luminescence did not fade on this occasion.

As I continued to meditate on this series of visions, I heard a voice commanding me to get out of bed and record the following prophecy:

> ***"I am the Lord your God, there are no other gods than Me. I am returning to claim My inheritance, My redeemed bride. I will strengthen and embolden you in order that you will be equipped to share the revelations given to you as your understanding develops. Over a period of time, I am going to reveal to you My timing of events to impose truth and grace on this fallen world, at which time you will eagerly share with all who will listen, the details of the restoration, renewal and redemption, of My creation. What all men have thought of as foolishness is the outworking of My wisdom.***
>
> ***You will receive more of My spirit and My peace as you die to self, to live for Me. You are to pray through each day, that your thoughts and your heart's desires might mirror My own desires, in order that your spiritual heart and mind might reflect My love for mankind. The more you pray and give thanks and offer praises to Me, and the more you meditate on My word, the more abundantly will you receive My Holy Spirit and the greater will be your understanding. As the moon reflects the light of the sun, so you will reflect My glory. I am the light of the world and as your own soul throbs and glows incandescently, receiving life, faith and illumination, you will receive more fruit from the tree of knowledge. You will also eat from the tree of life. Truth can only be seen through the eyes of faith. The combined lights of all believers will glow as living stones reflecting the image of My glory, in order that when I return My disciples will see Me through undimmed eyes. The unholy will be blinded in their helplessness bound by their own philosophies and judged by their own iniquities. For centuries the heart filled with faith knew that the foundation stone of the Church was in place. The cornerstone of My Church has been covered by deceit***

and hypocrisy, but the deception is washed away through the blood of the suffering Church that has continually flowed through the centuries, and is incalculably precious in its sacrificial worth in My sight. Hold firm to your faith; take counsel and comfort from your heart and realise My will for you is ordained to produce a more fruitful life. Satan has used the greed of man for wealth and advantage to besmirch legitimate trading through unredeemed capitalism. Satan believes that because depravity and lawlessness increases, the return of the Son of Man will be delayed. Indeed I will return to reign during the lifetime of the generation in which you are living51. Be ever watchful, for a political leader will arise from amongst the nations. He will enter into a pact52 with a religious leader and the world will wonder at the union. The liaison is not of Me but of Satan. I will cause you to reign in life now, despite the evidence of degradation that is ever presented to you through the media, and which greatly concerns your heart in the sufferings of others. It is at this time that I, the cornerstone, will be revealed to all those who are Mine. Many people, who have known Me, will be persuaded by the temptations of the evil one and will fall from grace. In the times of persecution that lie ahead, many people will find My way and My commands too difficult to follow and desert Me. Many who believe I will honour them for their service will come to realise that they have been deceived, but not by Me, for they have always been blind and have never fully understood the purposes of My life of servitude on Earth. The response of the self-appointed and unanointed, in seeking to control areas of Christian activity, has been unspiritual and unsuccessful. Such ministers have not been walking

[51] This prophecy does not mean that I will still be alive at the Second Coming. Without wishing to appear dramatic, it is quite possible that those who impose the New World Order will label me as a terrorist agitator. Perhaps a religious *fatwah* might be raised against me, but regardless, I must be true to the commission entrusted to me, as I understand it.

[52] This liaison between a politician and a religious leader will receive world acclamation. I believe that the politician of my prophecy could be a respected archetype who has not emerged out of the shadows as yet, although I am sure he is already established in office. It is logical to believe, but not necessarily so, that this man is a Westerner serving the committees who are yet to elevate him. I believe that the religious leader may well be a Muslim cleric, and these two men may be the two 'beasts' of Revelation Ch 13.

in the ministry that I gifted and called them into. I will honour many who have thought of themselves humbly as unworthy. Despite the heartache I have firmly decided to withdraw restraint of the evil that will rule the world prior to my return, that will result in My judgement, which will just as surely follow. Says the Lord your God."

The series ended at this point. Over the next few days and weeks, I wrote down what I had seen and heard, and pondered over why I had been given these revelations. Surely God had more able servants He could use to tell others of His plans?

Jewish historian Flavius Josephus (37-93 AD), in his ***Book of Antiquities* X.xi.1**, writes of King Nebuchadnezzar having besieged the capital city of Tyre for 13 years, finally sacking it and overthrowing the priest-King Ittobaal, in ***the same year that Solomon's Temple was destroyed***. The sentence of God over every nation was announced in the cursing of the citizens of the city of Tyre, who were named in Ezekiel Ch 27:2 as the '***merchants of the earth***', depicting them as the archetype of unredeemed commercialism (which I sense to be linked to my interpretation of the revelation concerning the final overthrowing of the earthly kingdoms depicted in the statue of the reigning King Nebuchadnezzar, lasting until Christ's promised Second Coming, when human rule will be replaced by divine rule). Christ warns his followers in Revelation Ch 18: 4-5;

"Come out of Babylon, for her sins are piled up to Heaven".

From Ezekiel Ch 28 it can be determined that King Ittobaal, a priest of Astarte, became the archetype of Satan (the bright morning star of Isaiah Ch 14:12-17). Over the centuries, Satan has, indulged the debauchery of his self-centred servants, even though they have not given homage to his sovereignty. In their rebellion against God, they have sought to be as gods themselves! Mystery Babylon[53] is a cryptogram for unredeemed capitalism or materialism. The personalities who are to become the ***two beasts of the unholy trinity*** during the Great Tribulation have not yet been revealed.

---

[53] I believe this ungodliness to be attributable to the committee behind the G7 bankers, the modern day '***merchants of the earth***', who together with the ten nations support the Pope's claim to govern the Temple Mount. The Pope will be the ***final antichrist***, alias the ***beast out of the sea***, being identified with the scarlet beast having seven heads and ten horns (Revelation Ch 17:3), motivated by wealth and power. The Pope is recognisable as the great prostitute wearing purple and scarlet, ***directing world affairs*** (in tandem) with the ridden beast. The antichrist is pictorially spoken of as a woman '***sitting on the seven hills***', and is identified with the city of Rome and the Vatican. I identify *Sheshach* as a cryptogram for Babylon, being spoken of in Jeremiah Ch 25:26 as the kingdom lastly suffering judgement among the nations. I identify '***mystery Babylon***' with unredeemed capitalism, as being the source of power of the unholy trinity evidenced from Rome.

The story of Nimrod typifies how much progress mankind can achieve by dint of effort, and God's reaction to Pharaohs, Caesars and rulers of empires in seeking to be as God is well documented. Although empires are not intrinsically evil (but only, at worst, self-glorifying and expansionary), they are certainly not godly regimes. The city of Tyre is the representation of Revelation Ch 17:16, the woman wholly given over to sinfulness, who rides upon Satan's back until the ***time of the Gentiles***[54] is fulfilled. I received the following prophecy:

> ***"Prepare your hearts; the Great Tribulation is upon you. I repeatedly told My people through the prophets that which I have decreed will surely happen. Heaven and Earth will pass away, but My word will endure forever. The time of waiting is over and yet, even yet, I love you and would have you seek My face. Turn and repent today, before I shake the Earth to its very foundations and the destroyer is judged. One thousand years in your understanding is an eternity, to Me it is as a single day. It is not only the fool who says that there is no God, but he is also a fool who says: If God exists His work is completed, and He is no longer involved in the functioning of this world. The fool will come to recognise his error and see the completion of My works in his own judgement. The wheat and the tares, the righteous and the unrighteous, are all loved by Me, but the full number of believers to be harvested into My eternal kingdom is already known to Me. Before this generation passes away, I will shake the earth mightily. I am a gracious and merciful God which is why I still seek to gather the strays, but I will not be ignored or mocked, nor will I accept other than heartfelt commitment. Those I have called will come to Me; those who do not respond to My word do not belong to Me.***

---

[54] The '***time of the Gentiles'*** was the sentence by God from the number of biblical days (the 2,520 years is an identical number of calendar years from Nebuchadnezzar's illness to the completion of the Gentile's period of grace). In Leviticus Ch 26:18,21,24,28, God decreed the number of years of cursings for rebellion by the Jews (2,520 years of the Diaspora). Daniel (representing Israel) was exiled in 606 BC, and 2,520 years later, in 1914, Britain declared war on Germany, with the objective set out many years before (by God) to protect the right of the Jew to live in their homeland unhindered. 2520 years also represents the period of time that unredeemed capitalism has been allowed to flourish, from the time of the original destruction in 520 BC, and will be completed with Babylon's final destruction during the Great Tribulation.

Foolish man you have coveted your neighbour's wealth, you gather from where you have not sown. Foolish man you have sold your own soul for profit by exploiting the weak and powerless. Where is your salvation to be found? Where is your dynasty? You have treated My world as a spoilt child treats an unwanted toy, breaking and despising it, whilst reaching out further for that which is beyond your grasp and forbidden to you. Your earthly yearnings are denied you for a very responsible reason. Perhaps you think you can reach heaven in your new Tower of Babel, the space rocket? Were you surprised that you could not see Me in the heavens? You sit in your ivory tower counting out your money and scheming how best to acquire greater power and wealth. You have no thought for the widows, the orphans and the aliens, but for your own comfort only. You scheme continuously how to best exploit your neighbour for your own advantage. To you, your ivory tower appears invulnerable, safer than the fortified bridge of a gunboat. You believe yourself to be strong and protected, powerful and poised for any battle, but your fortress is built on sand! Can you escape the judgement, which is prepared for you? Perhaps you will hide in your nuclear bunker believing yourself to be protected from My wrath. Do you think that I would let you destroy My creation? Rebellious proud child, your arrogance, built upon confidence in your own ability, has no foundations. Those fearful cries of torment you hear in the distance will come to dwell inside your own body. You the sinner, who is unconcerned for others and who pays Me scant attention, will soon come to a realisation of your own fallibility. Your remorse is not repentance and will not save you from judgement.

You have used false weights in your hypocrisy and you have been judged and found wanting! Did you think that I would let you destroy with impunity that which I have created? If you throw yourself naked, muddied and bloodied before Me and seek My forgiveness and the future guidance of My Holy Spirit, I will cleanse you. Come, My child, offer Me the sacrifice of a penitent heart. Many of you who have fallen away from a faithful life will want to renew your commitment to serve Me obediently.

In your weakness I will strengthen you. I weep for those who will surely come to curse Me in the times of testing that are even now occurring. Resist the enemy. Do not be faint-hearted. Be holy even as I am holy. Says the Lord your God."

The Lord revisited me saying:

"Oh you foolish, rebellious people! You cannot say you did not know or understand that there would be a day of judgement. You are aware of the history of the generations of your ancestors, who chose not to heed the warnings given in their own lifetime, which brought each generation of every nation into even greater spiritual poverty and condemnation. Each succeeding generation has transgressed into even greater iniquity, despite My warnings of an increase in natural disasters recorded in the Scriptures. The warnings are over and the sickle descends. Now the wheat is to be separated from the chaff, which will be burned in the everlasting fires. Did you think I would not hold you to account for your personal obedience to My word, My Son who became flesh to die in your place? I sentenced little Israel seven-fold for her iniquities, should I judge the Gentile less severely? I have sent so many correcting signs and powerful omens, yet you still turn your back and not your face to Me. In vain I have pleaded with you through My word and My prophets, whom you have killed, and the testimony of the saints through each generation, whom you have persecuted. There will be no delay, now the unbeliever will feel the rod of My anger. Even now you say you are innocent of all charges, that your motives are misunderstood. But I know your innermost thoughts and see your blackened stony hearts reflected in each of your faces. I have urged you so many times to change your ways; to have compassion and be merciful towards the orphan and the widow, the sick and the lame, the poor and the oppressed. You have hardened your hearts towards the dispossessed and closed your ears to their cries. Your haughty demeanour and unseeing eyes have been indifferent to their suffering. You have sought to do what is best for your own purposes, and only later shown regard for others who will repay you favour for favour, enabling you to

become more comfortable and powerful. I have weighed you on the scales and have found you wanting. Even now I would have you change your future behaviour, but you will ignore Me no more. Says the Lord your God."

In 1990, on the completion of my Diploma, I was invited to preach at churches and university campuses in Brazil. I enquired of the Lord on which subjects I should speak. I was instructed to preach on the '***end times***'. Signs and wonders followed the preaching and testimony of God's hand in the affairs of my life, as some people keeled over, slain in the spirit at the presence of God made manifest, and being healed of sicknesses, delivered of demons or saved from eternal death[55]. I have believed ever since that Christ's heralds are no longer saying: "***Prepare the way***", instead they are saying: "***Prepare your hearts; the Day of the Lord is upon us***", there is no more time to waste.

My first-born son Kerry died in December 1990. Whilst grieving, the Lord told me to set aside all my worldly ambitions, and whilst writing my autobiography to concentrate on Him through prayer and meditation. God was telling me, as he had similarly told Ezekiel at the time of his wife's death, that there was a greater significance than the grief of his personal loss. I sensed the curtain was being raised on God's final act of salvation, in which the present signs of disorder would rapidly deteriorate into greater depravity, which people should understand for themselves. In the light of the revelations and prophecies received, it was necessary for me to delve into biblical history, to explain how I have reached certain conclusions. There has been much conjecture over the Second Coming, owing to the lack of confirmatory written evidence! Archaeological and scientific discoveries, together with items of extraneous information, have confirmed or confounded every historian's particular hypothesis, but interpretation of signs and wonders are spiritually discerned, and may be equally obscure.

According to the *Talmud*[56], the Book of Daniel was transcribed from an oral tradition, handed down from the time of the Babylonian

---

[55] These supernatural occurrences happened long before the '***Toronto Experience***', I therefore knew that what a minority of church leaders termed as being '***conjured up by man***' or '***inspired by the devil*** ' were no such thing. I do accept that there were excesses of exhibitionism, but traditionalism is little different in its manifestations of pomp and ceremony. Later the initial 'enthusiasm' services became more orderly, but the congregations expected the Holy Spirits' presence to regularly manifest, even if services ran beyond scheduled length.

[56] The *Talmud* is the primary source of Jewish religious law, consisting of the *Mishnah* and the *Gemara*.

captivity, and compiled by men of the Great Synagogue[57]. The Book of Daniel was written in two languages, Ch 1-Ch 2:4 and Ch 8:1-Ch 12:13 were in Hebrew, whilst Ch's 2:4-Ch 7:28 were written in Aramaic. In addition the book is sprinkled with Persian and Greek words, the redactors having assimilated much of the lingua franca of the occupying forces stationed in Judah since 334 BC. A Qumran fragment from the Book of Daniel (one of the many well preserved scrolls that later became known as the '***Dead Sea Scrolls***' discovered in a cave in 1947), has led many modern scholars from both liberal and conservative schools of thought to believe that the Books of Daniel, Ezra, Nehemiah and Esther were written during the inter-testament years; concluding that all these books were of late composition, suggesting that the Book of Daniel was the final book to be included in the Hebrew Scriptures[58]. From the doubts over the authenticity and dating of Daniel, the author or the redactor either misinterpreted or mistranslated any oral or recorded account of Daniel Ch 5:20-21, either way presenting an incorrect picture to the readers of Scripture, that Nebuchadnezzar was no longer alive at the time of Daniel's '***interpretation'*** of the writing on the wall. If these books were written during the inter-testament years, then the original dialogue and the history may have been obscured.

In summarising my own deductions of world history I have drawn together eclectic threads of spiritual revelations, archaeological

---

[57] Some members of the Great Synagogue argued that there should have been a prohibition of prophecy received outside the Holy Land. I believe that God has allowed 'human interference' with what is written in the Scriptures, always providing any alteration was compliant with His supernatural code.

[58] The Persian Empire (the second beast of Daniel Ch 7) was overthrown by the Greek Empire (the third beast), which was in turn overthrown by the Roman Empire (the fourth beast). The decisive battle between the Persian and Greek armies was fought on the 7th June 334 BC, when Darius III was defeated in the Battle of the Hellespont River. The decisive battle between the Greeks and the Roman armies, in which the Roman armies emerged victorious occurred near Pydna, south of Thessalonica, at a lunar eclipse, which Faulstich determined as occurring on 18th of June 168 BC. I have come to realise that on the 7th June 1967 when the Israeli Defence Forces (IDF) liberated the Temple Mount from the Jordanian army, that the world was being shown something important. God emphasised this date by allowing the final king of Greece, King Constantine II, in the April of that same year, to be deposed in a military coup! There are exactly 2,300 years between these two battles occurring in 334 BC and 1967, which I believe points to the fulfilment of the prophecy of Daniel Ch 8:14! The first of those two battles won control of the land of Israel, whilst the second 'battle' was of coercing the minds of Jews through Greek Hellenism. Later the Roman Church claimed that God had rejected the Jew in favour of the Gentile! I believe that the prophecy of Ezekiel Ch 5:2, which amplifies Daniel Ch 11:34 (leading to God triumphantly proclaiming in Zechariah Ch 9:13, that He would take up the battle on behalf of the sons of Zion); that the time of the Gentiles was completed!

surveys, scientific discoveries, and the painstaking research of others. I have drawn from the research and conclusions of the gifted American Bible chronologist and computer buff, author Gene Faulstich, as expressed in his books ***History Harmony and Daniel*** and ***Witnesses for Jesus the Messiah***, as having particular merit. Faulstich is neither an Assyriologist nor an Egyptologist, nor does he hold a degree in theology or biblical languages, but that does not disqualify his biblical conclusions. The scholarly intellectual, the brilliant philosopher and the smooth-talking orator of no faith may be endowed with much worldly wisdom, but if that intellectual's mind is not illuminated by the Holy Spirit, any theological criticism he might submit is unlikely to convince or inspire any Spirit-filled reader. A clinical analysis of a non-academic's written work, previewed by a non-Holy Spirit-filled academic may prove to be as dry as dust in summary, and dismissive or disheartening to the author's theories or conclusions. Whereas a thoroughly investigated critique read, by a Holy Spirit-filled academic, through spiritual eyes, would prove stimulating. Provocatively, David Rohl in his book ***Legend, the Genesis of Civilisation***[59], writes, '***Academia generally does not attempt to answer vexing historical questions, for fear of being mocked or of being held to ridicule by other experts. The well-trained scholar, rather than attempting to penetrate to the heart of the investigation, tends to pick at the edges of knowledge***'. This statement implies that the intuitive imagination, combined with the thoughtful logic of the expert, would encourage further fruitful investigation, if only the expert would declare his conclusion! I believe that the most scholarly dissertations are invariably the summing-up of eclectic scholarship, based on presumptions, which are no more reliable than unscholarly revelation and intuition, which qualifies my own unscholarly suppositions as equally worthy of consideration.

<u>The rise of Babylon and Media, eclipsed by Cyrus the Great</u>

The ten tribes of Israel were deported over a 65-year period between 741- 676 BC (as prophesied in Isaiah Ch 7:8 (b)).

- The first deportation from Samaria occurred in 741 BC under Tiglath-Pileser 111 (745-727 BC), when the Israelites were deported to remote regions of the Assyrian Empire (2 Kings Ch 17:24), and absorbed into the local milieu.
- The second deportation under Sargon 11 (722-705 BC) occurred in 721 BC (2 Kings Ch 17:6).

[59] Where I refer to David Rohl, I am quoting from excerpts in his book.

- The third deportation occurred in 676 BC, when King Esarhaddon (681-669 BC) sacked Sidon, removing the invalids and the frail Samarians who had escaped the earlier deportations[60]. The people of Sidon were deported wholesale into the land of Samaria as a replacement society. Such action was a common practice in those times, designed to eradicate any thoughts of uprising. God had allowed the removal of the ten tribes from Samaria because of His anger that a temple of worship to Baal had been constructed in the Promised Land (1 Kings Ch 16:32).

I believe that the Samaritans, represented by Ephraim's stick (Ezekiel Ch 37:16 (b)), are the archetype of the Gentile believers. Ephraim, whose mother was a Gentile, was the Gentile son of Israel, fathered from the (spiritual) loins of Jacob (whose dying blessing was to include Jacob's two grandsons into the 12 tribes of the House of Israel). They will be eternally and inseparably joined as one, grafted into the one olive tree in the redeemed kingdom of God. Together they represent the 12 brothers of Genesis Ch 49, which included the two Gentile sons of Joseph, Manasseh and Ephraim, whose names I believe to be written on two of the 12 gates of Revelation Ch 21:12, in place of Simeon and Levi who, as tribes, became amalgamated into the other ten tribes.

I am confident of the inclusion of Gentiles in the kingdom of God, through knowing that Caleb, son of Jephunneh the Kennizite from Moab (Joshua Ch 14:6) was the first male Gentile to enter the Promised Land under the Israelite Covenant. The first female Gentile to enter the land was Ruth[61] (accepted as bride to the ***earthly kinsman redeemer*** Boaz); she also was from Moab, a nation born out of incest. Clearly the bride of Christ (the supernatural bride of the ***divine*** *kinsman redeemer* has been accepted as a substitution for Adam and Eve (who themselves represented mankind universal). No nation can expect to be dealt with any less severely than Israel over its lack of righteousness. I believe only those 'sinners' chosen by Christ will be 'covered' from 'original and personal' sin, by Christ's crucifixion, and will be saved '***from***' the nations. All Gentiles should

[60] It is possible to believe from 2 Kings Ch 17:27 that in the deportation of the ten tribes of the House of Israel, we are reading of the first occasion of 'ethnic cleansing'. Lions were killing the Sidonian exiles, and the provincial authorities were commanded by their king to send one of the deported priests back to the land to instruct the people in the traditions of the '***territorial god***' of the land. If there had been any old or sick remaining from the ten tribes still living in the land, they might have been asked how to appease this *territorial god*. It is highly unlikely that the lions killed every Israelite that had not been part of the deportations, whilst not mauling any Sidonians!

[61] Rahab the prostitute did not accompany the Israelites into the land, although through her we see a pagan recognising God', and being saved through repentance.

understand that believers are saved ***only*** by grace, and not by works or through an earthly family inheritance. In 1 Corinthians Ch 10:32 Paul speaks of only three races of people throughout the world ***Jews, Gentiles and the Church of God***. This means that for all practical purposes a follower of Christ has transcended his tribal or national background. The main body of Judeans over every generation since Christ's ministry on Earth forfeited salvation, through rejecting Jesus as their Messiah, saying: "***His rejection by us, be on our own heads***" but a merciful God foreknew this outrage and decreed in Jeremiah Ch 31:34 and 33:8:

> *"I will forgive their sins of wickedness and rebellion and remember them no more."* (paraphrased)

Gentiles who believe the lie of replacement theology, that God has divorced His olive-skinned bride[62] (Israel) and remarried a blue-eyed, fair-skinned (Western) Church must equally believe that God is not faithful to His word. Taking this analogy to extremes, because of outrageous Gentile behaviour, far more ungodly than that performed by God's first bride, Jesus would surely divorce His replacement wife! There is only one eternal bride of Christ and she is both Jew and Gentile. This wife has a separate identity, just as Jacob's wives Leah and Rachel had separate identities. This spiritual marriage is eternal (Hosea Ch 2:19). God's covenant with Abraham was irrevocable, unconditional and available to all Abraham's spiritual descendants (that is the ecclesia of the kingdom of heaven on Earth). Israel is the olive tree, it is the Gentiles who, as branches are grafted into the Jewish Church, which, although established at the covenant, was confirmed by Christ in Acts Ch 1:8[63], and by the manifestation of the Holy Spirit at Shavuot (also known as (aka) Pentecost, the Feast of Weeks or the fruit harvest). It cannot in any way be interpreted that the Jew needs to be grafted into a psuedo Gentile Church. The most thrilling revelation is that the salvation of **all *born again believers*** throughout ***Judah, Samaria and the ends of the Earth*** are inextricably bound together.

---

[62] In Ezekiel Ch 16:3, 45 God spoke to His unfaithful bride 'Jerusalem': "***Your father was an Amorite and your mother a Hittite***".

[63] While meditating on this passage, I was suddenly overwhelmed by a great feeling of merciful compassion, which I assume was the ache in the heart of God. I sensed that God would not sentence the non-believing Judeans of all previous generations, who suffered beyond belief, to the eternal fires of hell. I believe it will be the 12 Apostles who will (leniently) judge them throughout time (Matthew Ch19:28). It is because of the passage in Acts Ch 16:31 that I am hopeful of a second chance (see footnote 110) for all my loved ones, despite the compelling evidence of Ezekiel Ch 14:14, that, on judgement day, the actions of righteous men will not absolve an unrighteous nation, or even the unbelieving family of a righteous man.

King Sennacherib, appointed Deoces, a native born Median, to be his puppet or 'client' king. Deoces had the distinction of being the first king of a four-generation dynasty that ruled over Media for 150 years. Following Deoces' death in 637 BC his son Phaortes succeeded him, reigning for 22 years (637 – 615 BC). Cyaxares, who reigned for 40 years (until 575 BC), succeeded his father Phaortes. The last king of the dynasty, King Astyages, more familiarly known as Darius the Mede[64], reigned for 35 years until his death at 97 years of age in 540 BC. Following Sennacherib's assassination; his youngest son Ashurbanipal became king.

In 627 BC Addad Guppi succeeded his father Ashurbanipal, and appointed Nabopolassar, a native born Babylonian, as his viceroy of Babylon. Later Nabopolassar declared Babylon to be an independent country, and became the first of what became a 68-year long, four-generation dynasty, which mirrored the four-generation dynasty of Median kings. In 612 BC, both Crown Princes Darius and Nebuchadnezzar would have been in their twenties, and likely to have been Generals in the armies of their respective countries, who victoriously overcame the Assyrian Empire. As a young serving officer Darius married Vashti (whom he later divorced, Esther Ch 1:19). Amyitis (Darius the Mede's sister) married Nebuchadnezzar, which sealed an alliance uniting the two kingdoms. It was reassuring for the two kingdoms to know they did not need to deploy vast armies to protect their joint border. The two Crown Princes would have developed a healthy respect and a lasting friendship for each other, through their combined manouvres in defeating the Assyrian Empire, and through their relationship by marriage. Both of them would have been welcome guests at each other's royal palace.

The ***Midrash Rabbah*** states that Darius the Mede ruled Babylon prior to Cyrus assuming the Babylonian throne (which is logical as Darius was the grandfather of Cyrus). Greek historian Herodotus (484-430 BC) wrote of the extension of these royal family ties: ***Mandane**, **the only daughter of King Darius the Mede, married Cambyses**, **a Persian nobleman, who became King of Persia***. Historians Abydenus and Bishop Eusebius (262-339 AD), both wrote

[64] Throughout the Book of Esther the translator of the New International Version (NIV) of the Bible refers to Queen Esther's husband as King Xerxes, whereas in the NKJ version of the Bible her husband is named as King Ahasuerus. Faulstich is in agreement with the historian Jerome (342 - 420 AD), that it was the custom of the people in both Media and Persia, to affectionately or familiarly use family nicknames when referring to their kings. In the book ***The Companion Bible***, by E W Bullinger, Ahasuerus is identified as Astyages alias Darius the Mede. It would seem that the names Astyages, Ahasuerus, Xerxes and Darius were used interchangeably.

in confirmation of this. It would seem that Vashti (or an unnamed concubine was the mother of Cyrus) had given birth to Mandane, who in turn gave birth to Cyrus. It is not beyond the bounds of possibility that Esther became by marriage, the grandmother of Cyrus. Having been deposed as PM of Babylon by Belshazzar, Daniel was probably resigned to a life of obscurity. Without doubt Daniel would have considered the influence he might exert (in providing a strong governmental voice in support of his fellow Jews), before accepting the high position in Media as one of three overseers of the 120 satraps who ruled the provinces from India to Cush (Esther Ch 1:1). Daniel Ch 6:28 clarifies that Daniel was buried in Suza (not Babylon nor Judah), suggesting that Daniel, following the experience of being thrown to the lions, prospered ***throughout the reigns of Darius and Cyrus***. On Nebuchadnezzar returning to full health, Daniel probably accepted the post of personal priest to Darius in Media. My assumption is based on Darius' declaration in Daniel Ch 6:26-28 unequivocally publicly proclaiming that he worshipped the God whom Daniel served (together with his Jewish wife Queen Esther). Perhaps their daughter Mandane, and their grandson Cyrus had the passages of Isaiah Ch 44:28-Ch 45:13 recounted to them many times, that, when Cyrus became an adult, his armies would defeat Babylonia, when he would allow the exiled Judeans to return to their homeland.

The Deportations of the House of Judah

I was struck by the similarity of the revelations of the almond branch and the cooking pot of Jeremiah Ch 1:11, 13, to the visions and revelations of the oak tree and the cooking pot that I had received. In Israel the almond tree is the first tree to blossom, its blossom appears before its leaves, it is the herald or forerunner of Spring. The cooking pot I had seen concerned the events leading to the Second Coming. My vision pointed to an invasion of Israel by the surrounding Arab nations, in which the Messiah would intervene, in a measure to convince the most sceptical of Gentiles that Jesus is the only true Son of God, the kinsman redeemer of His earthly race. The invaders will be 'sucked' into a situation that they instigate but cannot control. The cooking pot of Jeremiah was a vision of a cauldron tipped over, pouring its contents towards Judah, signifying the destruction of the temple and deportation of the people. The cooking pot of Ezekiel's enacted prophecy (Ch 24:1-14), spelled out God's judgement on the House of Judah, initially leading to its ***deportation,*** and secondly to the ***desolation*** of the temple. These events occurred during the lifetime of these prophets; I am equally hopeful to be living at the outworking of my vision.

The first deportation[65] of the House of Judah (to ensure that the annual tributes would be honoured) occurred in 606 BC, starting the 70-year Babylonian captivity (the commencement prophesied in Jeremiah Ch 25:8-12 and its cessation in Ch 29:10). The armies of Prince Nebuchadnezzar, having defeated the Egyptian King Neco at Carchemesh, threateningly surrounded Jerusalem. For three years King Jehoachim pragmatically paid to Babylon the annual tributes of 'protectionism', formerly paid to Egypt (2 Kings Ch 24:1). Whilst resting his army in Judea, Nebuchadnezzar received news of his father's death. Nebuchadnezzar departed immediately for Babylon, taking an unknown number of hostages with him, but including the four highborn friends, who were given Babylonian names; Daniel was re-named Belteshazzar, Hananiah became Shadrach, Mishael became Meshach and Azariah became Abendigo. They each received a three-year course of education, specialising in Babylonian literature, astrology and divination of dreams, as part of a wider education, initiated in order to persuade the Israelites to accept Babylonian culture in preference to Judaism. Following the completion of their training, the four friends were presented to King Nebuchadnezzar, who accepted the conclusion of his officials, that the friends (whose spiritual gifts were endowed by God), were ten times better skilled than even the most experienced magicians and enchanters of Babylonia (Daniel Ch 1:20). It is reasonable to assume that all four friends received the interpretation of King Nebuchadnezzar's dream[66] and that Daniel acted as their spokesman. The three were each rewarded with positions as administrator within the province of Babylon, presumably for their contribution, whilst Daniel was promoted to PM of Babylon. Therefore the four friends were installed ***before*** the second deportation.

- Ezekiel was part of the second deportation of 10,000 souls in 599 BC (in the seventh year of Nebuchadnezzar's reign, Jeremiah Ch 52:28). With both Ezekiel the priest, and Daniel the prophet, being exiled in Babylon and both being godly Judeans, it is likely that the two men met on ceremonial occasions. Even if I am reading too much into their knowing each other, it is reasonable to assume that Daniel would have been informed of God's visitation to Ezekiel on the day

[65] It was also no coincidence that the House of Judah, similarly to the House of Israel, suffered three deportations. The 65-year period between the final destruction of the Jerusalem Temple in 70 AD, and the final dispersion of the House of Judah in 135 AD, was of identical length in the time taken to complete the deportation of the House of Israel.

[66] We have the supporting evidence that the Magi each received the same dream on the same evening (Matthew Ch 2:12), warning them not to re-visit King Herod.

Ezekiel's wife died, in the ninth year of King Jehoiachin's reign, on the tenth day of the tenth month (21st of December 590 BC, Ezekiel Ch 24:1, verified by 2 Kings Ch 25:1). Her death was to mark the date of the issuing of God's sentence of the temple's destruction (which took place some four years later). This event was recorded in the Bible to alert those of every generation, that God is very precise over the length of His sentences of judgement.

- The third and final deportation followed the destruction of the temple in 586 BC, when the remainder of the House of Judah were taken into captivity. At the destruction of the temple the less significant temple vessels had been taken as booty to Babylon, where the items had been meticulously listed (2 Kings Ch 25:13-17). The exile ended with Zerubbabel leading the remnant of the three deportations to Jerusalem in 536 BC. It must be emphasised that this was not the return of the 12 tribes of Hosea Ch 1, which is an '***end-time***' event, but a return of a remnant of Judeans and Benjamites only. Some of who were therefore in Babylon for only 50 years, whilst perhaps family farmers and their servants may not have experienced exile at all, but were retained to plant and harvest food for the armies of occupation.

The first of three episodic 70-year[67] periods of travail surrounding the history of the House of Judah occurred with Nebuchadnezzar deporting them to Babylon from 606-636 BC. I believe that God wanted future generations to realise that it was Israel's God who had decreed these deportations, which is why every period of judgement follows a similar period of time. It is written in Daniel Ch 9:2 that having analysed Jeremiah's scroll (which I believe to be Chapters 29-30 of Jeremiah), Daniel entered into a fast to seek God's will over the length of time before ***all*** of the House of Judah would be regathered in Jerusalem. Daniel was rewarded for his assiduous prayers by a visitation from the angel Gabriel, and was told (in verses 20-27) that Israel would return to Jerusalem ***at the Second Coming*** (of Christ), when the six conditions of Daniel Ch 9:24 would be completely fulfilled. There is no suggestion in the text that all Judeans would return to Israel at the end of the Babylonian exile.

- The second 70-year period divinely decreed by God (590-520 BC) ran from the initial besieging by Nebuchadnezzar's army, leading to the temple's destruction, until the rebuilding of its foundations.

[67] Seventy is a sacred number attributed to God. Seven is the number of God's seal of sacredness and ten is the number of ordinal perfection. When multiplied together, the significance is also multiplied.

- The third 70-year period (586-516 BC) referring to the ***desolation*** of Solomon's Temple lasted from its destruction until the completion of Zerubbabel's Temple.

The Times of the Gentiles

Nebuchadnezzar had commissioned a statue of himself 2m high, cast in gold, secured on a column 60 cubits high (27.4m) and 6 cubits broad (2.74m), presumably to mark the 25th year of his reign, as an act of triumphalism, in that he had defeated and made every known nation not ruled over by Media, into vassal kingdoms. The conspicuous statue was constructed on the Plain of Dura. It was symbolic of mankind's pride and rebellion against God, and represented mankind's fall into sin. One year after receiving his second warning from God for arrogant boastfulness, Nebuchadnezzar was struck down for seven ***biblical*** years of days (which is 7[68] x 360 days = 2,520 days, see footnote 55), with lycanthropy (a condition in which the afflicted person believes himself to be a wolf). Nebuchadnezzar proudly proclaim: "***Is this great city of Babylon constructed as my royal palace for my pleasure at my decree***, ***evidence of my mighty power***, ***signifying the glory of my majesty***?" Nebuchadnezzar was well aware that the nation of Media, the country of his wife's birth, shared the Chaldean religion with his own people, and he would not have wanted to jeopardise his country's treaty with Media by unnecessarily upsetting the priesthood of either country. In view of King Nebuchadnezzar's acknowledgement of Daniel's God, he may well have elevated his son to co-regent for no better reason than at the Coronation of his son Belshazzar, he could hand over the kingly high priest title of ***Pontifex Maximus*** (a title handed down in perpetuity to the latest reincarnation of Nimrod). Belshazzar is written of as '***the son of Nebuchadnezzar***' in both the Book of Baruch Ch 1:11-12 and Daniel Ch 5:11, 18, clarifying that Crown Prince Belshazzar was elevated as co-regent to the throne, to reign conjointly with his father. It is implied in Daniel Ch 5:21 that Nebuchadnezzar was dead at the time of Belshazzar's kingship. I do not think this could be true, owing to the fact that Belshazzar could offer only the ***third*** highest position in his kingdom to Daniel. This must surely have arisen because Belshazzar as co-regent held only the second highest position of authority in the land, ***behind his father***. Josephus wrote

[68] The digit '7' is consistently and repeatedly coded into every sentence of the Hebrew Scriptures and the Greek Septuagint. Both alphabets are numeric languages, every letter having a mathematical value. In Leviticus Ch 26:18,24,28, where God spoke of biblical ***years***, He repeated four times that a seven-times sentence of years would apply for retribution. As I understand this curse, God would relent after the sentence was served.

that ***Belshazzar died, 408 years before the profaning of the altar in 167 BC***, which clarifies that he was assassinated in 575 BC. Nebuchadnezzar finally died in 562 BC, nine years after recovering from his illness. Nebuchadnezzar's grandson, Evil-Merodach (Belshazzar's son[69]), was proclaimed king, and reigned for three years until his assassination in 559 BC. Neriglissar, King Evil-Merodach's Assyrian brother-in-law plotted the assassination of the Babylonian king and proclaimed himself as king in his stead. As followers of the Chaldean faith, the priesthood accepted Neriglissar as their new divine kingly priest.

Nebuchadnezzar's armies had taken 19 months from first besieging Jerusalem to overrunning the city (2 Kings Ch 25:1-2). It would have taken more than one night to overrun Babylon, a city with much stronger fortifications than those that protected Jerusalem! I fail to understand why anyone could be persuaded that a marauding army entering the land would not have been identified and its objectives fully understood, even weeks before a blockading siege of any capital city took place. If an invading army had been encamped within a day's march of the city of Babylon, King Belshazzar would obviously not have been throwing a party for his friends, but would have been checking his fortifications for weaknesses. It is much more likely that the apocryphal story recorded in the *Midrash Rabbah* is true, that Belshazzar, the son of Nebuchadnezzar, was assassinated by two of his own palace guards (***not an invading army***), the very night of Daniel's interpretation. There is an alternative view that the Babylonian army may have refused to fight for an unpopular king, but in view of the fact that a treaty was currently in operation, and of Darius' kinship with Queen Amyitis, such a belief does stretch credulity! Darius did not bring a triumphant army against his nephew King Belshazzar, but rather he had graciously responded to a request from his sister, Queen Amyitis, to honour the alliance between the two nations. This agreement also acted as a deterrent against any attempted assassination, by a usurper against the shared throne of Nebuchadnezzar and Belshazzar, which could have caused an internal revolution. Darius promised his sister to garrison a regiment of Median soldiers, powerful enough to protect her husband's kingdom, in the event of an aggressor's army invading (or to repel any internal unrest or uprising), whilst King Nebuchadnezzar was unable to command his armies.

---

[69] My reason for belief in Belshazzar having a son is through the '**third generation**' prophecy of Jeremiah Ch 27:7: *"**All nations will serve Nebuchadnezzar and his son and his grandson**."*

On Belshazzar's final night on earth, God interrupted the drunken merriment of a sacrilegious ceremony, during which Belshazzar profaned the Most Holy God. Belshazzar was a pre-figurement of the final antichrist himself, who would be summarily despatched to hell on judgement day. Having toasted his blasphemous speech, the assembled guests quivered in trepidation, as a finger of a disembodied hand wrote on the wall in a supernatural indecipherable language the words ***Mene mene tekel parsin,*** which Daniel '***interpreted*** as meaning that the Numberer's days were numbered ('Numberer' is another name by which Satan is known)'. Many scholars believe the words to have been Aramaic, but it is not believable that no one could be found to interpret the handwriting of such a common language. It is implied from the words of Daniel Ch 9:1, that Darius was ***made*** (recognised as), and not ***crowned*** king, He did not occupy Babylon by force, but rather was ***invited***, as the brother-in-law of the King of Babylon, to assume custody of the Babylonian Empire, until Nebuchadnezzar's health was restored.

The clemency of God, in restoring Nebuchadnezzar's sanity was granted, because he was the most highly esteemed archetype of Gentile kings, being equivalent in stature to King David, and was Gods' instrument in punishing Judah. Nebuchadnezzar duly humbled and repentant, became a follower of God. He proclaimed God's sovereignty and testified that his own worldly kingdom was temporal and of short duration, refuting all of his earlier boastfulness and no longer held regard for his former religious affiliations. Nebuchadnezzar now worshipped a god with eternal dominion declaring publicly in Daniel Ch 4:34-37:

> *"Now I Nebuchadnezzar praise exalt and glorify the King of heaven, because everything He does is right and all His ways are just. And those who walk in pride, God Almighty is able to humble."*

Josephus records a report by Berosus, ***Neriglissar died in 557 BC***, ***and his son Labashi-Marduk*** (aka Laborosoardach), ***who exhibited depraved conduct, succeeded him for less than a year. The conspirators who beat Labashi-Marduk to death appointed one of their number***, ***Nabonidus, to reign in his stead***. I imagine that the argument in Babylon over who was the more powerful god, Sin or Marduk started from around this time. Nabonidus never attended any religious celebrations in honour of the Babylonian god Marduk (the chief deity of the territory from which Babylon had developed), but rather spent considerable periods of his reign visiting every province of his empire, promoting the worship of the Chaldean god Sin as superior to Marduk. This practise had alienated any affection or loyalty the Babylonians may have fostered for their Assyrian overlords.

It is important for my argument to establish the year in which the decree allowing the Judeans to return was issued, in order to be certain who issued it. Cyrus became King of Persia in 559 BC, and of Media in 551 BC. According to the Babylonian Chronicles (Chronicle 7), Astyages of Media (alias Darius the Mede, during the sixth year of the reign of Nabonidus of Babylon in 551 BC) marched his armies against his grandson, Cyrus of Persia. The Median army rebelled against their autocratic ruler and refused to fight against Cyrus' army, handing their king (at that time 86 years of age) and his kingdom over to Cyrus, believing than Cyrus would prove to be less dictatorial than his grandfather had been. Although at this time the Judeans were under vassalage to Babylon, Cyrus, on becoming king of Media, declared his vowed intentions (in accordance with Isaiah Ch 44:28-Ch 45:5), of allowing the Judeans ***as a nation*** to return to Judah as soon as his armies had defeated Babylon. Cyrus allowed Darius, who he placed under house arrest, to retain his throne title until his death in 540 BC. Cyrus chose not to invade Babylon during the lifetime of Darius the Mede out of respect for his grandfather's own short but important reign over Babylonia, which confirms King Cyrus to have been an emancipated, egalitarian monarch. No death of any king is recorded in the Babylonian Chronicles around the years of the occupation of Babylonia. Berosus a Babylonian priest and historian wrote: ***When Cyrus became ruler of Babylon, Nabonidus was banished to Carmenia, where he lived out his life in peace***. Cyrus did not order the killing or maiming of any of the deposed rulers, He only banished them from the land. Neither did he impose his religion on his new subjects, as was the normal practise of those times, rather he allowed every citizen the right to worship the god of their choice. The Babylonian priesthood were banished, together with the deposed Babylonian co-regent kings, under threat of losing their lives if they attempted to reintroduce their unacceptable religion to Babylonia. It was a relatively simple matter for the priesthood to establish their mystery religion[70] in the city of Pergamum[71] in

[70] The earliest priestly ancestors of the Babylonian religion were an ethnic group called Hittites, who migrated from Anatolia and further eastward from India and the Orient to Mesopotamia and into Asia Minor c2000 BC, Over the years the Chaldean religion, as practised in Babylonia had assimilated the magic and the astral features of the Mithras cult of Anatolia, fused with the Indo/Iranian worship of Cybele, demonstrated by promiscuous sexual behaviour.

[71] Pergamum was written thus in Latin, or as Pergamos in the Greek language.

Asia Minor. This imported religion quickly developed into acceptable worship (for a more detailed study ***Mystery Babylon the Great*** by G H Pembor should be read).

In 539 BC, at the time of the invasion and occupation of Babylon by Cyrus' army, King Nabunaid (Nabonidus), was campaigning in Tema, to the north of his empire (and therefore not in a position to defend his capital city). His son, King Belshazzar[72], having heard reports that the cities of both Opis and Sippar had fallen to the invading armies, chose to be out of the city on manoeuvres with his troops in Akkad, rather than suffer a defeat in battle. Cyrus had no need to rule Babylonia with a rod of iron, for the Babylonians welcomed him as a beneficent monarch. Following the occupation of Babylon, Zerubbabel (Sheshbezzar), the newly appointed governor of Judah, although given permission to lead the Judeans back to Judah, had to take into account the wishes of the returnees, concerning the amount of time needed, to honour previously made contractual pledges, sell homes and any businesses etc. The Judeans returned by camel-train in 536 BC, and not on being given their freedom to return in 539 BC. Many Jewish families chose to stay in Babylon. Zerubbabel, in order to ensure adequate food provisions for the first Winter of the return of the remnant, would have had the foresight to ensure that the caravan train left Babylonia with sufficient time on arrival back in their homeland to sow seeds for the reaping of the Summer harvest in September, and for the priests to rebuild the altar of sacrifice, in order to recommence worship centred around the temple sacrifices, but with particular emphasis being paid to their first Festival of *Succoth* (aka the Feast of Tabernacles, or the Feast of Booths). Cyrus' successors were King Cambyses 11 (539-529 BC), and then King Hystaspes (529-522 BC), who fulfilled Cyrus' decree to allow all enslaved people groups to return to their homelands. The decree (allowing the Judeans to return, with emphasis to the rebuilding of the Jerusalem temple) was found in, Ecbatana (Suza), the capital city of Media buried in the royal archives. If the decree had been issued in Babylon it would have been found in the Babylonian archives.

The returnees did spend two years restoring the foundations of the temple, but then they concentrated their energies on building their own homes and establishing their own businesses. This may have been

---

[72] Belshazzar, the son of King Nabonidus, was co-regent with his father for the whole of his father's reign of 17 years (557 - 539 BC). Josephus highlights this discrepancy of history, concerning the truth of there having been two different co-regent kings Belshazzar, with many years separating their reigns, pointing out in Antiquities X.IX.4 that Belshazzar is inscribed on the Babylonian Cylinder as the ***son*** of King Nabonidus.

forced on the Judeans by anti-Semitic[73] Syrian Governor of Samaria and Judea Rehum, who had written a letter to the Persian king, warning him that the leaders of the recently returned Jews planned insurrection from a rebuilt, fortified city, and although they could have rebuilt the temple, they were forbidden to rebuild the city and its walls (Ezra Ch 4:21). I suspect that Rehums' long-term plans had been to overthrow Persia, but in the meantime he wanted to ensure that Jerusalem remained a city without walls. Tattenhai succeeded Rehum as Governor. On the elevation of King Darius 1of Persia to the throne in 522 BC, Governor Tattenhai had written a very naïvely worded letter to the recently crowned king, asking him to thoroughly investigate the claims of the House of Judah regarding whether King Cyrus had issued a decree restoring the right of the Jews to practise their religion centred around the rebuilt temple, drawing attention to the confiscated temple treasures, which had not been restored to the Persian Treasury, but rather had lain in the Babylonian vaults. In December 520 BC, the prophet Haggai rebuked Zerubbabel the governor, and Joshua the high priest, for not prioritising the rebuilding of the House of God. He advised these leaders that the returnees were not prospering because God was exasperated, not only with the people, but with the priesthood, for not urging the Judeans to rebuild the temple, following the completion of its foundations. Haggai in Ch 3:15-19 said:

> *"I struck all the work of your hand with blight, mildew and hail. From this day forth I will bless you if you concentrate your efforts on rebuilding the temple."* (paraphrased)

The leadership repented and instructed the people that the rebuilding would have to take precedence over all other priorities. This decision coincided with King Darius 1 commissioning the rebuilding, which took four years to complete. Scholar and archaeologist Hugo Winckler dates Ezra's mission to Jerusalem as commencing in 515 BC, and dates Nehemiah's rebuilding of the ***walls and city*** as in the 20th year of the reign of Darius I, that was in 502

[73] Some Jews have thought of anti-Semitism as a symptom of evil or ignorance, whilst others thought of it as a hereditary Gentile disease that manifests in psychic aberration. Because of the Gentiles' lack of compassion and mercy towards the Jew, I believe that the anti-Semitism practised towards the Jew, has manifested itself amongst Gentile tribes as aggressive xenophobia more recently recognised as 'ethnic cleansing', as a judgement from God.

BC[74]. Having found Cyrus' decree in Suza's royal archives, there is a greater likelihood for Darius I sanctioning the rebuilding of the temple and city walls of Jerusalem, than that King Artaxerxes Longimanus decreed the rebuilding of the city walls only.

The system of double dating (recording the date in both the Persian and Judaic kingships and calendar systems), was introduced ***during*** the reign of Xerxes in the 5th century BC. Faulstich is convinced that the Artaxerxes of Ezra Ch 6:14 and Ch 7:12-26 was really Darius I, for the earliest of the Elephantine Letters, written by scribes from the colony of Jews living in Egypt, were ***undated*** thereby identifying that they were written during the first half of the reign of Darius I in the 6th century BC. A letter labelled C17 Marcheswan 19 (11th November), Epiphi 7, double-dates the year of its writing as ***'year 37 of Artaxerxes'***, and must have been written during the reign of Artaxerxes Longimanus (464 - 423 BC), who was the only Persian king to reign for a full 40 years. It is a moot point, but Darius I actually reigned for 36 years and 7 months. King Xerxes (486-465 BC), the son of Darius 1, reigned for only 21 years.

If Esther had married the son of Darius 1, she would have been close to 100 years of age at her marriage! It is known from Esther Ch 2:5-7 that her elder cousin Mordecai raised Esther. They had been part of the second deportation. Bullinger has written of the amazing discovery (which is awesome in its magnitude), of a hidden skip code acrostic[75] that he decoded in the Book of Esther. Both Memucan and Haman were bewildered when their advice, which the king originally accepted, was rejected. From Esther Ch 3:8 it can be discerned that Haman did not disclose to the king the name of the race of people he

---

[74] The year 502 BC was the 49th year (being seven years 'squared' 7^2), following Cyrus' original decree. The late Ivan Panin, Russian mathematician and biblical scholar held a Masters Degree in Literary Criticism. He agreed with Winckler and Jerome that the rebuilding of the temple of Jerusalem, ***together with its walls and gates,*** is implied in the Scriptures, but Panin does not supply the dates of completion.

[75] The name Jehovah is repeated four times in the skip code, twice in ***reverse*** order when spoken by Gentiles, Memucan (in Ch 1:13-20) and Haman (in Ch 5:11-14) from whom the king sought advice, and twice when Queen Esther speaks in Ch 5:4 and Ch 7:3, the name 'Jehovah' is transcribed correctly (forwards) in the skip code, indicating that the name Jehovah is also found consistently repeated in the Book of Leviticus on selecting every seventh letter. Vowels were not introduced into the Hebrew language until the 6th century AD, which makes the coding of the EDLS system into the Scriptures even more amazing! Many mathematicians have attempted to write passages applying '***God's signature***' (coding), they have found it to be an impossible task, and even a paragraph cannot be written that reads coherently! This device was perfectly simple for the God of Creation to have coded into the Scriptures, but impossible for man to have designed in support of the Judeans, had overruled the king's earlier commands. (In Chapter 3, I write of more recent developments of code breaking).

proposed should be exterminated. Darius the Mede knew Mordecai to be a Jew (Esther Ch 6:10), but perhaps he did not know of her relationship with Mordecai. The king would not have agreed to Haman's proposal if he had known that his own wife's race was the proposed race to be exterminated. The highly unlikely unasked questions, who were this race of people to be exterminated, does make the Book of Esther more gripping, if hyperbolic! Esther disclosed her racial background in Ch 8:6.

The Books of Ezra and Nehemiah in the Hebrew Scriptures are one book, which is not so surprising, considering that both men were Jewish leaders and contemporaries in Israel (Nehemiah Ch 8:9 confirms this). King Darius 1 appointed both men into high office. In Ezra Ch 1:7-11, during 536 BC Zerubbabel was entrusted to return with the temple treasures to Jerusalem. During 516 BC, Ezra the priest, having received his instructions from King Darius 1, took the temple treasures to the rebuilt temple (Ezra Ch 7:15-20). Ezra's task was to ensure both the priesthood and the people were familiarised with the *Torah*, with regard to the correct procedure of ceremonial, purification and sacrificial rites (over which animals and on which occasions they were to be sacrificed). Facsimiles were made of the gold furnishings that had previously been situated in the Holy of Holies, with the exception of the Ark of the Covenant (Jeremiah Ch 3:16 (b). It has been suggested that the Ark was 'Raptured' into Heaven and is the same Ark referred to in Revelation Ch 11:19, I am not convinced.

I had retired to bed on the night of 21st December 1998, pondering over the reason why the temple treasures belonging to Jerusalem were given to two entrusted Jewish officials by two different Persian kings many years apart (first to Zerubbabel and then to Ezra). I was puzzled over why King Darius 1, early in his reign, seemingly without provocation, ordered the destruction of Babylon[76]. It was two years following the above insight that it was revealed to me that I had received the revelation ***on the anniversary of the night that God spoke to Ezekiel*** of the destruction of Solomon's Temple! Babylonia had been a peaceful, obedient and a productive people for almost 20 years, substantially adding growth and stability to Persia's economy. On my awakening the following morning, through a revelatory '*word of knowledge*', I knew the answer and found confirmation in Ezra Ch 5. On further investigation it was discovered that Rehum had 'restored' (or recovered) the temple treasures that had been entrusted to Zerubbabel, to the vaults of Babylon, where locally collected taxes of the vassal kingdom were deposited for 'safekeeping'. This treasure house would have financed a major uprising with the fortified city of Babylon as its power base. From Ezra Ch 4:9-10, and by reading the history of enmity between the House of Israel, whose leaders had entered into alliances with Assyria to overthrow the House of Judah, it became apparent that history was planned to be repeated. King Darius 1's advisors proved more perceptive than those of King Cambyses (or perhaps King Hystaspes) had been. A furious King Darius 1 sent a decree to Governor Tattenhai ordering the financing of a rebuilt temple in Jerusalem, to be paid for from the collected taxes stored in Babylon's treasury, under penalty of death for delay. Having anticipated the insurrection, King Darius 1 acted decisively and immediately by ordering the burning of the city of Babylon to the ground.

---

[76] The destruction of Babylon's fortifications carried out in 520 BC was not the ***final*** destruction of the city. Jeremiah Ch 50:9 had to be speaking of a later time in history following the ***rebuilding*** of Babylon. Jeremiah spoke of an ***assembly of great nations*** from afar attacking Babylon. This passage implied that weapons would be fired from safe positions with arrow-like accuracy. I consider that Jeremiah was referring to modern day missiles fired from aeroplanes, ships and submarines, and from land bases behind territorial boundaries of a neighbouring country. In 1898 German archaeologists discovered ruins of the once resplendent city of Babylon, some 110km south of Baghdad, which was overlaid by 2,000 years of accumulated sand. Iraq's renaissance was solely attributed to President Saddam Hussein who embarked on a visionary program of restoring the fortunes of Babylon to its former glory. Since 1982 uncounted millions of dollars from the US$100 million daily, received through the sale of petroleum from Iraq's vast oil fields, were spent in the restoration of the ancient capital city of Babylon having its former temples of worship rebuilt. National pride was restored to the 17 million Iraqi population who lived in the land. In 1987 Saddam introduced the lavish Babylonian Festival, as an annual event. It was during the second festival that clay bricks were produced, stamped with the symbols Saddam Hussein and King Nebuchadnezzar. Every fourteenth brick laid in the reconstruction of the Tower of Babel, by presidential order, had to bear this stamp, suggesting that Saddam considered himself equivalent to, if not the reincarnation of Nebuchadnezzar.

Following the Greek Empire overthrowing the Persians, many Jews emigrated throughout the Greco-Roman world. Even in Judah, many formerly observant Judeans embraced Greek Hellenism, as an improvement in freedom of self-expression. The Judeans became less devout, in that they no longer offered sacrifices or made the journey to any of the annual feasts at the Jerusalem Temple. They retained their 'Jewishness', preferring to settle in solely Jewish communities isolated from the endemic natives of their adopted country, which was resented and interpreted as aloofness. They would not eat with non-Jews (owing to dietary and purification laws), nor take part in any non-Jewish festivals. The Jews appalled the Gentiles further through their insistence in circumcision of their infant males, which aggravated hostility still further.

The Judean Tribulations

- The first of the three pre-Diaspora seven-year tribulations (humiliations) occurred with the humiliation of worshipping idols and the offering of offensive sacrifice imposed by Antiochus Epiphanes; these were identified with the abomination of which Daniel had written[77]. Antiochus ruled Syria 175-164 BC, and thought of himself as a ***manifestation of God***, but he accepted the Greek belief in a ***pantheon of gods***, for he recognised that mortality was ephemeral. M de Cheseaux believes this period of illegitimate sacrifice lasted for the 'sanctuary period' of 2,300 days (which he believes was the number of days that Antiochus Epiphanes reigned in Judah). Judas Maccabeus slew a priest who was prepared to minister an illegitimate sacrifice, before killing the Syrian overseer. It was this event that ignited the Maccabean revolt over the period 167-160 BC. In overthrowing the yoke of Seleucid oppression, Judea recaptured most of the land that King David had ruled over, and forcibly converted to Judaism all of the captives in those nations. In 140 BC Simeon declared himself to be king of the enlarged nation, commencing a national dynastic kingly priesthood; offering his nation as a Roman protectorate, in effect becoming a buffer zone in the event of attack on the Roman Empire from the east.
- The second period of Judean tribulation commenced on the death of Queen Salome in 68 BC, who had succeeded her husband Alexander Janneus as ruler. He had ruled as priestly king over Israel

---

[77] To support my understanding, I refer to 1 Kings Ch 11:5-7: "***Solomon built a high place for each of the gods his wives worshipped. The worship of which was an abomination to God's sensibilities.***" Antiochus IV Epiphanes imposed radical Greek Hellenism into Judean culture, by introducing the illegitimate sacrifice of unclean animals (pigs) in order to destroy the pietistic obedience of the people to the rabbinical law.

from the turn of the 2nd century BC, until his death in 76 BC. Queen Salome's eldest son John Hyrcanus II served as high priest. At her death, John proclaimed himself priestly king, which resulted in his younger brother, Aristobulus, raising an army to contest John's claim to the throne. I sense this 'seizing of the throne to be an allusion to the servant Jesus returning to reign as Messianic King of the Earth, on His being recognised by the Jews of Israel (Matthew Ch 24:39), as the divine[78] *kinsman redeemer* of His people. I received a '*word of knowledge*' that God spoke (through the Scriptures) to John Hyrcanus II. He believed (from reading in 1 Kings Ch 11:31, that the prophet Ahijah had told Jeroboam that the break-up of David's kingdom was ordained by God), that he should offer no resistance to his brother's claim to the throne. John abdicated and seceded the joint role of king and high priest to his younger brother Aristobulus. It was Aristobulus who prefigured Jesus as the '***anointed one***' of Daniel Ch 9:25, who wrested power from his brother in 68 BC

General Pompey's army rested in Jerusalem prior to invading Syria, at which time Pompey reviewed the new status of Aristobulus. On receiving a present of a copy of a vine carved in gold (valued at that time as being worth 500 talents), General Pompey acknowledged Aristobulus as governor and high priest but refused to grant him kingship. In 64 BC, 3½ years into the appointment, Pompey's army having defeated Syria, invaded the city of Jerusalem, ruthlessly slaughtering some 12,000 ill-equipped but religiously loyal Jews, including the priests on duty in the temple, before ordering the cancellation of the daily sacrifice of the defeated priesthood. The reason given for the invasion was that Aristobulus had unwisely chosen to populate part of Syria previously conquered by the Roman army. Aristobulus was imprisoned in Rome, where he died. He was cut off from his previous high calling, retaining nothing of value or esteem (as prophesied in Daniel Ch 9:26). This degradation was an allusion to Christ's immaculate conception (Philippians Ch 2:6-7). Judea had become a subject nation, and Jerusalem became a Roman garrison. General Pompey and General Crassus colluded with Julius Caesar (whose own army was more powerful than the armies of his fellow conspirators), to subvert the Roman Republic into becoming an empire, through forming the first unofficial Roman triumvirate, in effect by imposing their authority over the Republican Senate, the former

[78] Today in the USA there is an established movement whose intention is to change Catholic dogma into accepting that Mary (mother of God the Son) is divine, and was herself given the role of mediator between mankind and God the Father. But it is clearly written in 1 Timothy Ch 2:5 that Jesus Christ is the only mediator between man and God.

governing body. The military coup was too powerful to be resisted, and would have resulted in a bloody civil war. In 63 BC Julius was elevated to Emperor of Rome, and became the supreme civic and religious ruler of the empire.

The people of Asia Minor, who, since the banishment of the Babylonian priesthood, had been thoroughly indoctrinated with Middle Eastern syncretic practises, revered Julius Caesar as a god. King Attalus III of Pergamum[79] inherited the divine title of *Pontifex Maximus* legitimately from the successors of Belshazzar (the son of Nebuchadnezzar). At his death in 133 BC, King Attalus III (who had no family successors) bequeathed his dominions and title to the Roman Republic. A century later it seemed fitting to Julius and his family to assume the defunct title. Julius' family could trace their lineage back to Iulus, the son of the goddess Aeneus, whose legendary mother was believed to be Aphrodite (aka Venus). Julius introduced the worship of Aeneus as the divine mother with the corollary that he himself was the divine son (the worship of a divine mother and son had reached Europe!). In 61 BC (3½ years following John Hyrcanus' re-appointment to the office), Rome reintroduced the post of high priest as a political appointment. Daily sacrifices were resumed, and Rome tried to impose 'Emperor worship' (first instituted by Alexander the Great), through icons of Julius Caesar being prominently displayed in the temple. The priesthood agreed to offer daily sacrifices to God for the protection of Caesar, but refused to recognise him as divine.

General Pompey finally took umbrage at the divine title of supremacy assumed by Julius, which was resolved at the Battle of Pharsalus in 48 BC, where Julius Caesar's army triumphed over Pompey's army. Julius' victory was short lived, for he was assassinated three years later in 45 BC. Julius was posthumously honoured by his successors with the title 'Perpetual Imperator'. A second triumvirate was formulated between Mark Anthony, Lepidus and Octavian. Mark Anthony was chosen to become Caesar but he was slain in battle by his adversary and pretender to the title, Octavian (Augustus) who became the undisputed ruler. The cult of worshipping ***Rome and the Emperor*** became prevalent from 29 BC, by which time Augustus had discovered ways to secure even greater authoritative powers over his subjects, without infringing the letter of the Roman Constitution.

---

[79] Jesus refers to Pergamum, where a huge statue of Zeus had been erected dominating the city (in which the Church had successfully established itself), as the '***Throne-room of Satan***' (Revelation Ch 2:13), because of the licentiousness of the inhabitants.

- The third seven-year period of Judean tribulation occurred after Jesus' death, during the period 67-74 AD. Syrian General Cestius, under orders from Rome, fought to overcome the insurrectionist guerrilla groups, known as ***zealots***, who adopted the strategy developed by the Maccabees against the Seleucids during the Maccabean uprising. The zealots organised surprise ambushes against the occupying forces, and then melted silently back into the community, until the occupying army's security became less vigilant, when the zealots would mount further attacks. It was Caesar Vespasian who 3½ years later in 70 AD ordered his son General Titus to destroy Herod's Temple. The zealots were finally forced into the open, and then remorselessly hunted down. The last group held out in the fortress of Masada where the Roman Army besieged the zealots and their families until 74 AD, when the brave insurrectionists chose to take their own lives rather than submit to Roman rule.
- It is because of those earlier times of tribulation, that I believe a fourth 'mirror image' event will take place, coinciding with the third appearance of the 'horns', during a reoccurrence of the fourth and final period of tribulation.

It was Sir Isaac Newton who noticed that when converting the year of 536 BC from the Hebrew calendar into the Gentile calendar it was possible to ascertain when the Jews would finally be allowed to return unhindered to Israel. By multiplying the number of **biblical days** in a **biblical year**, by seven years (the number of years of insanity imposed on Nebuchadnezzar), a sum of 2,520 years is obtained[80]. On the multiplication of 360 years by 2,520 days, the sum results in 907,200 days, and by dividing the resulting 907,200 days by 365.25 (the number of days in a **calendar year**), a sum of 2483.8 years results. Therefore if the 2483·8 calendar years are added to 536 BC, a date in 1948 AD is arrived at! The first elected government of Israel, on the 14th May, announced the Law of Return to the Promised Land. Israel was reborn in 1948 supernaturally and protected from annihilation on the following day, when the land was invaded by the neighbouring Arab nations. Consider carefully that on the 29th of

---

[80] This procedure is quite legitimate because we read in Numbers Ch 14:34: "***According to the 40 days in which you spied out the land, you shall bear your iniquity for 40 years***". In Ezekiel Ch 4:5-6 God says in metaphoric symbolism " ***I have assigned you to lie on your left side for 390 days, to bear the sins of House of Israel. I assign you to lie on your right side for 40 days, facing the model of the city of Jerusalem, each day representing one year, for the sin of the House of Judah***."

November 1947, through resolution 181, the United Nations[81] (UN) voted to establish the right of the Jews of the Diaspora to be restored into nationhood in Israel (unfortunately neither the areas of land nor the cities were specified, in what had become Palestine).

The only sacred year of jubilee (50 years of autonomous government in Israel) to occur, since the days of the Caesars, commenced on *Rosh Hashana* (aka the Feast of Trumpets, celebrating the Jewish New Year's Day) at 5:30^{PM}, on the 17th of September 2001. The fig tree of Matthew Ch 24:32 was figuratively replanted in 1948, and reintroduced the cycle of years leading to the final jubilee in history, with the fruition of the fig tree. For those who protest that God has washed His hands of the Jews, think again. If you have hardened your heart against the Jews' return to the Promised Land, then you are rebelling against the purposes of God. It was of this day that Isaiah was speaking in Ch 66:8, when he prophesied rhetorically:

"Can a nation be born in a day"?

[81] On the 1st of January 1942, the 26 national governments, at that time at war with the Axis powers, embodied the Atlantic Charter, more familiarly known as the United Nations Declaration. On the 25th of April 1945, delegates from 50 nations met in San Francisco and formed themselves into the powerful successor to the disbanded League of Nations. The UN flag depicts planet Earth surrounded by olive branches. Israel's flag depicts the five-pointed Star of David. Apocalyptically, both flags (emblems) are written of in Isaiah Ch 11:10-16, before Isaiah prophesied the result of the abortive attempted invasion of Psalm 83, the drying up of the Euphrates River (enticing the kings of the East to attack Israel); together with the mass conversion of former Muslims who have yet to suffer the 'plagues of God' in their homelands, following the fruitless invasion by the Islamic nations on Israel. I embrace all these pointers in Chapter 7 in my explanation of the '**end times**' scenario.

Chapter 3

UPON THIS ROCK I WILL BUILD MY CHURCH

In the opening Chapter, I gave a broad overview of the creation and ultimate destruction of the world. In the Second Chapter I précised my understanding of the events surrounding the destruction of Solomon's Temple and gave my understanding of Daniel's prophecy concerning the four beasts. In this Chapter I have concentrated on the development of the Church, from the ministry of Jesus until the impending Second Coming, using the tools of modernity, computer science and theomatics, as researched by others.

The Dating of the Birth and Death of Christ

Using computer science, Faulstich plotted two solar eclipses occurring over Jerusalem encompassing a seven-month period, *Tishrei* in 7 BC and *Nisan* in 6 BC, pointing to the birth of the two cousins John and Jesus. Both eclipses occurred on the first day of the two most holy months; *Nisan*, which marks the first month of the ***religious*** calendar, and *Tishrei*, which is the first month of the ***civil*** calendar. Faulstich plotted the two wandering stars, Saturn (which Israelite astronomers had designated as representing the ***city*** of **Jerusalem**) and Jupiter (the king of the planets, which represents **royalty**). Saturn and Jupiter remained uniquely in alignment with each other's orbits ***for more than one year*** of the Zodiac calendar. The 12 houses (known as 'constellations' of the Zodiac) are equal 30° segments of the 360° circle.

In July of 5 BC a nova (an exploding star) was recorded as having taken place in the constellation of Aquilla (the Eagle). Possibly this nova was a sign to celebrate the successful escape into Egypt of Christ's parents, from the impending threat of a massacre of all babies born in or near to Bethlehem during the previous two years. The poll tax census in 6 BC was the motivation for Joseph taking his pregnant wife Mary to Bethlehem. Tertullian wrote in ***Against Marcian*** that Jesus was born during Sentius Saturninus' governorship of Syria (for the period 9-6 BC). Quirinius served two terms as governor of Jerusalem (6-4 BC and 6-9 AD), which may have added to the later confusion of dates surrounding Jesus' birth. Clement of Alexandria dated Jesus' birth from the Egyptian calendar as *Pachom 25* (14th May in 6 BC) in the 28th year of Augustus (Stromata 1,xxi), on *Iyyar* 28 (14th May 6 BC). Faulstich believes that the conjunction of the planets, together with the solar eclipses over Jerusalem, combined with the biblical and extraneous historical facts, establishes his own dating of

Christ's royal birth as being correct. In the Spring of 6 BC, following Mary's vision of the angel Gabriel, the planet Mars (the third wandering star) came into conjunction with Saturn and Jupiter[82] and may well have produced the effect in the sky, familiarly known as the '***bright Morning Star***'[83], that faded from view following Venus crossing the path of Jupiter at Christ's birth. Christ was circumcised on *Sivan* 6 (Pentecost) eight days following His birth (when His blood was shed for the first time).

Josephus records (in **Antiquities XVIII.iii.I**) that Pontius Pilate commenced his appointment as governor of Jerusalem in the autumn of 26 AD, on the first day of *Succoth.* Faulstich believes this was the same day that Jesus commenced His ministry, which is supported by Luke Ch 3:23 saying that Jesus was ***about*** 30 years of age when on the occasion of the calling together of His apostles. If Faulstich were correct, Jesus would have been approaching his 32nd birthday and not the age of 30 years that rabbis and priests usually entered their ministry. The date and year of Jesus' death is another area of conjecture. Until 30 AD Passover did not occur on any Friday close to the year in which Jesus was thought to have died. Christ ascended on *Iyyar* 28 in 30 AD on the 35th anniversary of His circumcision. Clement of Alexandria dated Jesus' death as occurring on *Nisan* 15 or *Pharmouthi* 25 in the Egyptian calendar (Friday 5th April 30 AD). Faulstich found that a solar eclipse had occurred over Jerusalem on that date, which encompassed the hours spoken of in Matthew Ch 27:45-50, suggesting that this was the date that Jesus died.

---

82 Robert W Faid refers to a conjunction (a sign?) appearing in the heavens on the evening of the 29th May 7 BC, when the Zodiac calendar moved into the 30□ segment represented by the constellation Pisces (Pisces represents the **nation of Israel**). This conjunction was unusual in that they occur every 804 years. In this instance two further conjunctions occurred in quick succession (on the 3rd October and again on the 4th December).

83 If Faulstich's assertions are correct the star sign may have been visible in the sky for a whole year, until Venus entered the constellation. The Magi knew from the star signs that the nation of Israel had received their kinsman redeemer born to rule from Jerusalem. If Faulstich's assertion is right, the Magi would have had plenty of time to follow the star, from Babylon to Bethlehem. Astrologists have recently realised that during 6 BC when Herod was king (he was represented in the astrological circle as Aries the ram), the planet Jupiter entered into the house of Aries on the 17th of April, on the same evening that a lunar eclipse occurred over Jerusalem. Jupiter may have appeared as a bright morning star; perhaps the Magi were able to plot the planets position over Bethlehem.

The Dark Ages

Following Jesus' ministry, and through the evangelism of Christ's Semitic apostles and disciples, the Good News of the Gospel of grace was proclaimed, throughout the Roman Empire, despite the Jew being despised by Gentiles. At the time of the destruction of the Herodian Temple, the Church consisted of several million Jews and *c*100,000 Gentiles. The churches in the nations to which the Judeans emigrated became increasingly reliant for growth in membership, and spiritual guidance on the earthly wisdom of their Gentile congregants. Increasingly anti-Semitism became widely practised. The ten 'horns' warned of in Daniel Ch 7 became recognisable to some scholars as the first ten Caesars, who ruled the Roman Empire from the first Caesar Julius, to the tenth Caesar Vespasian. With the cessation of altar sacrifices the priesthood became teachers of Judaism. The Judeans were forced into an imposed exile in 135 AD, which remained in force until 1947.

More influential male Gentile citizens became Christians, mainly converted through the exhortations of wives and mothers, who had been thoroughly converted through overt evangelism by Jewish ladies (in market squares, and at the water wells etc). Many such converts were recognised as people of importance by their fellow congregants, in their respective communities, and as such were invited to hold positions of leadership in the local church. Christ had warned that the Gentiles would try to impose their leadership qualities and authority over the mainly Jewish congregations (Matthew Ch 20:25-28). No new Jewish apostles or prophets arose to replace those who had died having faithfully served the church from its formation. A widely held view that gathered increasing support was that God had rejected the Jews as '***Christ killers***' in favour of the Gentiles. Anti-Semitism mushroomed in the churches (that very predictably had become predominantly Gentile), into replacement theology.

A letter known as ***1 Clement***, written in the name of the Roman church to its sister church in Corinth (*c*90 - 100 AD), supported the suggestion of church order through a three-tiered structure of church episcopacy (bishop, presbyters and deacons), together with the introduction of a distinction between the 'professional churchman' and the laity. Many advocated that each church should have its own bishop, the appointment of which would be approved by Rome to ensure orthodoxy and correct practises. Another ecclesiastical policy was that only the episcopacy should demonstrate spiritual gifts. In later years any layperson in the Roman Church exhibiting the spiritual gifts was put to death as being in league with the devil! The papacy even forbade the laity from reading the Bible under threat of death for disobedience.

Bishop Ignatius of Syrian Antioch (writing *c*110-115 AD) maintained that a Roman monarchical episcopacy must administer the churches in every country in which the Roman Empire ruled. Rome claimed that Peter's power was absolute, and that he had held the office of Bishop of Rome (43-64 AD). During the bishopric of Cyprian of Carthage (248-258 AD), Cyprian advocated that the 'throne of St Peter' formed the foundation of the Roman Catholic Church, a throne that had been entrusted in perpetuity to the incumbent of the Roman Apostolic See. The Eastern Orthodox Church never accepted the Pope as having been elevated by Christ as His successor. Most Catholics accepted as fact the myth that the apostle Peter had been the first Bishop of Rome, and, as he had been given the keys to the kingdom[84] by Jesus, they would automatically be passed on to his successors on their appointment. These early Gentile church fathers claimed that as Peter had been the Bishop of Rome, then this was a sign of the seniority of Roman bishops, over every other bishop, I am baffled at such a deduction.

Ignatius claimed that the Jewish prophets had lived according to Jesus Christ's teachings and not in accordance with rabbinic instruction, which was therefore in error. Ignatius went further, providing the wedge that opened the door to tradition being as important as scriptural truth. He urged his readers to oppose all things Jewish, and advocated replacement theology[85], which other scholars expanded upon. This and other of his writings disinherited the Jew by transferring the promises to the Church, which he promoted as the new or true Israel. Irenaeus (Bishop of Lyons from 178-195 AD) in Book 5 of his work, ***Against Heresies*** applied four Old Testament prophecies of promises of the restoration of Israel, to the gathering into the Gentile Church of the nations. Irenaeus introduced the 'Rule of Faith'[86] to counter the teaching of Gentile heretics (the Gnostics, Docetists and Marcianites) that taught heresy. Origen (185 - 254 AD, the head of the catechetical School of Alexandria) took

---

[84] The so called 'keys' was the 'prize' given to Peter initiating the reception of the Holy Spirit first on the Jews in Jerusalem (Acts Ch 2:14-39), and then on the Samaritans (Acts Ch 8:14-17) and finally on the Gentiles in Caesarea (Acts Ch10: 25-44). ***All authority*** was then passed on to ***every believer, <u>not</u> only to the Bishop of Rome***.

[85]Replacement theology is the replacement of the promises of God to the Israelites, being transferred to the Church as the bride of Christ. Origen also supported this theology. Ronald E. Diprose in his book ***'Israel in the Development of Christian Thought'*** has given greater detail of Roman propaganda from his research into this subject.

[86] The Rule of Faith was the first Christian Creed or Statement of Faith.

the replacement theology propounded by Ignatius and Irenaeus a stage further by allegorising a three-fold meaning behind the Scriptures[87]. Origen introduced a theory of a physical, a psychic, and a spiritual meaning in every passage of Scripture. He emphasised that the promises of God were not made to '***physical***' Israel, because Israel was unworthy of them, but rather they were made to the '***spiritual***' Israel (the Church). If Peter ever went to Rome he would have met regularly with Paul, and the Bible is silent over such meetings.

The belief grew that Christian leadership had been assimilated into the Levitical or Aaronic priesthood, but this supposition was based on an incorrect understanding of Malachi Ch 1:10-12. It is true that Judas Maccabeus appointed his brother Jonathon as high priest, thereby breaking the Zadokite tradition of Aaronic priesthood. Nowhere in the New Testament is it suggested that elders are invested with the priestly function gifted to the Levites, or that a remote (always absent) third tier of ecclesiastical leadership should be appointed as this functionary. Of course elders were elected ***by their flock***[88] as paid leaders, and as such should lead, teach and minister their flock (Hebrews Ch 13:17). From my understanding of James Ch 5:13-16, elected elders are pastoral visitors who exercise some part of the five-fold ministry (Ephesians Ch 4:11-13), or might demonstrate other spiritual gifts such as those mentioned in 1 Corinthians Ch 12:28. Elders are to anoint the sick with oil and pray for the flock in their care to love each other, and the community in which the church was planted.

God will deal with each person from every nation individually, as He dealt individually with His first two anointed kings, Saul and David; for each individual is responsible for their personal walk with God[89]. Following the Diaspora Jewish believers worshipped mainly in churches administered by Gentiles, but their attendance became spasmodic and later ceased owing to overt anti-Semitism. Over the

---

[87] It is not wrong to apply to the Gentile Church the Scriptures that were written for the Israelite nation, but the Scriptures have been spiritualised and allegorised by Bible expositors to a point where the truly inspired meaning may be overlooked. Biblical hermeneutics are concerned with correct exegesis, interpretation and appropriation of the text.

[88] It was a common practise for communities of ten Jewish families to appoint one from among them to act as their rabbi, and administer the education of all the children, each family contributing a tenth of the wage earners income.

[89] God says in Ezekiel Ch 14:14: '***Even if these three men Noah, Daniel and Job were living in* a nation, *they could save only themselves by their righteousness***'. Apart from Daniel living in Judah as a child, these godly men lived their lives outside of Israel.

years, most of the believing Jews (who were powerless against the tyranny practised against them and their families) had deserted what had become the established church; they chose to worship independently, and were then accused of '***particularism***' and thought of as being part of an Eastern sectarian movement. Wherever the Diaspora Jews sought to settle in Europe, they were treated as a pariah people (worse than cattle), by the endemic people. Martin Luther (1483-1546 AD) believed that he would be able to influence the misguided Jew, back onto the paths of righteousness, but like so many others before him, he did not fully appreciate the Gentile position in Christ, or the place of the Jew. Luther fanned the embers of hatred against the non-conformist Jew into fire, and anti-Semitism increased.

The Edict of Toleration was promulgated in 311 AD, which, throughout the Roman Empire, legally allowed freedom from persecution to followers of the Christian faith. ***Christianity was received into Rome and not Rome into Christianity***. Pagan religions were openly practised throughout the Empire. Generally people who followed any faith proved to be peaceable and did not oppose Roman rule. It was for this reason that in 313 AD Constantine introduced the Edict of Milan, which allowed for religious freedom for all faiths.

Persian religious charismatic Mani (216-276 AD) immigrated to Rome where he became popular with many residents in the application of his own particular faith, which blended elements of worship drawn from Zoroastrianism, Mithraism and Buddhism and early forms of dualistic Gnostic Christianity. Mani's followers were known as the Manichees; they used symbols in their worship that depicted the mythical primeval conflict between light and darkness, good and evil. Black magic was practised, and the teachings of Jesus, through His disciples, became the target of the Manichees' curses. Manichaeanism had many devotees in Europe and developed widely and quickly throughout the Roman Empire, particularly as Emperor Julian the Apostate (361-363 AD) was himself a follower. Before making any important personal or political decisions, Julian would consult soothsayers, diviners and astrologers. Julian died whilst leading a military campaign in Persia in 363 AD, and was succeeded (for less than a year) by Emperors Jovian, and then by Valentinian 1 (364-375 AD), both of who were Christians.

In 366 AD, on the death of Bishop Liberius, Damasus (366-384 AD) disputed with Ursinus for the vacant position of Bishop of Rome. In the ensuing bloody battle 137 followers of the two protagonists died, which resulted in Damasus becoming bishop; truly a baptism in blood.

It was a notable achievement for Damasus to fuse together the established Roman civic and imperial pride with Romanism. Bishop Ambrose of Milan 373 - 397 AD supported Damasus in his policies. Damasus spoke of his fellow bishops as being his sons rather than his brothers, and assumed the title of Patriarch, Bishop of Rome. Damasus' declaration that the Emperor had jurisdiction only in temporal matters, and not over the papacy on matters spiritual, was accepted without protest, because both Emperors Gratian (375-383 AD) and his successor Valentinian II (375-392 AD), were practising believers, who deferred to Damasus over spiritual matters. Gratian became Emperor of both Eastern and Western empires on the death of Emperor Valens (364-378 AD), the younger son of Valentinian. Gratian decided he could not successfully govern both empires, and appointed Theodosius, a Westerner and a noted soldier, to become the Eastern Emperor (375-395 AD), surely the two legs of iron and clay of Daniel were an allusion to the two warring powers within the empires[90]? Early into his reign, Theodosius outlawed the Manichaeans and banned their public processions, forcing its devotees to worship in secret. In 380 BC, Theodosius passed a decree introducing the '***infamy of heretical dogmas***', imposing the death penalty for dissent. On one occasion he ordered the slaying of 7,000 citizens of Thessalonica, for the murder of his appointed governor. The death occurred during the rioting incited by his Governor's refusal to grant the freedom of a popularly acclaimed slave who had gained the favour of the Thessalonians by his horsemanship in the Coliseum.

Theodosius was a strong-minded leader, but was overawed by the charismatic Bishop Ambrose of Milan (previously a Roman aristocrat, with equally noble and powerful friends), who wrote vituperatively and spoke consistently against the character of the Jew, insisting that they were '***irrevocably perverse and incapable of any good thought***'. In 388 AD the Bishop of Callinicum in Syria ordered a local synagogue to be burnt down. Theodosius had ordered the rebuilding at the bishop's own expense. Ambrose refused to continue a church service that he was conducting, and which Theodosius was attending, until Theodosius rescinded his order! It must have been this success that had given Ambrose the encouragement to threaten Theodosius with excommunication soon afterwards. In 390 AD, in fear for his life, Theodosius publicly repented of his ill-judged reaction and renounced his title of *Pontifex Maximus,* which Pope Siricius (who succeeded

[90] The dissimilar materials of the statue's legs being the Eastern Empire, and the other being the Western Empire 'spiritually' administered by the Roman Catholic Church; alternatively the materials may have represented State and Church.

Damasus as bishop) immediately assumed, a title assumed by successive popes ever since[91]. Siricius was the first Pope to use a *decretal* letter similar to that familiarly used by the Emperors. In adopting this method of decree, Pope Siricius declared for himself the same binding authority that the previous Emperors (beasts or horns) had formerly exercised. Successive popes were a different kind of 'beast', not themselves being soldiers bearing weapons (Revelation Ch 6:2), but claiming to be God's spokesman on earth, as the earthly mediator between man and God. Following Theodosius' death, his two sons, Arcadius and Honorius, reigned as Emperors in turn. In 410 AD Honorius reiterated the decree of the death penalty for heresy.

Ambrose was the mentor of Bishop of Hippo Augustine (354-430 AD), who wrote disparagingly of the impious curiosity of the ***'kingdom of the Jews'*, *which drew them to strange gods and idols*, *and led them to kill Christ***. Augustine believed that the Judeans no longer had any claim for restoration in the land of Israel. He held to a doctrine known as non-dispensationalism and wrote: ***Any 'special place or purpose' for the Jew was completed by their inclusion into the body of the Church***. It was Augustine that introduced the doctrine of '**two swords**' (based on Luke Ch 22:38), in which the disciples said to Jesus "***here are two swords***", and He replied, "***It is enough***". It was through his doctrine of the two swords that Augustine justified the persecution and murder of all who did not swear allegiance to the Roman Church. He chose to ignore the fact that Jesus rebuked Peter for using a sword to fend off Malchus, in effect saying He did not need carnal help (Matthew Ch 26:53), as His battle was spiritual. The blood of millions of devout Christians, as well as Jews and Muslims is on Augustine's hands. The Irish monk Pelagius, a man of impeccably fine Christian virtue, visited Rome to seek the support of the Pope to rescind succeeding Emperors' hardened attitudes concerning the death penalty for heresy. Augustine's reply was that '***free will' would undermine the foundation of the newly constructed Holy Roman Empire***. Pelagius was excommunicated for his publicly expressed opinions[92]!

John Chrysostom (347-407 AD, patriarch of Constantinople from 398 AD) was as equally vitriolic as the Jew haters before him. Chrysostom accused the Jews of murdering their offspring, and of

---

[91] Theodosius reigned for a further five years until his death, but no longer held the spiritual title that had formerly been attributed to him as Emperor. The Western empire became (loosely) Westernised Christendom, with imperial and political authority being assumed by the papacy.

[92] Pelagius advocated liberty as being the vestibule of virtue. He wanted the Roman Church to recognise humanely the personal choice over evil, being available to all men.

worshipping devils rather than God. Chrysostom maintained that God now hated the Jews, who had become a rejected people because 'they' had murdered God's Son. Complete ostracism of the Jews was decreed by the Council, which met at Trullo in 692 AD. A totalitarian political State, administered by the Roman Church was now firmly in place.

The NKJ version of Daniel Ch 7:12 speaks of a '***season and a time***' (450 years) passing before the '***beasts***' lost their dominion. It was not understood that it was not the empire that would be overthrown, but the spiritual authority of the Caesars, who would eventually defer to the episcopacy. The 90 years 'season' started in 61 BC, and ended in 30 AD, the year of Christ's death. Daniel's prophecy of the Pope succeeding the Caesar was fulfilled 450 years *a 'season and a time'* after 61 BC, following the completion of Daniel's ***seventy times seven weeks*** prophecy. A 'time' of 360 years from Christ's death (in 30 AD) ended in 390 AD, which was the year in which ***Pope Siricius*** (384 –399 AD) ***assumed the divine priestly title of Pontifex Maximus, on the overthrowing of the fourth*** '***beast***'. ***The mathematics and the logic are irresistible***! The archetypal 'Vicar of Christ' now held the office and title of Pope, which to my understanding nominates the pope in power at the time of the Great Tribulation, as being the final antichrist. It was the ***office*** of Pope to which the angel Gabriel of Daniel Ch 8 was alluding, not a particular figure. The Pope had emerged as the triumphant horn and undisputed spiritual leader of Christendom. In the introduction to his well illustrated and well researched book entitled ***The Two Babylons***, the Reverend (Rev) Alexander Hislop, writes: ***Finally the Pope himself is truly and properly 'recognised' as the lineal representative of Belshazzar***.

In 410 AD the Goths sacked Rome, and Emperor Honorius fled to the city of Ravenna[93], which became the new headquarters (hq) of the Empire. In 476 AD, the barbarian officer Odoacer overthrew the last of the Western Emperors (although the Eastern Emperor was still received as ruler of Rome), and declared himself as king. In 606 AD, the Pope was acclaimed as 'Universal Bishop' by the ten most powerful and firmly established European kingdoms. All these kingdoms embraced the Catholic form of Christianity, accepting spiritual authority through the coronation of future kings from Rome[94].

[93] Ravenna was the capital city of the Byzantine Government, the main route from Rome to Constantinople passed through the city.

[94] In an age when the divine right of kings was unquestioned, the very fact of receiving a 'divine blessing' from the Pope was tantamount to acquiescing spiritual authority to the Pope.

It made political sense for the kings to pragmatically recognise the Pope as Christ's Vicar on Earth. Every king realised the Catholic Church was a stabilising and uniting influence over a volatile society, for their subjects were warlike people exhibiting barbaric behaviour. Under the temporal and spiritual guidance provided by Romanism, the energy of their citizens could be channelled into peaceful purposes.

In 711 AD Emperor Philippicus, as head of the Eastern (Greek Orthodox) Church, spoke out against the practice of the Western (Latin Catholic) Church of iconoclasm[95] (the worshipping of images of pious Catholics, who had been raised to sainthood by papal decree). His successor Emperor Leo Isaurus in 726 AD, in an effort to force a change in papal policy against this liturgy and on advice from the Greek bishops, promulgated an edict denouncing the edict of Pope Gregory II. He also wrote to Pope Gregory demanding that a General Council of both Eastern and Western bishops be convened to discuss the removal of this objectionable papal instruction. Instead, Pope Gregory convened a Council in Rome of only the Western bishops, which confirmed the institution of the worship of images, and excommunicated Emperor Leo Isaurus! The bishops of the duchies of Rome and Ravenna, Campania and Pentapolis, were appointed by the Greek Orthodox Church, which accepted the Eastern Emperor's spiritual authority. Pope Gregory promulgated the excommunication of the Eastern Emperor's heresy thereby withdrawing his patronage (protection from assassination).

The Exarch Paul who had spiritual oversight of Rome and Ravenna was killed during the ensuing rioting and Eutychius was swiftly appointed by Emperor Leo Isaurus to succeed Paul. Duke Exhilarates of Campania unsuccessfully attempted to enlist a supporting army of allegiance, but the majority of the citizens were loyal to Rome. Pope Gregory, realising he was more popular with the people than were the Greek bishops, raised an army and invaded Campania, whose citizens welcomed the invaders with open arms. Duke Exhilarates and Hadrian, his son, were slain in the ensuing battle for control of the duchy, prior to its becoming part of the papal dominion. The Bishop of Pentapolis offered no resistance and the duchy accepted the spiritual leadership of the papacy. Meanwhile Pope Gregory let it be known that he regarded the Exarch Eutychius as a traitor. Duke Peter of Rome had been blinded in retribution for his disloyalty to the papacy, and Eutychius fled from the

---

[95] The Medieval Church ignored the prohibition of icons (Deuteronomy Ch 27:15), and considered protesters as 'those who ***thought like a Jew***'.

region in fear of his life. The Lombards attacked Ravenna, overthrowing Eastern control of the State and handed the duchy (cleansed of its supposed former 'unrighteous leadership') over to Pope Gregory. It appears to me that Pope Gregory II, by the deposing of his rival, was pointing to his namesake Pope Gregory XIII who changed the ***times and the law*** and persecuted Christ's followers as confirming that this was the man who spoke boastfully (see Daniel Ch 7:8). The passage may equally have been referring to Pope Siricius through his acting in presumption, in posturing as God's representative on earth. This was a mirror image scenario to that earlier enactment of the little 'horn' and the ten 'horns' surrounding the final destruction of Jerusalem. These latter three 'horns' were the three kingdoms that had been under the authority of the Greek Emperor that were uprooted by the little 'horn' (perhaps a play on the story of the four 'horns' being spiritually united and overthrowing truth, Daniel Ch 8:12).

In December 753 AD Pope Stephen II crossed the Alps to meet with Pepin, king of the Franks in order to secure a new Western political alliance that would recognise papal sovereignty. The Pope produced an infamous fraudulent document, dated 30th March 315 AD, known as the 'Donation of Constantine', which purported that Emperor Constantine had bequeathed the western half of the Roman Empire to the papacy, on his conversion to Christianity, supposedly ***instantly*** granting the Bishop of Rome supreme temporal and spiritual lordship of the West. Constantine had relocated the capital and the hq of the Roman Empire to Byzantium, (which he renamed Constantinople), linked the two Empires, apparently gifting control to the Catholic Church. Pepin was persuaded that former Byzantine territories, recently occupied by the Lombards, including the duchy and environs of Rome, legitimately belonged to the papacy. Pepin liberated the territories of central Italy from the Lombards, and handed them to the Pope. The concluding act in freeing the papacy from the Eastern Empire and the Greek Orthodox Church, took place on Christmas Day 800 AD with the Coronation of the Holy Roman Emperor Charlemagne (founder of the Carolingian dynasty and son of King Pepin) by Pope Leo III. Charlemagne drew up a charter acknowledging the papacy as both temporal and spiritual ruler over 'all the regions of Italy and the West' and in so doing initiated the formation and acceptance of the Papal States. The Papacy had found another human saviour to bale them out! Over his 14-year rule, Charlemagne conquered the whole of Western Europe, and forced conversion to Catholicism in the occupied lands. It was not until

1453 AD that the Ottoman Empire overcame Spain, shattering the uneasy concordance of the Western 'Christian' Empire.

The Foundation of the New World Order

During the period 1231-1235 AD Pope Gregory IX initiated what became the 700-year Inquisition (intimidation of Jews[96]). He wrote to the French bishops foreswearing to repress any alternative to the Vatican's version of Jewish admission into Christianity (the rejection of former devotions, of which he named as heresy, witchcraft, alchemy and devil worship). I believe that it was in ***322 AD*** that Emperor Constantine probably first contemplated making Christianity, the State religion with himself at its head. I realise that I am stretching a point to serve my argument (for which I make no apology!), but by taking the ***1,260 days*** of Revelation Ch 11:3, Ch 12:6 from 1582 AD (the date of Pope Gregory XIII authorising the change of calendar dates[97], the ***altering of time*** (***s***)), it can be seen that the year ***322 AD*** emerges.

The Fourth Lateran Council passed anti-Jewish legislation in 1215 AD. It was required that henceforth Jews were to wear a distinctive badge on the back of a coat or a dress, and they were forbidden to appear in public during Holy Week. Unless the Jew renounced his ancestry, he was denied entry into the Church and society, and even then the gesture was only a palliative. In 1252 AD Pope Innocent IV authorised torture as acceptable in extracting confessions from 'deviants'. In 1478 AD, Pope Sixtus IV authorised the Spanish Inquisition, leading to tortuous suffering. By the time the Inquisition ended in 1909, 300,000 Jews had been burned at the stake. Today Christians may think it peculiar that such prejudice was widely accepted, for this philosophy does not recognise the necessity for Christ's death, or the fact that it was the Jewish followers of Christ who formed the first Church, and took the Gospel of grace to the Gentiles. Modern day Western society has rejected the Church

---

[96] The Fourth Council of Toledo (631 AD) decreed that Jews who had accepted baptism, but subsequently had their children circumcised, were to have their children taken from them, to be raised as Christians. The Council of 787 AD required that all Jewish converts must renounce all Jewish customs and ordinances.

[97] On 1st January 45 BC, the inaccurate Julian calendar was introduced to the Roman Empire. Adjustments were authorised in 8 BC by Augustus Caesar but not widely recognised until 8 AD. On becoming emperor, in 312 AD, Constantine imposed his authority to adjudicate in Church disputes. Emperor Constantine initiated and summoned the churches to the Council of Nicaea, held in 325 AD, where the decision was made to recalculate the Julian calendar to correct accumulated errors. In 1582 AD Pope Gregory XIII implemented further changes to the Julian calendar and abolished the extra ten days that had accumulated since the earlier amendments. He renamed the calendar as the Gregorian calendar seemingly confirming the angel's words of Daniel Ch 7:23-25, prophesying of a time when a future empire would govern Israel, whose ruler would impose yet another calendar.

wholesale as being hypocritical, old-fashioned and out of touch with reality. Gentiles have responded to the lessons of the Scriptures and Jewish history, turning to Christ in repentance, despite the vitriolic anti-Semitism of the early church fathers. In Isaiah Ch 42:6-9, God says (repeatedly and forever) to the people of Israel:

> *"I will make you* (the Israelite nation) *to be a covenant for My people and a light to the Gentiles."*

The Vatican maintains that the Catholic Church alone is the one and only true church, which is patently untrue. Since the Council of Trent (1545 – 1563 AD) the Vatican has advocated a 'one-world religion', with the Pope being God's representative on Earth. It is certain that God has not given sole authority for flocks to be shepherded by the Roman Catholic Church. Many Catholics are evangelical and charismatic, but this does not diffuse the fact that the Vatican teaches 'another gospel' (2 Corinthians Ch 11:4, Galatians Ch 1:6-7). All actions, arising out of assumptions and tradition, will be judged before Christ's millennial reign. The papacy promotes:

- The veneration of images
- Atonement for one's own sin in purgatory
- Sacramental cannibalism (transubstantiation)
- Necromancy calling in prayer to evoke the spirits of dead saints
- Belief that Jesus' mother Mary as bearer of God, is co-mediator between God and man
- Salvation is by sacraments that work *ex opera operato* (meaning that the ritual itself is the means of obtaining salvation).

Among the various effects of replacement theology, three are listed here:

1. The Church decreed that the Jews were no longer or ever had been special to God, in establishing its own identity in anti-Judaic terms
2. Christendom's way of interpreting the Old Testament, based on prejudice, has made it very difficult for Jews to take seriously the claim that Jesus of Nazareth is the Messiah of Israel.
3. With the fall of the second temple in AD 70, Westernised Christian writers have written of biblical Israel in the past tense, and of having lost their inheritance.

On the 1st May 1776 AD, Adam Weishaupt, the son of a Bavarian lawyer, who had been educated as a Jesuit, formed a secret society, which he named, '***The Order of the Illuminati***'. He had planned its formation a year earlier in Munich with fellow anarchist, Knights Templar Baron Von Knigge. The express purpose of the organisation was to gain control of world power, through forming and controlling public opinion. The *Illuminati* would amalgamate religions by dissolving all the differences of belief and ritual that kept them apart; it would replace the Pope with an agent of its own into the Chair of Peter. A further project was to bring down the French monarchy, second only in influence to the Papacy, in maintaining coexistence between all the European nations. The Bourbon monarchy was subtly undermined by mastermind Joseph Balsamo (Cagliostro), a well-connected charlatan, who was sponsored by the House of Rothschild; as most anarchists have been, according to Piers Compton in his book, ***The Broken Sword***. The leaders of the Freemasons were persuaded to amalgamate with the Illuminati, forming a central committee based in Rome. The rank and file members were not informed of this executive decision. It is from Rome (the centre of the spider's web) that such motions were approved, and issued to the Masters of the various Lodges, for any appropriate action to be initiated. The result of this liaison was that the two tributaries were fed from the one secretive source. Many powerful leaders of industry, commerce and statehood held joint membership, ensuring the task of assimilation was not difficult. Senior Mafia leaders were welcomed into membership, probably because the executive knew that most members, if dissenting, would be intimidated into conforming. Speculative rumours of a reign of terror against society, introduced through unidentified but supposedly authoritative sources, were spread through the rapidly expanding network of international Lodges. Calamitous events that would destabilise good order, leading to discontent and rioting were ominously prophesied. The objective was to overthrow world leadership, replacing egalitarian order with an oligarchic world order. The Illuminati are credited with promoting the French Revolution (1789-1794 AD), first through Robespierre and later Babeuf. Misinformation was spread in 1786 AD that the Illuminati had been disbanded, but only the most gullible would have believed this lie. The leopard (of State control) had disguised his spots, and re-appeared as Communism. My conclusion is supported by Historian Professor John Robison, who wrote in 1798 AD, that he recognised six propositions in Weishaupt's programme of destruction, which were incorporated by the Communist Party:

1. abolition of all ordered government
2. abolition of inheritance
3. abolition of private property
4. abolition of patriotism
5. abolition of family
6. abolition of religion

In 1847 Carl Marx (1818-1883) founded Communism, which was funded and promoted internationally by the *Illuminati* from New York, where leading Freemason Arthur Pike, the principal leader of the *Illuminati* in America, launched the Communist party's banner. Pike wrote: ***Lucifer*, *god of light and god of gods*, *is struggling for humanity against Adonay, the god of darkness and evil.* He later wrote**: ***The world will soon turn to Freemasons to appoint both its sovereigns and pontiffs*. *We shall control the vacillations of the world rulers and establish equilibrium in the universe*.** In 1887, a well-meaning idealist, whose vision was to reconstruct society, in order to remedy the evils of poverty, founded Fabian Socialism. Once again, the Illuminati laid a false trail, moving into leadership of the Fabian Society. The leadership hid their association from the Society, whilst influencing governmental and European policy, in the name of philanthropy. Amongst those prominent in the formation of the Fabian Society, were Frank Pudmore, a Spiritualist; William Clarke, a Luciferian and senior Freemason; Mrs Charlotte M Wilson, a member of the Anarchist Movement, and Mrs Annie Besant, President of the Theosophical Society.

By far the greatest number of Jews, who had earlier assimilated into the Russian Empire, had been herded together in an area of Poland that later became known as the 'Pale of Settlement'. It was during the following decades, with fear of persecution meted out to the Jews, and hardship as common fare, that a groundswell of opinion amongst the non-religious developed. It became the plea for the leadership to appeal to the Sultan of Turkey for an allotment of land in some part of Palestine as a homeland. These were the nascent stirrings of non-religious Jews to restore their right to rule themselves, in a land of their own. In the early 1800s, devout Jews from Eastern Europe began to receive spiritual stirrings to return to the land of their forefathers. The journey on foot from the Russian steppes was often fraught with uncertainty and danger, mostly the migrants travelled through Babylonia or Syria, perhaps over many months. These early pioneers founded the agricultural settlements in Palestine, thereby providing employment and food for those who later joined the increasing numbers making *aliyah*.

In 1822 God provided an unlikely sponsor in Britain, in the form of the London Jewish Society (LJS), who sent a representative to Palestine. This sponsorship later provided a reason to secure military control of what was to become a vital foothold through Britain's self -appointed assignment[98]. The LJS 1823 opened a mission station at Christ Church in Jerusalem. In 1837 Lord Palmerston the British Foreign Secretary of State, who was related through marriage to the President of the LJS, Anthony Ashley Cooper (who became Lord Shaftsbury), saw the wisdom offered by his Christian relative, to provide full support to any Jews wishing to return to Palestine, a neglected, but important crossroads of international trading. In 1839 the British government established a consulate, which was built on land owned by purchase from Christ Church. The vice-consul's main function was "***to grant protection to the Jews***". In 1840, having overcome the Turkish Army in Palestine, Lord Palmerston, had put in motion an inexorable movement for the restoration of the Jews to their homeland. With the opening of the Suez Canal in 1869, the Middle East assumed greater political significance. France claimed Palestine as part of Syria, whilst the British claimed that as the major shareholder in the Suez Canal[99], Britain was entitled to protect her interests on the east bank of the Canal, in order to protect her self-appointed assignment as protector of the Jews in Palestine.

The Sultan of Turkey was not enamoured by the expansionist policies of his erst-while allies, and because the Ottoman Empire had practically disintegrated[100], he entered into a warm friendship in 1898 with the new Kaiser of Germany, Wilhelm 11, to whom he freely gave acres of land. Although National Socialism (Nazism) had not been widely expressed in Germany; the Muslims and the Aryan Germans were anti-Semitic, anti-democratic, and anti-intellectual, and placed power before justice[101]. It was in 1898 that the Zionist movement was founded, but when the British Government withdrew their protection of the Russian and Polish Jews returning to Palestine, it appeared that

[98] In 1798 Napoleon's army occupied Egypt. He knew that to defeat Britain he would need to cut off the lifeblood from their colonies of goods and manpower. He realised that if a canal was cut between the Mediterranean Sea and the Red Sea, it would provide swift transportation of troops across the world, that could counter the grip of Britain on its large empire. Napoleon was a Protestant who believed the Jews should return to their Promised Land.

[99] As a serviceman in the Middle East in 1956, when Colonel Nasser of Egypt declared the liberation of the Suez Canal, I was privileged to fly (uneasily) over the formidable American Sixth Fleet, as it steamed to Egypt to protect it from the intervention from Britain. The fact of Britain being the major shareholder of the Suez Canal Company (plc) was no longer considered valid in the political climate being experienced.

[100] The Empire had been in decline from the 17th century. The Young Turk Party attempted revival and reform, but the regime crumbled when Turkey supported Germany in the First World War. The sultanate was abolished in 1922.

[101] British politicians and bankers around this time were well aware of the vast oil fields in the Arab lands, and their potential wealth. They adopted a more favourable attitude to the Arab nations; even though it meant treachery towards the Jew.

the dream of a Jewish State would founder. Concurrently the face of Europe was changing: The papacy had controlled and taxed the Papal States of central Italy until 1861 (except during the Napoleonic period), when the Papal States were annexed by the newly founded United Kingdom of Italy[102]. In 1870 the Italian government paid to the Vatican restitution for the loss of revenue; whilst instituting the ***civil*** power of Catholicism over the Vatican City State in Rome. At the end of the 19th century the Southern Slavic States, together with Poland, had provided the buffer zone between European Catholicism and Communist Russia. Czechoslovakia and Yugoslavia were given their independence by the League of Nations. The two Balkan wars of 1912 -1913 greatly enlarged Serbia's territory at the expense of Turkey and Bulgaria. Serbia's designs on Bosnia Herzegovina, supported by Russia, led to friction with Austria, culminating in the outbreak of the First World War.

Overnight spiritual control of these emergent nations was shared between the Greek Orthodox Church and the papacy. Communism began spreading its influence throughout Europe. The Vatican, alarmed by their loss of control, decided to embark on another 'crossing the Alps' adventure. In order to restore their former power the Vatican allied themselves to some extremist groups, including the 'White' Russian intelligentsia who had fled from the Bolshevik Revolution. The Fascist Movement of Italy, and the Nazi Movement of Germany (1921-1945), were both anti-communist, nationalistically authoritarian and Catholic. Both Movements would have had difficulty in obtaining power without the support of the Vatican, who in return would be re-established as the head of the only true Church. In order to seal the concordat of the Lateran Treaty of 1929, it became necessary for the Pope to forbid all Catholics from participation in national party politics. As most Italian politicians opposed Mussolini, the Pope's strong statements of support for General Benito Mussolini, practically handed the government of Italy over to the fascist dictator. Pope Pius X1, in an address to the Roman Cardinals hailed Mussolini as '***an eminent statesman appointed by divine providence***'. Once more the anti-Semitic Vicar of Christ relied for redemption upon a human saviour in the mode of the Caesars, *Il Duce* Benito Mussolini, Catholic Croatian Ante Pavelic, an international terrorist, who later was elevated to Cardinal, was appointed to lead what became the

[102] The Italian national unity and independence movement was formed in 1815. The Risorgimento instituted the Italian Kingdom in 1861. The unification was completed with the addition of Venetia in 1866, and the annexation of the Papal States in 1870.

infamous Uštaše[103] guerrilla forces. Pavelic's partner in crime was Archbishop Aloysius Stepinac[104] of Croatia; between them they masterminded numerous assassinations, including members of the nobility and government officials who opposed the formation of an independent Catholic Croatia. The concordat was extended in 1933 to include Adolph Hitler's ***Third Reich***, most of whose supporters were German Catholics. The united objective of the conspirators was to 'liberate' the region, bounded by the Adriatic, Aegean, Baltic, Black and Ionian Seas, as a theoretic buffer zone between the Communist East and the Catholic West. Following the declaration of war, Hitler's armies marched through Yugoslavia and into the Croatian capital of Zagreb, declaring Croatia to be an independent nation. The one million Muslims of Serbia colluded with the Nazi regime[105], in their efforts to exterminate the Jew. In the process, 750,000 Greek Orthodox Serbs out of 900,000 living in Croatia were imprisoned, tortured into becoming Catholics, or exterminated, choosing to die rather than recant of their faith. Pavelic was appointed head of the puppet regime, and with bloodthirsty ferocity, liquidated, or transported to the Nazi death-camps, 94% of the 50,000 Jews resident in Croatia, and all Romany living in the land. The evil spirit behind *Pontifex Maximus* was aroused yet again!

Dave Hunt has written a book ***A Woman Rides the Beast***, which details the involvement of the Vatican, USA and Britain in the abandonment of the European Jew to the forces of evil. David Yallop has written ***In God's Name***, of a high level of corruption and intrigue, currently practised or condoned by the top echelons of the Catholic Church. These books reveal the sickening hypocrisy practised by those entrusted with the task of advancing human rights. Yallop maintains that the P2 Masonic Lodge established in the Vatican City State, together with the other Lodges throughout Italy, have

---

[103] Croatian Catholic Pavelic formed the Uštaše in Italy in 1929, under the patronage of the Vatican. Pavelic had been sentenced to death in absentia by the Yugoslavian government. He was hidden in the Vatican, which after the war arranged his passage to Argentina.

[104] After the war Stepinac was imprisoned for war crimes, but Pope Pius X11 successfully engineered his release. Stepinac was later elevated to Cardinal. As a Cardinal in his German homeland before the war, Eugenio Pacelli was a close confidant of Hitler. Pacelli was well aware of the slaughter of the Jews, and the Vatican's insistence that the Cardinal, who became Pope Pius XII (1939-1958), should be beatified as a saint is being strongly resisted. John Cornwell's book, '***Hitler's Pope***. ***The Secret History of Pius XII***', enlarges on my brief outline.

[105] Perhaps the nursed hatred of the Serbians, violently expressed during the ethnic cleansing of Bosnia-Herzegovina in the 1990's can be understood, particularly in view of the support given to the Croatians by the EC, the UN and NATO (see Chapter 6).

among their membership more than 100 prelates, some of whom are Cardinals. In Vatican Law, it is written that anyone found to be a Freemason should be excommunicated, but the Vatican has ignored this law.

The atrocities perpetrated by Hitler's Third Reich against the millions of European Jews, by the confiscation of their jobs, homes and valuables before the declaration of the Second World War is well documented. Millions of lives would have been spared without these unholy conspiratorial liaisons, but I believe that God allowed the outcome to fulfil His purposes. Although there was apparently no collusion at the 1938 Evian Conference (masterminded by President Franklin Roosevelt), there was no willingness to solve the emigration difficulties of would-be Jewish migrants from Germany by the nations represented. Hitler's advisors, who had attended the conference, reported that no ***nation has any interest in the welfare of the Jews***. The villainy of the Holocaust was diabolical and unimaginable; it included the extraction of gold fillings from the teeth of those who were slaughtered in their thousands. Their progenies have been denied access to the bank deposits of the previous generation.

Uri Lubrini, an Israeli government official, is the son of a Russian immigrant, whose family testimony is truly supernatural. His story is similar to many other testimonies to God having guided families back to Israel. Uri's grandmother lived with her husband, daughter and two sons on the border between Poland and Russia. In 1902 unaccountably she decided to take her two sons aged 11 and 9 years to Jaffa in Palestine, when, having paid for one year's accommodation and schooling for them, she returned to her homeland, never to hear from her children again. Uri's father met and married his wife in Vienna, where he qualified as a doctor, before making *aliyah* to Israel in 1924. He was filled with a driving desire to evacuate all of his 310 relatives to Israel, which he accomplished before the commencement of the Second World War.

During 1911, in Warsaw, Messianic Jews were permitted to worship Jesus Christ in Hebrew (at separate services) in an Anglican church[106] (effectively allowing the church to 'double' as a Jewish 'synagogue'). In 1923 the Bishop of Stepney advocated that Christian synagogues should be purpose-built in Britain, and incumbent leadership of Anglican churches should be encouraged to emulate the Warsaw experience. In 1929, an article was published in ***The Times***

[106] This is not a new idea, from Acts Ch 6:9 we are informed that the Synagogue of the Freedmen were separate from the traditional Jewish congregation of followers of 'the way'.

newspaper, which stated that 15,000 Messianic Jews living in east Poland had formed themselves into a sect, and were determined to build their own church, in which to worship Jesus of Nazareth, to baptise their members, and to study the New Testament. In March 1937, an article published in '**Immanuel's Witness**' (a publication by the Barbican Mission), reported that 200 Jewish families, anxious to worship in Hebrew together independent of Gentile influence, approached the Eastern Orthodox patriarch requesting to be baptised into Christ. They yearned to build their own church, and be recognised as part of the one body of Christ, and not as some new sect. The article also reported that 97,000 Hungarian Jews had recently been absorbed into the Catholic Church. This number of new converts was more than thirty times the number that turned to Christ at the first Pentecost!

The rabbis of Poland had taught that there would be no restoration to the Promised Land until their Messiah came, at which time they would be redeemed (a philosophy first expounded by the renowned 12th century theologian rabbi Maimonides). This Judaic group of religious Jews became known as the 'ultra-Orthodox'. They identified the passion of the patriotic zealots of a bygone age by disparagingly naming the agitators for return to the Promised Land as 'Zionists'. Prior to the Holocaust, the ultra-Orthodox rabbis were thought by their followers to be in the line of succession to the prophets, and their dictates of equal worth. These sages had quieted the fears of their flocks concerning Hitler's malevolent speeches. These rabbis taught that both the Jewish believers in Jesus and the Zionists were children of the devil, and that fleeing an imaginary Holocaust, by facing an uncertain and ungodly existence in Palestine or the USA was not an alternative to remaining in fellowship within their synagogues. However, when Hitler's speeches became a reality, many rabbis did flee without informing their flocks, which decade's later still caused pain.

As a Premillennialist I believe that the Second Coming will follow the Great Tribulation, and then a millennial reign will follow ***before*** the judgement of all people. The papacy promoted the postmillennial[107] theology of Bishop Augustine, who taught of a symbolic reign of 1000 years of the king's consort (the Church), ***until*** Christ's Second Coming. However when 1000 AD passed without the Lord returning, the Roman Church then taught the ***totally unscriptural*** theology that the millennial reign of the Church was of indeterminate duration,

[107] The term **millenarianism** is used as a synonym of ***premillennialism***, whereas a similar term '**millennialism**' is a synonym of ***postmillennialism***.

lasting until the world becomes fully Christianised, when Jesus will be invited to return, after which time will come the judgement. Many Protestant eschatologists believe that the Catholic theology on this issue has merit, that Christ will not return until the world has been fully evangelised. Revelation Ch 14:6-11 states that an angel, flying in 'mid-air' will proclaim the eternal Gospel of grace to both the ***living and the dead*** of every nation, during the hour of God's judgement. Two other angels, one reporting mystery Babylon's demise, the other warning his listeners not to accept the '***mark of the beast***' will follow. Every listener will hear the message in his or her native tongue.

I find it difficult to believe that since the innovation of radio satellites, that the gospel has not been heard by the ***living*** in the native tongue by every tribe, but of course even this sophisticated method of communication cannot reach those who have ***died*** in the womb, or in infancy, or who died before they could reason intelligently for themselves, prior to satellite communication. We are surely reading of a ***supernaturally delivered*** message. It is possible that John envisaged a satellite dish, exploded into the ionosphere (the mid-heaven), for radio and camera waves bounce around the circumference of the world. I believe that the spiritual kingdom of God descended to earth at the ascension of Christ Jesus, and that His subjects have lived in Christendom, since their declaration of reconciliation to Christ. It is reported that at the end of the 20th century, half of the world's population had not heard the Gospel! None of us have the capability to continue the Great Commission ***outside*** of our own lifetime, other than through our writings or through those believers we may have led to Christ, who themselves lead others to Christ after our death. No proclamation can reach the ears of previous generations other than supernaturally, as happened when Jesus Himself entered Sheol[108], and spoke to the inhabitants of God's redemption offered through Christ's personal sacrifice (1 Peter Ch 3:19). I am also hoping that every foetus that died in the womb, and every person who denied Christ in his or her lifetime for whatever reason will be granted a

[108] The underworld abode of the dead.

second chance of 'new birth' lived solely under Christ's reign[109]. This extra lifetime will be a form of 'custodial sentence'. God says in Acts Ch 17:26, that He knows of every circumstance of our birth.

The elect of the first resurrection, in their imperishable bodies, will reign with Christ throughout the millennium (Revelation Ch 5:10, Ch 20:4). I do believe that although there will be many changes following the Second Coming, Church life, like community life, will continue. Hebrew Temple worship will be reintroduced, but the anathema of sacrifice perpetrated through transubstantiation will be stopped. Initially there will be little difference in the unbeliever's way of life, those of other faiths will still continue to live their 70-year life expectancy, as they have since the Flood.

Pretribulationists believe that the Holy Spirit will be removed at the same time as the Rapture of the Church takes place. This will be prior to the Great Tribulation, and will leave only non-believing Gentiles and all Jews remaining on Earth; a very comfortable but unscriptural scenario[110]! They support their argument from the passage in 2 Thessalonians Ch 2:6-12, which they take to mean that I believe that the Holy Spirit will remove that thin veneer of civilised and compassionate behaviour, from those who regard themselves Christians, but are not 'born again' of the Holy Spirit. A compilation of Matthew Ch 10: 21 and Ch 24:10-13 says:

---

[109] I am praying for a 'second chance' on behalf of my unsaved loved ones and friends, and for non-believers and worshippers of other gods, from every generation, to experience Christ's kingdom on Earth for themselves. The reason for my hope is contained in John Ch 20:20-29, where the words of Jesus may have implied that those who have believed without seeing and touching Him are to be better blessed than those who do not have sufficient faith to believe in His resurrection as the 'first-fruit' and of His followers in the Rapture as the completion of the resurrection. I am reading (and hoping) that behind the words of Jesus is an implication that there will be a second opportunity to turn to Christ. I have shared my predictions of Christ's next appearance on Earth with a few non-believing friends, whose main concern is that they are given a 'normal' life expectancy and that their death will not be hastened by the Second Coming. The certainty of impending judgement after death, lasting throughout eternity, does not appear to concern them. Extraordinarily my friends have not been interested in changing their lifestyle by repentance. Can it be that Satan has persuaded the 80% mass of humanity (from the final and previous generations), who will not find salvation, that 70 years of earthly life, lived out in the manner acceptable to oneself, is more to be desired than a life submitted to God that will endure forever? If God chose to, He could snatch from Satan's grasp all those who have rejected His Son's salvation, but God has given mankind ***free will*** to choose how one leads one's life.

[110] The ***Rapture*** is the catching away in the air of the elect (the redeemed) mostly at the Second Coming of Christ. The original Greek word for Rapture is '***harpazo'***, which means 'snatched up'. On translation into Latin the word was translated rapturos, which means 'an ecstatic catching away'. The elect, who are saved from eternal damnation, are those disciples who believe Jesus Christ is the Messiah (***Yeshua HaMashiach***).

"In the last days, many will turn from their faith, hating and betraying even members of their own family." (paraphrased)

God will consign to eternal suffering those with sinful minds, who short-sightedly choose to betray even their loved ones to prolong a very short lifespan on Earth. The thin veneer of civilisation, like beauty, is only skin deep; the blood that courses through the veins of an unregenerate heart that beats in a synagogue of Satan (a hypocritical heart), is not sanctified by the Spirit of God. Nominal Christians are familiar with the ministry ***of*** Jesus, but they do not accept or ***obey*** Him, they are not 'born again' by the spirit of God. Jesus will not withdraw His Holy Spirit at any time prior to the Second Coming, for, if He did, how could the uncountable multitudes find Christ for themselves (which is what is prophesied to happen in Revelation Ch 7:14)? In Hebrews Ch 13:5 Jesus said:

"Never will I leave you or forsake you."

I have found that the believer knows the 'why' for existence and is able to accept without fear the trials and tribulations of life[111]. Mid-tribulationists believe the 'Rapture' will carry all Christians away from Earth before the '***Day of the Lord's wrath***'. Post-tribulationists believe that Gentile believers will experience Christ's Second Coming in the air, prior to being 'Raptured'. Many of my non-redeemed friends have wanted to know how my faith gave me the confidence in my salvation and the certainty that I had found the meaning of my life, and how the obvious changes in my character had arisen.

The Year of The Lord's Return

The 'Millerites', were followers of a 19th century American Baptist preacher, William Miller who calculated that the Second Coming would occur in 1844. Miller believed that the cleansing of the sanctuary foretold in Daniel Ch 8:14, represented the purification of the planet Earth by fire, ***prior to the millennial reign of Christ***. He correctly reasoned from Daniel Ch 9:24, that the prophecy of 70 weeks of seven years was a continuous period concerning only the Jews. He concluded from Ezra Ch 7:12-26 that the kingly decree allowing the Jews to rebuild the city walls of Jerusalem was issued by Artaxerxes Longimanus, during the seventh year of his reign in 457 BC. By adding

---

[111] Shortly after becoming born again, feeling not only unworthy, but wretched and condemned, I beseeched the Lord for some weeks, for confidence over my personal salvation. I received a picture of my bookshelf, full of study books of theology. Suddenly some books flew off the shelves with the leaves acting as wings, descending and hovering in front of my eyes. The open page of one book, which I was told was the Book of Life, had highlighted my personal details. The columns of entries written on either side of my details were blurred; I was not granted the opportunity to read any other names.

on 69 weeks of 7 years (69 x 7 = 483 years after 457 BC) a date of 27 AD is arrived at. Miller's conclusion was that the last week of seven years (completing the 70 weeks of years) were a combination of 3½ years of Christ's ministry to the Jews, and 3½ years of His disciple's ministry to fellow Jews, ending with the stoning of Stephen in 34 AD (27 AD plus seven years = 34 AD). The 490 years that related to the Jews when deducted from the 2,300 years of Daniel meant (according to Miller) that 1,810 days of years remained for the Gentiles to receive Christ (that is 34 AD plus 1,810 years=1844 AD). Miller's deductions were widely accepted when on 13th November 1833 a large meteoric shower of stars cascaded over the USA, which Miller claimed was in fulfilment of Revelation Ch 6:13:

> *"The stars of heaven fell to the earth as a fig tree drops its late figs."*

A New York newspaper featured Miller's conjecture and wrote on the following day the 14th November, that Jesus had prophesied this last sign concerning His return 1,800 years earlier in Matthew Ch 24:32-33:

> *"Learn from the fig tree, know that My return is near."*

As 1844 approached, many thousands of Gentiles throughout the world became members of the Church through Miller's hypothesis. When 1844 passed without the Lord returning, 50,000 souls in the USA, who had received Christ through Miller's teaching, stopped attending church. Many who accepted that Miller's interpretation had been broadly correct, formed themselves into a denomination, which became the Seventh Day Adventists (SDAs). The leadership of the newly formed SDA's, pragmatically announced that the 1844 date was the occasion that Jesus ***entered*** the heavenly tabernacle to ***prepare*** for His Second Coming (at some unspecified time in the future). They maintained that God was giving just one last warning to repent or suffer His ***non-avoidable judgement*** for rebellion against His sovereign decrees. Miller, like many of today's leaders, made no allowance that the nation of Israel would be restored to the homeland ***promised by God to the Jewish race***. Amos Ch 9:15 states:

> *I will plant Israel in their own land, never again to be uprooted from the land I have given them.*

Other prophets record similar words[112]. I cannot accept the view, taken by some scholars, that Israel must once more be exiled from their homeland.

---

[112] A Jewish restoration is prophesied in Isaiah Ch 11:11, Ch 49:19-23, Ch 60:15-16, Ezekiel Ch 34:28, Joel Ch 3:1-2, Zechariah Ch 14:16.

If the cascade of meteorites did signify that Christ was shortly to return as the SDA's claimed, then it is not so remarkable that a period of 153 years between 1844 (Miller's year of the Second Coming), and the commencement of the year of restoration to the land in 1948 (the jubilee, which was completed on the 30th of September 1998[113]), was signposted. The number of years between the two dates reflects the full draught of 153 fish, miraculously caught at Christ's beach barbecue (John Ch 21:11). Additionally, 17 (the number for ***perfection*** or ***spiritual order***) multiplied by 9 (the number representing ***finality*** or ***judgement***) amounts to 153. The 153 years are separated into shorter, but significant, periods of years (70+25+9+49 = 153 years). Seventy years following Miller's projected year of the Second Coming, Britain declared war on Germany, as happened again in 1939 (that was with 25 (5^2) years intervening). The European Jews were officially allowed to return to Israel as a nation in 1948, nine (3^2) years after the commencement of the Second World War.

Mathematical Significance of the Bible Codes

Devotees of theomatics[114] (numerics or numerology) believe that this science is a gift from God, specifically revealed to the final generation in which Christ will return. Del Washburn with the co-operation of Jerry Lucas has expanded upon Ivan Panin's system of numerics, which is detailed in their book entitled ***Theomatics***, where the mathematical designs used by God are analysed and decoded. By counting the repetitions between repeated letters, it is possible to decode God's hidden messages.

The numeric symbol representing ***resurrection*** is '8', and the number 888 (which may be divided into 8 x 3 x 37) enumerates the name of the coming king. Three represents the ***Trinity***, and 37 for the ***Very Word of God*** and is the sum total of the value of the Greek letters that spell the name Jesus. In the Greek alphabet Jesus is spelled *IESOUS*. I=10, E=8, S=200, O=70, U=400 and S=200 (IESOUS) = 888. On the numerical value of all the letters used in the alphabet being added together they amount to 1,369 (37^2). This is very

[113] It must be remembered that this significant 50-year period, did not coincide with the sacred 50-year jubilee recognised as being completed in September 2001. But May the 14th 1948 is an important pointer, in that the date coincided with the anniversary of Jesus' birth.

[114] Theomatics depend upon ***factoring***, which is a numbering system all mankind uses in every day life, to form linkages of time, events or themes (memorabilia). In order to complete a game of darts, where a score of say 133 is required; the thrower would calculate that (using all three darts) in order to win the match finishing with a double 19, he must score a multiple of 7 x 19. God has used the same method of deduction, but in a much more complicated coded system.

much God's design, being present in every page of both the Old and New Testament, supporting the belief that God indeed inspired the authors of the Bible to record His every word in strict sequence, syllable by syllable. To my simplistic understanding God has chosen to keep hidden until the end times many of the biblical truths that have no corroborative evidence of support outside of Scripture.

It has long been a view of mathematicians that the Bible had a hidden code[115] woven throughout its fabric. On the 4th August 1985, the ***Mail on Sunday,*** (a British newspaper), reported that a rabbi, David Ordman, with the help of 19 other rabbis, using the American Prime mainframe computer at a University in Jerusalem, programmed in the entire 125,000 words comprising of 304,805 letters of the *Torah*, placed in one continuous string. The object was to search for a system of equidistant letter sequences (EDLS), a sophisticated system of skip coding that might be hidden within the words. The research proved conclusively that there was a hidden code contained in the text. Taking the first Hebrew letter '*T*' in the first line of Genesis, and following it with every 49th letter, the word *Torah* emerges. The same pattern occurs in the Book of Exodus, whilst in the Book of Numbers and Deuteronomy the word *Torah* occurs in the same fashion at every 48 letters, but written in reverse[116]. The EDLS codes of letters are not necessarily consistent, and in some cases have apparently been written in reverse or even as an acrostic. That the number sequence is not identical, might suggest that a human originator designed this dysfunctional repetition.

Further research into decoding God's hidden code has been undertaken by American Messianic leader, Yacov Rambsel, who has written two intriguing books entitled ***His Name is Jesus-The Mysterious Yeshua Codes***, and ***Yeshua-The Name of Jesus Revealed in the Old Testament*** in which he has discovered Christ's signature encoded throughout every prophecy in the Old Testament.

---

115 I was thrilled to read in ***The Daily Mail*** of the 28th May 1997 that computer researcher and mathematician, Dr Eliyahu Rip also working from Jerusalem but using a more sophisticated computer, had discovered the existence of at least one hidden system of skip coding contained in the Bible. Michael Drosnin, the author of the book, entitled ***The Bible Code,*** explains that the results of dividing all 304,805 letters into a two-dimensional array of letters with rows of equal lengths has verified the dates and locations of birth of 34 secular Jews born between the 9th and 18th century AD, whose names were taken from ***The Encyclopaedia of Great Men in Israel*** and to find that their names, births and localities of their birth were all pre-ordained and written into the Scriptures.

116 An 18th century sage, affectionately known as the *'Gaon* (Genius) *of Vilna'*, was quoted as saying: "***The rule is that all that was, is, and will be, unto the end of time and is included in the Torah, from the first word to the last.***"

Jesus said that those Jews who did not believe in the Law and the prophets would not be convinced by anyone who rose from the dead. Of course on Christ's feet descending on the Mount of Olives, the Jews (of every generation?) will witness the event and repent (Zechariah Ch 12:12) and their punishment will have been fulfilled. Daniel Ch 12:4 makes it clear that in the last days the Scriptures will be fully revealed (understood?), by both Jew and Gentile. I am sure there is yet more to discover in the fruitful field of investigation of biblical decoding; for example a date of Damascus becoming a ruinous heap of rubble (as prophesied in Isaiah Ch 17:1), or the date of the ten nations of Psalm 83 invading Israel. During the Iraqi/Kuwait War, Mossad and the IDF determined, by using the EDLS system, that an Iraqi Scud missile attack was likely to occur on one of three dates, one of which was Friday January the 18th 1991, which proved to be the actual date of the first Scud attack. It is possible that there may be other yet undetected codes hidden in these supernatural Scriptures, written under the guidance of a supernatural God, that speaks of all major events in every nation and of every generation throughout history; the total number of EDLS codes computed have just not been deciphered as yet. The particular encoding method employed so far emerges only where the date of an event or a person's name is fully known, and is the result of one of a series of options selected by divine providence. I believe that if a researcher received a supernatural revelation of what he was looking for, he would interpret successfully any date from a sign that God revealed to him. Unexpected relationships between ***chance, human choice*** and ***predestination*** (which I believe is also true of ***prophetic insight)*** exist within the Bible codes, as was reported in the book ***The Truth Behind the Bible Codes*** by Dr Jeffrey Satinover.

The author Edward Chumney points out in his book ***The Seven Festivals of the Messiah*** that the third of the four annual agricultural feasts, the 'wave' offering[117] (the festival celebrating the wheat harvest to be stored into barns to provide food for the coming Winter), following the death of Christ, was ***fulfilled*** with the arrival of the Holy Spirit at *Shavuot*, when Jesus became the ***first fruit*** of the resurrection. The wheat harvest, is an illusion to the final '***ingathering of souls***' into God's barn, more familiarly known as the Rapture).

[117] The 'wave offering' featured a single sheaf of the first fruits from the current harvest (representing Jesus). A priest blessed the offering on the day following the Sabbath (Leviticus Ch 23:9-14). The annual festivals are a prophetic illustration, foreshadowing the purposes of God for His people, first the Jew through the barley planting and harvesting and then the Gentiles through the Summer harvesting of the wheat, and the final Summer harvesting, will mark the ***fulfilment*** of the Feasts.

The other festivals are ceremonial and all occur during the Hebrew month of *Tishrei* (when they occur varies between September/October). *Rosh Hashana* is not only a ceremonial occasion, it is a biblical feast day in that this day also celebrates the first day of Creation, and looks forward to the completion of that Creation. *Rosh Hashana* is celebrated over a two-day period, and is preceded by the 30th day of *Elul*; the only day that the *Shofar* is not blown during the 40 holy days of this special season known as *Teshuvah* (repentance and return to God). Historically the reason given for the trumpets being silent on this day is because the day is hidden from Satan, who is caught 'off guard' by the absence of any warning. Throughout the world there are 24 x 2-hourly time zones, the full moon takes a two-day period to complete its cycle. For this reason this two-day celebration of *Rosh Hashana* is often called the '***long day***' or the '***hidden day***'.

God draws mankind's attention to His determining of events, by causing events to be repeated on anniversary dates. The 9th of *Av* is one such date, and on the anniversary of that date in other years, other significant events occurred:

- The worship of the golden calf in 1461 BC (prior to the tablets containing the ten words being broken)
- The destruction of Solomon's temple in 586 BC
- The destruction of Herod's temple in 70 AD
- The destruction of Simeon Bar Cochba's army, and final deportation of the Jews from Israel in 135 AD
- The issue of the decree by King Edward 11 banishing all Jews from England, by the 1st of November 1290 AD
- The expulsion of all Jews from Spain decreed in 1492 AD.

Another set of anniversary dates fall on the 25th day of the ninth month (*Chislev*)

- The foundation stone of Zerubbabel's temple laid in 520 BC (Haggai Ch 2:18-19)
- The cleansing of the temple on the third anniversary of its desecration by Antiochus Epiphanes in 165 BC on the Jewish Feast of *Hanukkah* [118](aka Festival of Lights or Feast of Dedication) introduced by Yehuda ben Matthias (Judah the Maccabean, 1 Maccabees Ch 4:59)

---

118 *Hanukkah* occurs close to the winter solstice, when daylight hours are at their least and the waning moon is practically invisible (the shortest day and the darkest night).

- The capturing of Jerusalem by General Allenby from the army of Turkey in 1917.

The attention to anniversary dates of feast days being repeated is evident from the earliest books of the *Tanach* (the Old Testament). The 10th and the 14th day of *Nisan* are two such dates:

- The Passover lamb was selected on the 10th day of *Nisan* (Exodus Ch 12:3, Passover night, Exodus Ch 12:6)
- The Israelites crossed the Jordan River and entered Canaan on the 10th day of *Nisan* when all males were circumcised (Joshua Ch 5:2)
- The Passover lamb was slain on Passover night, celebrated four days later (on the 14th day of *Nisan*, Joshua Ch 5:10)
- Israel (Jacob) had entered Egypt 430 years earlier on 14th of *Nisan* (Exodus Ch 12:41)
- Hebrew sages believe that Abraham entered Egypt on 14th of *Nisan* (Genesis Ch 12:10)

The evidence of God's timing of events is overwhelming.

Chapter 4

A PENNY FOR YOUR THOUGHTS

In Chapter 1, I examined explanations of Creation history and the ultimate destruction of planet Earth. In Chapter 2, I wrote of Israelite history and the place of the Jewish race in God's heart in her redemption. In Chapter 3, I explored and summarised the history of the Church, and its fulfilment as the 'bride of Christ'. In this Chapter, my concern is to convince the reader that God is not allowing further time than He has decreed to usher in His kingdom, and that this current generation are to be witnesses to the '***Day of the Lord***'[119].

The Hole in the Ozone Layer

Dr Dale H Peterson of the Oklahoma School of Medicine has found that more than 60 diseases may be caused or aggravated by the constant intrusion of harmful electro-magnetism and chemical combinations of radiation since the removal of the protective ice-canopy. Dr Peterson has researched the effects of atmospheric gases penetrating the Earth's atmosphere when combined with ultraviolet radiation, which is increasing year on year, as the suspended molecules of water in the atmosphere are incinerated by the intense direct rays of the sun, causing the ozone layer to evaporate to such an extent that holes (perforations) are very visible to modern scientific equipment. Global warming and ozone depletion are accumulative and may be exacerbated by industrial pollution, which has mushroomed since the 19th century. Throughout the world the acreage of burning jungles and forests in 1997 was double that of 1996. The measured sulphuric contamination was equivalent to the pollution arising from industrialisation by the **whole of Europe** in that same year. The effect of industrial pollution and deforestation over the whole Earth is the result of man's greedy exploitation of resources. Toxic wastes may prove to be the contents of the second bowl of wrath suffocating all life in the sea (Revelation Ch 16:3), whilst in Revelation Ch 16:8 we read of men being scorched by the sun's great heat, on the fourth angel pouring the contents from his bowl[120]. These two events will be fulfilled before the Second Coming, probably as part of the Great Tribulation. I will paraphrase selected verses from Jeremiah Ch's 2-5:

---

[119] Joel Ch 2:31 speaks of the signs appearing ***before*** the 'Day of the Lord', but Obadiah verse 15, Zephaniah Ch1:14, Zechariah Ch 14 1 and Malachi Ch 4:5 point to ***that day*** finally manifesting.

[120] Jesus warned his disciples in Luke Ch 21:11, 25-26 of violent extra terrestrial activity, which will occur during the Great Tribulation.

"The senseless foolish people are not ignorant of My authority because they have not been properly taught of My sovereignty, but because they prefer to pretend I don't exist. The priests and rulers have also defied My expressed will. My people will be as disappointed with the outcome of promises of prosperity that the gods of the Gentiles worship. Faithless Israel was more righteous than unfaithful Judah. If the nations had only sought to be obedient to My righteous laws instead of following the stubbornness of their evil practises, I would have relented. The sky grows dark and the earth is stained with blood. I curse the mountains and the hills and they are quaking and shaking (famine, pestilence, floods, droughts and earthquakes etc, fruitful plains become wastelands and former towns and cities lie deserted and in ruins). I have pleaded in vain so many times for My people to repent of their ways, and return to Me. In My mercy I have been very patient, but I will no longer tolerate unrighteous behaviour. I have spoken and will not relent."

During 1987 I repeatedly received a complimentary vision to that of Jeremiah:

> The appearance, as an incandescently glowing golden ball of fire, of the rising sun on the horizon, that could only be seen clearly through the early morning mist by shielding my eyes from the glare. My eyes drank in the barren, apparently lifeless sand. On closer inspection I could see a reed and a ground-hugging open flower, some small creeping insects, and the sand rippling away into the distance. The height from which I observed the scene gave me the impression that I was patrolling the outer walls of a city and because of the time of the day being experienced, I knew myself to be a night duty watchman. A slight wind moved the sand and the reed continuously, almost imperceptibly.

My plea for revelatory discernment was not answered until 1988. An unseen angel reminded me that the television (tv) viewing public had earlier that week been watching on their screens, an attempt by the Russian and American seamen to rescue three drowning whales trapped in the pack ice of the Arctic Circle. I was told that the whales had chosen to separate from a large school. This to me, was likened to the reluctant Christians who choose not to share responsibility wholeheartedly with their fellowship, because of the commitment to live and love and work within the body of believers, which they consider too demanding of their time. The uncommitted Christian drifted away from church life, analogous to the whales in their loneliness, searching for a deeper meaning to their lives, in unfamiliar waters (circumstances), but resulting in certain death. The whales had swum to this area to escape the contamination (evil) that pollutes every ocean with toxic chemicals.

Shortly after receiving this revelation I tuned in to a tv programme in which the narrator was reporting that owing to all of the pollutants present in the atmosphere, a hole had appeared in the ozone layer over Iceland and was enlarging, causing a greenhouse effect by warming up the cosmos. It had been detected that pollution in Antarctica had entered the food chain through mammals (seals) that had developed irreversible liver disease, and were passing the disease to their suckling pups. The disease had become endemic and was transferable to the Eskimos who relied on seal meat as their staple diet. Autopsies confirmed that some Eskimos had died of liver poisoning. A picture was then flashed on to the screen of a member of the British Scientific Expedition, who was floating a measuring balloon into the atmosphere to determine how large the hole was. It was at this point that my blood ran cold. A shot was panned of the surrounding countryside and there was that same orange ball of sun rising above the horizon that I had so often seen in visions of the desert, when I had been a watchman on the walls of a fortressed city. The difference in the two pictures was that now I was looking at snow and not sand, with no apparent sign of life in this wilderness. That night I received a further confirming revelation.

A great number of tanks were entering Earth's atmosphere through holes in the ozone layer. The gun turrets of the tanks were swinging around freely and firing shells indiscriminately. Some tanks developed several barrels and in unison shelled the terrain in many directions. Some of these tanks then turned upside down, their gun barrels became flexible metal legs allowing the tanks to travel menacingly and easily over the terrain like giant spiders with a deadly and unstoppable purpose. This vision was accompanied by the following prophecy:

> ***"Oh you foolish people! How much destruction did you cause in your haste for knowledge and profit? Your pesticides and pollutants stain the earth and discolour the deepest sea. Even the firmament is tainted by your efforts to acquire greater wealth. Nations great and small make war on each other, leading to the richer nations growing richer at the expense of the poorer nations. Each nation is living in a state of hostility and mistrust. Each nation is fearful of its neighbour's power; each one***

> ***enters into alliances with others and later break their treaties. The captors bind the captive nations in slavery, poverty and ignorance, by charging their prey a high interest rate for goods and services rendered. You have not paid the right amount for what you have taken from these poorer nations but in your haste for wealth you have cloaked your greed by calling it assistance or relief aid. Oh child, do you not see what a monster you have created? You hoped your problems had been exported, but now you see that your exploitation of others has returned to your own lands, even to your own homes. A weapon you once controlled has been turned against you. Says the Lord your God."***

An Arabian Nights Dream

Following Iraq's invasion of Kuwait, I received a vision that led me to prophesy that once all peaceful avenues had been explored, there would be a short but bloody war in which the UN Forces (the Allies, from 28 member nations) would force an Iraqi withdrawal from Kuwait:

> I was transported over a huge military camp in the desert into a war planning and strategy bunker. Military men, dressed in camouflaged battledress, were examining a map of the Middle East. It was as if I was invisible, or a fly on the wall, for no one was aware of my presence. One of the officers was illustrating the current deployment of troops, weaponry and the terrain of the land, with a pointer to explain the strategy decided upon by High Command. The pointer accidentally struck and overturned an opened bottle of red ink, the contents of which spread across the map indicating to me that there would be much bloodshed in the forthcoming battle areas.

I was told that in the same way that errors of military judgement would reveal many mistakes surrounding political manoeuvrings, a news-hungry media would expose other political indiscretions of the subversive undercover work of the Western nation's diplomatic corps. Also politicians and statesmen from around the world, not directly involved in the relief of Kuwait, would demand a return to the *status quo,* with an early end to what was seen as imperialist aggression. There was to be no resolve to the short and sharp shooting war that later took place, which would paper over cracks but solve nothing.

Following an Arab League meeting some two years before the invasion of Kuwait, Saddam invited President Hosni Mubarak of Egypt to be part of a small band of conspirators in a plot to overthrow the sheikhdoms of Saudi Arabia, Kuwait, Bahrain and the United Arab

Emirates. Jordan was to be given the western provinces together with Mecca and Medina, whilst Yemen would also receive two provinces as plunder. Mubarak was promised all of the oil that Egypt would ever need, in return for his complicity. Mubarak declined Saddam's overtures owing to Egypt's dependence on American aid and supplied the Central Intelligence Agency (CIA) with details of Saddam's plan, a strategy of sheer military brilliance in its simplicity. Basically the plan was to invade Saudi Arabia, the only nearby Arab nation having friendly relations with the West, with sufficient land to accommodate supply and ammunition depots, a well-equipped force with all the necessary support groups, and large enough to launch a counter-invasion. President Bush had been furnished with a military plan of responsive strategy to be used, once evidence of any significant troop movement was detected. Three months were needed to transport sufficient men and munitions to a large enough area of land capable of supporting a sustained war effort. The American Forces occupied a landmass large enough to accommodate the back-up supplies needed to fortify a huge army. No effective counter-invasion could have succeeded, if launched from a country further away from the theatre of war. I cannot understand why Saddam did not invade Saudi Arabia at the same time as his armies occupied Kuwait; it must have been God's interference that confused Saddam's mind. Within five days of the attack on Kuwait, two American airborne divisions were airlifted to Saudi Arabia.

Over a ten-year period leading up to Iraq's invasion of Kuwait on the 2nd August 1990, US$50 billion were spent in equipping Saddam's militia with sophisticated armament and weapon systems. Iraq's army was acknowledged as being the fourth most powerful in the world. Saddam is a totally evil man, who exercises a reign of terror over his nation, cold-bloodedly ordering the death of Iraqis who have the temerity to protest against his dictatorial authority. The late Syrian President Hafez al-Assad was determined to remove the Jews from Israel, which was why Syria was not included with the conspirators, for Saddam intended that the distinction of driving the Jews out of 'Palestine" was to be his[121]. Within two weeks Iraq would have captured almost two-thirds of the worlds' oil supplies. The intervention by the UN was not a simple matter of ***good*** standing against ***evil***, but of one group's self-interests opposing another. Many Arabs saw

[121] It is significant that Assad's life was taken from him on the *Shabbat* of *Shavuot* in the year 2000, the anniversary of the Law of Moses being given, and the anniversary of the first coming of the Holy Spirit following Christ's death (do you hear the sound of trumpets, or sense the arrival of the wedding invitations?).

Saddam as a patriot, and the man behind whom all Arab nations could unite in overthrowing the yoke of *infidel* oppression, and reclaiming land belonging to *Allah*. Muslim extremists have been eager to repay this affront against *Allah*, a subject to which I will return in Chapter 7.

My ministry to St Matthew's Church in Cambridge (where I had worshipped as an elder for several years) had been discerned as prophetic and evangelistic. I have always taken very seriously the injunction contained in 1 Corinthians Ch 14:15-16 and Colossians Ch 1:9-12:

> *"I will pray and sing in my spirit for understanding, in order to be properly informed over what issues to pray for. I will pray to God for all spiritual wisdom and understanding of His will."*

The Lord spoke to me again:

> ***"It was for times such as this that I appointed you to St Matthews. I want you to advise the congregation of My purposes in the current world affairs. Through prayer, you seek My guidance on what to pray for as a parish church. Do not be fearful, nor deceived or deflected, turn the eyes and ears of your heart towards Me, and look to Me for your enlightenment. A one-world government, a one-world religion and a one-world economy are the three strands that are plaited together by money, power and authority and are not easily broken. I have repeatedly demonstrated to the nations that I am a merciful God. Long ago I scattered the people and confused their language when they sought to deny My incontestable authority. By this humane measure, I delayed the day in which the people of the nations would once more aspire to behave as gods themselves, but that day is now here. My wrath will precede My judgement, for I will not allow My authority to be challenged with impunity. You are witnessing the removal of My restraining hand on evil. The true believer need not fear My vengeance and judgement. My wrath is reserved for those who deny Me. They did not look upon My creation with the eyes of their hearts, but with veiled faces, choosing to go their own way in rebellion. Do not weep for the world, but rejoice that I am coming to claim My bride, My redeemed people. The time of waiting is over and preparations for the wedding are completed. None of those who are invited will fail to be there, none for whom***

there is no invitation will attend. Says the Lord your God."

The Iraqi forces were successfully pushed out of Kuwait during Operation Desert Storm, launched by the allied armies. Saddam threatened the UN General Assembly that if the Allied Forces invaded Baghdad, Scud missiles, armed with biological war-heads, would be fired into Israel. The General Assembly therefore refused the demands of President George Bush (senior), British PM Mrs Margaret Thatcher, and French President François Mitterand to overthrow President Hussein and replace him with a puppet leader. Ironically out of all those leaders only Saddam remained in power into the 21st century.

A Summons to Jerusalem

During August 1992, whilst on holiday in Norfolk, I had been meditating on God's purposes in allowing Israel to be invaded in every decade since her rebirth. I recalled a revelation received in 1991, in which I was told that, during the final generation, the two kings of the North and South of Daniel Ch 11, would not represent earthly kingdoms, but would manifest as poles ***apart*** ideologies of extreme Islamism and libertarian *laissez faire* (apostate) Christian churchmanship. The message that God does not choose sides is hard to accept to the western mindset, but a glance at Joshua Ch 5:13-14 confirms my contention. I realised that the theme connecting my meditation, prior to retiring to bed, and the earlier revelatory dream, concerning the Allies' response against Iraq, was '***war***', connected with God's protection of His land and His people during those invasions It is well documented that the 'hits' or 'scores' accomplished by the IDF during all wars against Israel since 1947, had to be supernatural, for they were three times as effective as those used by the invading forces.

I awoke the following morning experiencing a high-pitched humming in my ears, both awakening and alerting me. I knew from past experiences that I was about to receive a revelation in trance form. The sun was shining through the four windowpanes, which were covered in condensation. Owing to the early morning sunlight I was squinting through half-closed eyes, blinking to clear my blurred vision. Suddenly the digits 1, 9, 9, 9, appeared very clearly seen (each about 200 mm in height and as thick as a man's finger), with one digit in each of the four panes. I received a '*word of knowledge*' that that the '1' was Christ and the three 'nines' were the amalgamation of the accumulated judgements of the ungodly, that would soon be effected on the citizens of the world. The suggestion was impressed upon my mind that during 1999 a major earthquake would occur in the

Middle East, in an Islamic country, as an indication of that judgement. A man-inspired disaster would also occur in a 'Christian' western nation, which was also to indicate the coming. I was told that the unholy covenant, of Daniel Ch 9:27, would be realised between the blowing of the *Shofar* (ram's horn) announcing *Rosh Hashana* (in 1992 and 1993[122]). One month following the notification of the coming judgement, on the morning of my 58th birthday, I was told to present myself at the Wailing Wall (western wall of the destroyed temple) on the following *Yom Kippur*, on Friday evening the 24th September 1993, at which time I would receive further revelations. In obedience I reserved accommodation at Christ Church[123] in the Old City of Jerusalem. On the day I received confirmation of my booking, my Bible readings were from Luke Ch 24:49:

> *"I am going to send you what My Father has promised; but stay in the holy city until you have been clothed with power from on high."*

---

[122] On the 13th September 1993, the world had witnessed on tv the much publicised signing of the Oslo Accord by Israel's PM Yitzak Rabin and the leader of the PLO, Chairman Yasser Arafat.

[123] Christ Church is the flagship Anglican Church in Israel, as it has been since the restoration of Israel has been preached; I will identify this sanctuary henceforth as Christchurch. Read the book by Kelvin Crombie ***For the Love of Zion*** to warm your heart towards our brother the Jew, and to provide a comprehensive history of the Promised Land.

I was aware that I was being summoned to Jerusalem at the time of the 1993 Yom Kippur (aka the Day of Atonement), to hear further from God regarding the approaching 'Day of Judgement'[124].

While in an airplane on its flight-path over central London (during which time I was reminded of an earlier revelation, given whilst flying over Jerusalem on Christmas Eve 1994, of which I write in Chapter 7), I received a '*word of knowledge*' that mayhem and devastation could result, if a cold-hearted fanatical pilot chose, to use his aeroplane as a missile against a 'significant target'. Equally any citizen in control of a crop spraying plane could spray a deadly chemical over a city, just as easily as planting high explosives in a crowded shopping centre, as the Irish Republican Army (IRA) had done on occasions. In September 2001, documents were found in Missouri USA outlining details of delivering just such a chemical attack, as I had spiritually seen! I envisaged how migrants, having been granted rights of citizenship, could infiltrate a fifth column into the structure of their enemy's homeland, integrating into the community as an espionage cell that might remain undetected until an atrocity was committed that might be

---

[124] At 3:02AM on the night of the 17th August 1999, Izmit, a city in Turkey was struck by an earthquake, in which 18,000 people died; its magnitude measured 7.0 on the Richter scale. Perhaps the revelation was not startling, for the numbers of earthquakes of this severity have doubled throughout the world since 1970! I had received a similar word some years earlier that God intended that night to kill one million Muslims, who were attending the Hajj pilgrimage. I was told to spend the night in prayer for a relaxation of His decree. It transpired that 'only' 100,000 lost their lives or homes, it seems that my prayer time was rewarded. On January the 26th 2001, 50,000 people died in the earthquake in Ghandidham in India. Many Indian pastors have said that this was God's judgement, on the pilgrimage made one month earlier by Hindus to the River Ganges, to pay homage to their many gods. It is possible but unlikely, that God struck down a representative group of idol worshippers, but many Christians also died in this incident. It is true that the collapse of the Tower in Siloam resulted in the death of both guilty and innocent; a justice beyond man's comprehension is involved (Luke Ch13:4-5). Following the unsuccessful attack on the World Trade Centre in 1993, I received a word of knowledge that a quiver of arrows was to be fired by fanatical Islamists at the heart of capitalist America, resulting in an international meltdown of economic and religious order. One of these arrows was to be fired at a nuclear plant, causing huge devastation. I was to pray that these events would not take place. The fact that a nuclear plant was not attacked was an answer to prayer. The earthquake in Izmit resulted in many more deaths than the destruction of the World Trade Centre, but because the suicide attack was carried out with cold-hearted precision, humanity has recoiled in horror and loathing and unfortunately will exact revenge. Unredeemed mankind can only shake an ineffective fist at, what is perceived as God's judgement. On reflection it seemed strange to me that I was told that the earthquake of 1999 would occur in an Islamic nation, and not an Arab country, which Turkey is not! I decided not to record in the earlier edition of this book all that God had told me in all its baldness, partly because I hoped God might relax His allowance of evil activities about to happen, as He had done on earlier occasions. I disguised my words in imagery, but in view of events I can no longer hide anything revealed to me to share.

traced back to them. It was the thought of all these possible disasters that I was to pray against coming to pass. I am compelled to say that God set in place spiritual laws governing what appears to be a benevolent 'mother nature'. He also limited His own control over mankind's ***free will***, to act as their universal heart and mind dictated. I heard the words: "***A penny for your thoughts. Write them down so that when you share your understanding with others no salient points are forgotten***."

> *This commission was like receiving a special sought-after birthday present! I have searched the Scriptures for confirmation of the various revelations received, and meditated over their meanings, becoming more confident in my interpretations, which, together with my discernments intersperse this book, I offer to you the reader to weigh and to judge.*

Will the Ark of the Covenant be found?

I arrived in Jerusalem at 3:00^{AM} on the 16th of September, and spent the day prayerfully meditating in my room. That same evening at the Wailing Wall as *Rosh Hashana* commenced, I received two further prophecies (of which I have written in my autobiography), and during the remainder of my visit, the Lord granted me an unforgettable second episode of nightly dreams, accompanied by revelations. I was also commanded to visit the Church of the Nativity, in Bethlehem, on the Christmas Eve of 1994 (the following year), as this would be the last Christmas that Bethlehem would be under the supervision of the IDF. I was to revisit the Wailing Wall at this time, when I would receive further revelation.

I befriended three ladies from the USA, who were also lodging at Christchurch. They had been conspiratorially told that the Ark of the Covenant was located amongst the underground passages, and the rabbis were aware of the Ark's location. Public knowledge of the Ark's whereabouts might cause civil unrest, or even a religious uprising; therefore the entrance to its resting place had been concreted over, for what are termed *'security reasons'*. The Rabbinate were content that this most sacred of treasures should remain hidden until the temple was rebuilt[125]. That night I received an extraordinary vision:

> I was watching a kneeling priest offering supplication to God over the likely outcome of King Nebuchadnezzar's armies carrying off the temple treasures to the vaults in Babylon. I was told that the praying figure was Jeremiah, and that God Most High was instructing him to secretly hide the most sacred items in an underground cave in a quarry outside the city walls. Amongst these most sacred treasures were the six-stemmed golden Menorah with seven lamps, the Ark of the Covenant, the Table of Shewbread, the Incense Altar and the Tent of Meeting. The vision continued with a pseudo burial procession in which the mourners carried the coffin, containing the sacred treasures from the Holy of Holies. Under cover of darkness these sacred items were silently transported to the quarry entrance by way of an old but well-used pathway, outside the city walls of Jerusalem.

In times of peace, boulders of all shapes and sizes were quarried from this place, to build walls and homes, but during the siege the besieged Judeans used the boulders extracted as ammunition. I read later in 2 Chronicles Ch 26:15 of some skilful war strategists who had built giant catapults mounted on to mobile platforms, as defensive deterrents that could be moved to reinforce weaker positions being attacked. Nebuchadnezzar had developed a healthy respect for these earliest of missile launchers and established base camp for his armies to a position behind a siege wall, out of range. The area between adversaries was a no-man's land. My vision continued:

> The sacred items were carried into an underground catacomb with many large caverns off the main passageway in which all manner of items were stored. Only a few especially trusted confidantes were invited to help Jeremiah transport the heavy

---

[125] The Temple Institute of Jerusalem has manufactured copies of many of the sacred items necessary for daily temple sacrifice to be re-established. All that is needed is a continuously burning fire on an altar prepared from uncut stones, on which no iron tools have been used, upon which the four corner horns may be sprinkled with the blood of a red heifer (in accordance with Numbers Ch 19:1-9 and Ch 8:31). In 1996 at Qumran a 2,000 year old clay flask containing anointing oil was found, that scientists confirmed as being composed of the precise ingredients described in Exodus Ch 30:25-26. This is the anointing oil with which to anoint the high priest and the officiating priesthood written of in verse 29. An unverified report of a publication in circulation inviting their Jewish readership to offer their newborn sons for adoption into the priesthood for an upbringing in a place of security and tranquillity, free from worldly influences, where the children would be trained. The object being to purify these boys, so that at 13 years of age, they will be qualified to (blasphemously) sacrificially slaughter and incinerate a red heifer.

> and bulky sacred items to the cave in which the treasures were to be hidden. After his friends returned to the city, Jeremiah bricked up the entrance of the cave camouflaging its presence.

I read later from the Apocrypha in 2 Maccabees Ch 2:8:

> *Jeremiah sealed up the entrance.*

The passage continues that Jeremiah's fellow conspirators (motivated by greed) tried unsuccessfully to locate the whereabouts of the cave. Jeremiah confronted his unreliable servants, giving credence to my visions, declaring:

> *"This place shall remain unknown, until God gathers His people together, having forgiven them. Only at that time will the Lord allow these items to be revealed again, when God's glory will be seen by all."* (paraphrased)

Whilst resting in my room, I received a vision:

> I was observing a familiar early evening Middle Eastern scene, in which I was standing in a narrow pedestrian street. The scene was idyllic and one which has occasionally returned to me during the night hours. Everybody present had responded to my invitation of drinks and nibbles. Many guests sat relaxing on the stone steps leading to the first floor entrance of the house. Guests, who chose to wander through my home, threaded their way between those sitting on the steps without difficulty. At no time did the space we occupied appear to be overcrowded, nor did it seem that there were just a few of us partying in a cavernous echo chamber[126]. I have always believed that there were more than the three dimensions of length, height and width, and of course Einstein[127] proved 'time' to be a fourth dimension (he also suggested a fifth dimension in which good and evil forces opposed each other). I circulated from group to group, greeting new arrivals, reminding them of earlier shared

---

[126] It was a peculiar sensation to experience areas of space alternately widening out and narrowing, as my spiritual (subconscious?) mind, and my eyes focused on the scene. I recalled other visions in which I had the freedom to see over horizons and around corners, and walk through solid objects such as rock faces, or alternatively pass through closed doors, as if my body had dematerialised, whilst my body and mind had been in a '***disembodied state of existence***'. I had also been able to walk through solid objects.

[127] Albert Einstein had postulated of greater numbers of dimensions occupying the ***same space***, but was unable to prove his theory. Hebrew sages wrote of ten dimensions, six of which collapsed at Creation to a size so small that they became inaccessible. The sages wrote of the Earth being formed from a ten dimensional micro-pellet, loosely connected as if threaded on a string, that exploded outwards at the speed of light on God's original command for light to appear.

experiences in our lives. As we spoke of absent friends, so those friends materialised to join us. Many of my friends chose to stand on the lounge balcony overlooking the street, where a cool evening breeze circulated. They called out to my neighbours, who were taking advantage of the cool evening breeze, on the balconies of their homes. Although we were in a congested area, the space we occupied expanded to allow for the extra guests arriving, whilst the space contracted, as some groups dispersed, similar to the action of a lung inhaling or expelling air when breathing deeply.

I became very excited on reading of the calculations made in 1984 by two physicists, John Schwarz and Michael Green. Using a complicated mathematical formula, they were able to prove that each of the three known dimensions of '***space***' were shared by two further dimensions, which, combined with the dimension of '***time***', added up to ten separate dimensions occupying the same area. Their theory proved that all four natural forces present in the universe, that is, gravity, electromagnetism, and both the strong and weak nuclear forces, which although fluctuating in their mass or presence, are strictly governed in their combined total force. Every particle of matter and energy that God initially created (the fundamental building blocks of matter and energy) was limited by the combined strength or presence of the other natural forces (always accepting the scientific presumption that there has been no increase in availability of matter or energy since the world was created). The two scientists concluded that although the particles may change in shape, size or effect, the remainder always add up to the same ***total availability***. It is possible to pass through one dimension to another through infinitesimal ***points*** and not through infinitesimal ***strings***. I believe that when Jesus answered Pilate's questions of John Ch 18:36 by stating that His kingdom was not of this world, He may have been implying that part of His kingdom was existent ***in other dimensions***, of this world. I was greatly reassured that I was not suffering from an over-active imagination, for these scientists have confirmed my spiritual experiences to my satisfaction.

I received a videotape of a lecture delivered by American evangelist Henry Gruver, who spoke of a breathtaking archaeological discovery, made in January 1982, by American archaeologist, Ron Wyatt. Wyatt maintained that he had located the Ark of the Covenant by painstakingly clearing an 8m depth of rubble accumulated over the centuries, covering an area of land in Jerusalem above where he believed the cave was located, in which Jeremiah had hidden the items of my vision. He uncovered an alignment of nine-inch square slots, each about 1m deep, spaced equally apart. Wyatt deduced that the slots followed the track leading past the city's refuse dump, along a stretch of pathway outside the city walls of Jerusalem, which were made during the times of the Roman occupation, to act as a deterrent to other protestors, who were tempted to rebel against their Roman masters. Having searched around Wyatt found the opening leading to a series of tunnels, some of which were blocked by debris, or were too small for Wyatt to crawl through until he enlarged them.

Wyatt broke into a hidden cave, 3m in height, 4m wide and 7m in depth to the back of the cave from its entrance, in which were located the sacred treasures from King Solomon's Temple, together with the Tent of Meeting (Exodus Ch 26:1-37, Ch 27:9-18). The sacred items had been covered with animal skins prior to their storage to prevent deterioration or damage. Wyatt claimed that he found dried blood on the lid of the Ark of the Covenant (aka the Mercy Seat) that on analysis proved to be of human origin, but with some ***'identifiable differences'***, leading Wyatt to insist that this was Christ's blood. He noticed a fissure in the rock ceiling immediately above the Mercy Seat, which connected with a square slot, having a fissure in its base. Wyatt was convinced that this was the very slot into which the spigot (or upright member) of the Cross of Jesus fitted. He reasoned that following the spear being thrust into Christ's ribcage, His blood flowed from the wound down the vertical spigot and through the fissure in the split granite roof (which Wyatt concluded was caused by the earthquake of Matthew Ch 24:5) and on to the Mercy Seat directly beneath. Assuming Wyatt reported accurately, then the events of Psalm 85:10-11 are fulfilled; mercy and truth (God the Father, and Jesus the Messiah) have met together (on the Mercy Seat); Righteousness and Peace have kissed. Truth shall spring out of the earth (resurrection) and Righteousness (God) shall look down from heaven (observing the outworking of His purposes).

During the 1994 Feast of Purim at the Tomb of the Patriarchs in Hebron (now renamed as the Ibrahimi Mosque) Dr Baruch Goldstein gunned down 50 worshippers before being overpowered and killed. Goldstein had been a member of the Kach Movement, dedicated to the defence of Jews everywhere. A little over a year later (between the dates 4th-14th November 1995), I was one of a team of evangelists ministering on the Mount of Olives. The mission was unforgettable in that Yigal Amir, a 27-year-old right-wing law student; assassinated PM Rabin on the night of our arrival. He insisted at his later trial that he was not part of, nor acted on behalf of, any organisation. I received a *'word of knowledge'* that *c*2000 AD the UN will declare Jerusalem to be an international city, this being an allusion to the division of Christ's clothes (Psalm 22:18, Luke Ch 23:34). It was on the 13th October 2001 that I received a 'word of knowledge', that one of the instigators of the Oslo Accord would die before a year was completed, and that others involved in plotting the division of Jerusalem would die before the Feast of Dedication in 2004 was over. Just before the Oslo Accord was signed almost without the notice of the world's media, Jewish leaders from around the world appended their signatures to a declaration that the City of Jerusalem would never be divided again. This resolution surely represents the nations standing in unison against Israel, as spoken of in Jeremiah Ch 25:26-38 that every nation will drink from God's cup of wrath, with God sending a sword upon them, ***in their homelands***. Psalm 2:1-4 says:

> *"The nations rage and plot against the Lord's appointed, but He sits and laughs at their futile endeavours, which will come to nothing."* (paraphrased)

Because El Al Airlines had overbooked I had to fly home *via* Athens, where I was delayed owing to a knife-wielding hijacker, who had demanded to broadcast his protest on a Greek radio station. Having boarded the aeroplane, a tyre burst on taxiing onto the peritrack as we prepared to take-off. I received a '*word of knowledge*' that the trauma surrounding this mission would have a greater significance to me in the future. In view of the destruction of the World Trade Centre, and the revelations received, I would warn the IDF of a *word of knowledge* I received in 1994 whilst flying over Jerusalem, of which I write in Chapter 7, that in order to avoid the Al Aqsa mosque being dive-bombed (whilst Muslims were at prayer in a copy-cat attack, the IDF may have to shoot down an aeroplane.

Chapter 5

BRITAIN IN THE DOCK

The unwritten Constitution of Britain was introduced by godly King Alfred, and enshrined principles founded on God's Law. One only has to look to the inhuman treatment meted out during the Crusades[128] against both Jews and Muslims, (in which Catholic Britain was involved), or more latterly to the natives of the British Crown Colonies to recognise Britain's deepening sinfulness. King Edward expelled all Jews from England in 1290 AD, under the penalty of death for non-compliance[129], which is probably when the speed of acceleration into unrighteousness increased. The term 'British' only emerged after the Act of Union with Scotland in 1707 AD. Royalty, parliamentarians and esteemed leaders from every walk of life will be at God's courtroom (the great white throne of judgement), together with those Britons who did not protest against the unrighteous government of the statesmen who administered justice in their homeland. I am of the opinion that, owing to ungodly stewardship by government, church, and society's shameful self-indulgence and cravings, God has given society over to Satan (Romans Ch 1:24-32), be by judgement will follow. Judgement Day will arrive one day, when all who are not covered by Christ's blood of righteousness, if their names do not appear in the Books of Life, will be thrown into the *lake of fire* (Luke Ch 16:8-9).

The city of Nineveh did receive a 150-year reprieve from judgement[130] prior to its destruction, but it is not known what percentage of the 120,000 people repented, I suspect repentance was mostly confined to the King's officials, who were responsible for carrying out the king's now enlightened righteous decrees. Nowhere in the Bible is a prophecy given that would lead any serious investigator to believe that whole nations will turn to God in repentance. Currently the country of Argentina is midway through the second decade of

---

[128] Approximately one-third of all Jews in Germany and northern France were murdered at the outset of the first Crusade, and 969 Jews were burned to death in the main synagogue of Jerusalem.

[129] Altogether 16,000 Jews were expelled, many of who died in straightened circumstances.

[130] Faulstich confirms that a total solar eclipse occurred over Nineveh on the 7th of June 763 BC, which is referred to in the Assyrian eponyms (or Canon), where it is also recorded that a national plague (the huge earthquake of Amos Ch 1:1), occurred in 759 BC. The judgement of ruination of the city was deferred until 613 BC (of which Nahum, more than 100 years earlier had prophesied in Ch 3:18-19). The deportation of the House of Israel occurred in between these two 'outside' dates of 763-613 BC.

'***awakening***', but not every Argentinean or foreigner who lives in Argentina has become a believer. There is not, and has never been, a totally Christian nation, just as there are no righteous persons (no, not one. Psalm 143:2). We read in Genesis Ch 18:16-32 of the story of Abraham's negotiations with God. Sodom would have received a reprieve if only ten righteous men lived in the town. It is clear from Ezekiel Ch 14:14 that only the righteous believers living '***in***' a nation shall receive salvation, they shall be saved '***out***' of the nation in which they reside. Many British believers hope that if they pray fervently for long enough then revival will result, with first the whole town and then the whole country coming to Christ, which is not a true understanding of Scripture. God's kingdom will be populated by a small percentage from every nation. During the end times, God will not grant a 'Ninevehian-style reprieve, even of short duration. If He should, which nation would He select? God's time scale will not be adjusted in order to reap a greater harvest. True Christians are 'foreigners' in an alien society and culture, whatever country they were born in. I do wish to witness the collapse of the wall of implacable Islam, Maoism, fascism and communism, all of whose philosophies are totalitarian utopian dreams that inevitably mean the subjugation of all opposition by force. Western Catholicism, Protestantism, dogmatism in the body of Christ will need to be repented of by all who believe themselves to be Christians. New Ageism, humanism and terrorism are all expressions of individuality that are part of the realm of Satanism. Such esoteric authoritarian regimes will impose themselves into national and international dominance, in ***ideological wars of confrontation***, during the next seven years but when events become too murderous for the elect to bear, Christ will return. The Christian's fight is not against people, but against principalities and powers in the heavenlies.

Following the enthroning in Britain of Protestant Queen Elizabeth 1, Catholics were forced to practise their faith in secret, as Catholicism was banned in England until the 17th century. The ban was initiated because the Vatican urged British Catholics to overthrow the Protestant oligarchy established by King Henry V111. On the defeat of the Spanish Armada in 1588 AD, the people of Britain were characterised as pompous and superior beings, nursing an overweening pride. ***Erastian***[131] ***Christianity*** as perceived by the public became identified with '*Colonialism*', nobility and the Establishment. What has been called the 'great Protestant missionary movement' came about through missionaries accompanying the Queen's armies in their programme of expansion of trade and of the

---

[131] Erastianism is the subordination of ecclesiastical to secular power.

British Empire. The East-India Company (a privately owned trading company), which was seeking to expand its commercial markets overseas, was a faithful accomplice. Many natives accepted British control owing to dependency on employment or out of fear or reprisal for resistance. Brian Mills and Roger Mitchell, in their well-researched book ***Sins of the Fathers***, corroborate the view I hold over such matters. In 1834, the British Government of the day, realising the scale of revenue being generated through the sale of opium into China, assumed control of the East-India Company, whose licence to trade had expired, and became the commercial arm of the imperial power. In 1657 AD the British Empire flourished after Republican (anti-monarchist) Oliver Cromwell, as Lord Protector of England, granted Jews the right to settle in Britain. Parliamentary legislation was passed into the Statute Books through the Licensing Act of 1662 AD, to limit the effects in His Majesty's Protectorates at home and abroad from heretical, seditious or schismatic opinion. Britain now ruled the waves; the boast was soon to be that the sun never set on the British Empire. Puritanism (which was basically a continuously evolving form of Protestantism), was perceived by the newly formed Church of England as a danger to its very foundations, and as a movement, was marginalized and eventually lost its following. It became 'politically correct' to accept and proclaim the faith which the leaders of the land declared themselves as following. In God's eyes it is righteousness that exalts a nation (Proverbs Ch 14:34), and not the vastness of its empire, or indeed the astuteness of its leaders in government and industry.

Following the Glorious Revolution of 1688 AD, a Coronation Oath was introduced which extended oaths undertaken by earlier monarchs, with the intention of extending to all citizens, regardless of station or circumstances, a just and righteous Constitution, supported by the combined authority of the Monarchy, State and Church. The nation should acknowledge the debt owed to many enlightened high profile Christian politicians, philanthropists and churchmen, who, since that time, have sought parliamentary legislation to correct inequalities, such as the introduction of the Poor Laws, the abolition of slavery, free education for all children, votes for women, a national health service available to all etc.

Following the worldwide depression, which occurred between the two World Wars, after suffering 30 years of struggle, the electorate of Britain were generally in favour of a freer more relaxed standard of Statute Law. Lord Reith, in his 1948 Declaration of Intent as Chairman of the British Broadcasting Corporation (BBC), recognised that Britain had ventured on to the slippery slopes that leads to godlessness. He sought to reaffirm Britain's Christian heritage by setting out four important standards:

- To maintain standards of truth, justice and honesty in private and public life
- To explain what the Christian faith is, and to demonstrate its relevance during his tenure of office
- To lead the unchurched into the body of active believers
- To develop an evangelistic outlook to challenge non-believers.

The 1990 Broadcasting Act not only removed the teeth of the 1948 Declaration, but also swept away many Christian principles to which lip service was previously paid. Democracy is not the granting of freedom of individuals to do as they wish (which is secular humanism), but rather the duty of the State to enforce God's eternal laws, which are essential for righteousness, for the common good of humanity[132]. Britons today are ***legally*** able to break, any or all of the Ten Commandments, without fear of prosecution.

- In 1959 amendments to the Obscene Publications Act were passed by Parliament, and in 1967 amended further, removing the barriers of censorship and rendering the previously enshrined law as toothless.
- In 1965, the abolition of the death penalty was enforced, leading the way for greater trespass. Many murders are premeditated through violence in or outside the home; in most cases, the murderer is known to the victim.
- In 1967 the Abortion Act was passed, and amended in 1995, to allow for babies conceived up to 20 weeks, and handicapped babies up until birth, to be aborted. Five million British babies have been aborted since 1967. This legislation has in turn led to the availability of free contraception advice for schoolchildren in Britain. From the findings of a recent survey, 20% of 15 year olds admitted to be sexually active. Britain has the highest rate of teenage pregnancy in Europe. Our nation has been badly advised by sociologists and educationalists, and a media that continuously urges greater freedom from restriction, resulting in a slackening of governmental laws, insidiously undermining the moral mores of Britain. Satan has been very successful in convincing our society that to preserve one's virginity until marriage is prudish and old fashioned.

---

[132] French philosopher Jacques Maritain (1882-1973) argued that nationalism expressed as State engendered Fascism, Nazism, Communism or xenophobic triumphalism was unrighteous government, against the will of God and the common good of mankind. Not a popular position to take, but one I endorse emphatically.

• In 1967 the Sexual Offences Act legalised homosexual acts. The age of consent was lowered in 2000 AD leading to a rise in the number of paedophiles and atrocities committed; again it was the threat of prosecution and imprisonment that had acted as a deterrent[133]. The homosexual lobby would have society believe that homosexuality is egalitarian and emancipating.

Disturbingly some of Britain's leading statesmen and church leaders are practising homosexuals. Pressure groups actively promote the acceptance of homosexual orientation and practice, as another form of lovemaking in the rich tapestry of life. Advocates of homosexual relationships fail to recognise that, when given free rein, their sexual orientation is confirmation of fallen disorder, an issue to be confronted and confessed as an abomination in God's sight, and not something to be celebrated. The sins of Sodom and Gomorrah were of pride, self-centredness, greed, sloth, and unconcern over the poor and needy, and only lastly their permissiveness. The sins were listed in Ezekiel Ch 16:49, and confirms only that the ***increasing manifestation of homosexuality*** is the ***final straw*** in exhibiting the breaking of God's covenant with mankind, ***resulting*** in the '***day of God's wrath***' leading to judgement.

I would warn my reader that he who judges another for their misdeeds invites the same measure of judgement on his own head for his own unrighteousness. The Bible condemns all unrighteous behaviour (or thought, including homophobia, xenophobia or racialism) as unholy. But if a believer holds to high ideals, he will accept that 'no fault' divorce has made it easy to walk out on a marriage, although only half of today's society goes through the formality of a marriage, which is why the Law governing divorce has been rendered almost ineffective. The children of broken relationships are traumatised and often brutalised by a new partner of the one parent who acts as the guardian. On a steady relationship breaking down, a succession of unsuccessful relationships often results. A study by anthropologist

---

[133] In 1967 Britain endured a national outbreak of foot and mouth disease of cattle, which was thought by many prophets as a warning from God. This is being repeated in 2001, following a series of other signs, such as BSE (bovine spongiform encephalopathy), swine fever, train derailments (Railtrack's profits rose from £190 million in 1966 to £428 million in 1999, confirming that profit is the motivating force behind trading, ***not the safety or consideration of the user***), severe flooding, united public protests over fuel prices etc, Surely our leaders can see that that there is a spiritual dimension in unrighteousness that has to be paid for in retribution? Are the words of Deuteronomy Ch 28:16 irrelevant in our modern society? "***Your basket and kneading trough and your crops, and the fruit of your womb will be cursed***", and in verse 18-20. "***Confusion will be your portion***. ***Your cattle will be slaughtered***, ***but you will eat none of it***". (paraphrased)

Professor John Unwin, showing that sexual promiscuity had destroyed 80 civilisations, caused him to conclude that: "***An advanced society that permits premarital sexual behaviour will degenerate into a backward society of the lowest cultural level within three generations.***" Unwin may be in error only over the length of time necessary to pass for degenerate behaviour to be tolerated without protest, by the majority of any country's citizens.

In Romans Ch 13:1 Paul said that every citizen should be peaceable and law-abiding, because God has established the governance of his or her leaders. Also believers are urged to pray for kings, and all who rule in every hierarchical system (1 Timothy Ch 2:1-4). This I understand to mean that resorting to violence, with the intention of overthrowing the government of the day, is ungodly despite any altruistic intentions. ***Terrorists will be answerable to God for their actions on judgement day***. Over a period of time, people power exerts itself, resulting in the overthrow of regimes and hastening community improvements. However quite often internal revolution results in a more unjust society, but in the long-term God's word is proven to be true. Paul continues in verse 2:

> *"Therefore whoever resists the authorities resists the ordinance of God and those who do resist will bring judgement on themselves."*

Jesus did not advocate other than peaceful protest to seek change to unrighteous government in any nation. If obeying God's laws in contradiction of nationally imposed laws means imprisonment or death for disobedience, then that is the pathway to the kingdom of God; Jesus demonstrated this in His own death.

In 1992, 1,247 votes **in key marginal seats** of Britain, ensured the Conservative Party were elected to govern with a majority of 21 seats. In 1997 the votes of just 168,000 in the marginal constituencies ensured a landslide victory for the Labour Party. The under-privileged 20% of society, tend to live in ghetto-style community groupings, within a highly populated city, which means that their grievances are well down the pecking order of priorities of the main political parties! The introduction of proportional representation is not in the interest of the two major political Parties, but this is the ***only*** true form of voting, ***acceptable*** in a '**just**' (compassionate and incorruptible) society. Having formerly sought election as a candidate for the Green Party. The main Parties 'steal the clothes' of minority specific issue Parties, with no intention of pursuing minority, potentially vote-losing issues.

Nations reap what their leadership sows. In the name of political correctness, Local Authorities readily approve planning permission to build shrines to other gods. Permission for Christian organisations to improve facilities are often rejected, which is why in Britain today, mosques and temples of worship to the gods of former colonies abound, whilst Christian enterprises become redundant and Church membership declines. In 1990 it was calculated that actively religious Muslims outnumbered active membership of Baptist and Methodist Churches combined; this does not surprise me! As Britain enters into the 21st century, Muslims attending mosques were close to exceeding the total number of attendees of all 'established' Protestant denominations, including Anglicans, but excluding the Pentecostal denominations and the 'charismatic' House-Church movement[134]! During the 1990's, 467 mosques were built in Britain, but at the approach of the 21st century, mosques were built at the rate of one every two weeks! ***The consequences are writ large on the wall for those politicians and Bishops, who have allowed the relaxation of Britain's more godly laws***, ***out of humanistic principles or personal preferences***. It was Edmund Burke who said: "***The only thing necessary for evil to flourish is for good men to do nothing***." Unfortunately British Christians have never been part of a majority other than the silent moral majority, and have not persuaded any government to change policies. Queen Elizabeth 11 at her Coronation on 2nd June 1953 said she would do her utmost to maintain the laws of God and the true profession of the Gospel within the nation. Unfortunately the Head of State is now little more than a figurehead, and can do no other than announce, without comment, her

[134] In 1970 across the world there were 3.79 million individual charismatic Christians within the established churches, this number increased to 123 million by 1988! During that same period, the growth rate of Pentecostals within their various church denominations grew from 64 million to 176 million! The growth in the 1990s was estimated to be in the region of 224% mainly from the Third World countries that encompass 70% of the charismatic movement. The Christian Research Association has estimated that there are 2.1 billion out of approximately 6 billion people across the globe that claim to be Christian. There is no reason for self-congratulation over the increase in numbers of one denomination whilst the numbers in other denominations are diminishing. A survey conducted by the Christian Research Association revealed that between 1979-1989 church attendance in Britain had dwindled by 13%, and between 1989-1998 attendance had fallen by an alarming 22%! Over that same period the Pentecostal and House Church movements, have increased in numbers attending, by a staggering 50%! Perhaps the worship featured on radio and tv, or the teaching experienced at cross-denominational bible-camps and conferences have been the main reason to become dissatisfied with one's former place of attendance. Whatever has caused the migration away from institutional churches; the mass exodus has certainly shaken out any previous complacency!

Government's agenda (at the opening of Parliament for the forthcoming year).

I believe God has placed revival and eternity in the hearts of every believer in every generation. Most revivals have been localised and of short duration. But revival of the established Church during the Great Tribulation is a contradiction of what is written in 2 Thessalonians Ch 2:7-12, an increase of wickedness and apostasy may be expected. We should not deceive ourselves on this matter; a falling away should be expected (Matthew Ch 24:10). According to Revelation Ch 16:16, the subjects of rebellious kings will cooperate with the antichrist (now totally possessed by Satan) to overthrow Jesus Christ, who they have been persuaded is the false Christ, in the final battle of Armageddon on the Plains of Megiddo. Even following the millennial reign of Christ, there will be countless numbers, who have professed with their mouths faith in Christ, but who have not accepted Christ in their hearts, for we are told in Revelation Ch 20:7-11 that countless millions will join forces with Satan in a further concerted attack against sovereign King Jesus. Together with Satan they will be thrown into the lake of fire for eternity, confirming that not everyone will be redeemed.

My heart bleeds over the malnourished, African orphan, socially inconsequential, educationally deprived, regularly abused physically or sexually, and often born handicapped, or suffering with Acquired Immune Deficiency Syndrome (Aids[135]), but I can only offer up prayers to God that such tragedy will be shortened, owing to Christ's Second Coming, when all pain and sorrow will be dealt with. I am more mindful of every persecuted minority grouping closer to home, each of which needs to experience the love and acceptance of God in their lives. I am concerned for the children of one-parent families, and the problem of becoming unwanted stepchildren on their sole parent setting up home with a new partner, or if the single parent takes a lover, or even a succession of partners. I hate the indifference shown to the socially exploited and the deprived, whose needs are overlooked as being of less significance than the satisfactory handling of our own problems. Local government officials and leaders of communities, often do nothing to correct unrighteousness, claiming to be powerless, or of not having enough financial muscle to correct anomalies. I am appalled at the conduct of cruel and bestial molestation of children by paedophiles, and the wanton brutality of

---

[135] In an effort to put tragedy into an international perspective, I would point out to Westerners should be aware that twice as many people die of AIDS ***each month*** in South Africa alone than died in the World Trade Centre horror.

sadistic burglars who rape or murder their helpless, often aged victims in their own homes. The author of a book entitled ***AD 2000 Together*** would try to persuade his readers that only after the Church has imposed its authority over world governments, will the Lord return, perhaps many centuries into the future. The population might just as well put its trust in the tooth fairy as the established Church! The world will continue spiralling into further evil until the Second Coming. I see clips on tv and read in the newspapers of gangs of youths who rob or batter passing pedestrians, or who incite others to mindless thuggery in the streets of our cities, causing damage to private property with seeming impunity. Perhaps my reader has been the victim of such an assault.

It was whilst meditating on God's impending and inevitable judgement of Britain, that I fell asleep. Awakening on the morning of the 21st of May 1985, I found myself experiencing a vision in the form of a trance:

> I switched on the engine of my car, and fastened my seat belt before deciding whether or not to turn on the sidelights as dusk was approaching. A small wooden cross was suspended from the roof lining above the windscreen of my car, as a notice to any interested observer that the owner of the car was a Christian. I displayed my cross similarly to other car owners suspending accessories, such as dice or dolls, or more often by the pasting of a fluorescent strip on the windscreen over the driver's seat signifying the owner's name. The wooden cross began to hum and glow, changing in material and appearance (just as the tree trunk of my earlier dream had altered in shape and material), becoming a huge diamond of many facets, which revolved slowly whilst glowing incandescently. I sat in awe, delaying the release of the handbrake, drinking in the effects of shades of colour on the circulating diamond, now reflecting the lights from the illuminated row of shops where I had been shopping, and the dipped headlight beams of the passing cars. I became aware of what I mistakenly thought to be a leaflet, advertising a sale or an event, placed under my windscreen wipers. I got out of my car in order to remove the obstruction and saw that the 'leaflet' was a huge black bat, wings outstretched that had flown into the windscreen stunning itself. A smaller bat was clinging to, and biting the flesh from the body of the larger bat. I waved my arms frantically and shouted loudly in order

to distract the bats from their ghastly performance. The bats flew into the night squealing.

I meditated on the symbolism of the trance and concluded that the larger bat represented the Church, which although it has sought to change society for the better, has patently failed, and could not deny the criticism levelled at its performance, which was why it chose to sacrifice itself. The smaller bat represented society. A '*word of knowledge*' revealed that the procrastination of leadership had been practised on the body of the Church by deferring to the dictates of British Law, and not vehemently protesting at times when God's righteous laws have been rendered toothless in the name of public opinion. I was reminded that wild animals, even domestic pets, often bite and scratch when provoked or disturbed. Whilst outside of my car, I observed what the passers-by (non-Christians) had seen, which although sickening was not uncommon in the natural (secular) world. The shoppers could not see the glowing diamond, nor draw the strength from it that was available to all Christians; they saw the wooden cross as my talisman, a good-luck charm, and were going about their daily business, keeping themselves to themselves. Some window-shoppers were retired couples, strolling as exercise and companionship in the open air, with their families or friends, whilst those with jobs were travelling to or from their place of employment. No group of people exhibited any interest in any other group.

The loitering bored youngsters grouped together were unemployed, aimlessly passing the time, totally disinterested in pursuing leisure activities or hobbies. They were oblivious to the needs of others less able than themselves, the old and infirm, the widows and orphans. Each of the groups had become inured to suspicion and hostility concerned only for their own circumstances, being sullen and resentful of what was perceived of as an alienated Government. Through frustration, or to find some excitement, some of these groups developed into unruly packs intimidating vulnerable individuals and weaker groups. These disturbances led to repeated and more unlawful activity, from which mayhem often resulted. These groups defied those in authority by robbing, looting, mugging, raping, burning and killing, costing the community dearly in the time spent in monitoring and moving on gathering groups, to deter likely trouble. I likened the gangs to packs of animals (hyenas, jackals and vultures), feeding off the vulnerable and the unprotected, prepared to eat the carcasses of dead animals (that had been killed or wounded by larger predators), rather than attempt to hunt for themselves. Many of those who joined the packs were from deprived groups: orphans, children from broken homes, abused children, the children of one-parent families, prostitutes and ex-convicts. The collective expectations in this life were not high for the disillusioned and disenfranchised unemployed, who had been pacified by rhetoric of better days yet to come, as hollow platitudes by church leaders and politicians alike. The Church had patently failed to act as watchmen guarding the walls of the cities in which they ministered. The white-skinned members of gangs were resigned in the knowledge that, owing to consolidation, automation and obsolescence, the jobs available during their parent's working life were not available to themselves. The hopelessness of the second and third generation black-skinned unemployed youths (children of former 'colonials'), well knowing that they had fewer possibilities of finding gainful employment, resulted initially in resignation and then in angry demonstrations of protest. The occurrences of disorder mushroomed in intensity and duration, into racial disorder as resentments surfaced.

The smaller bat represented the silent, but often resentful, underprivileged groups of law-abiding citizens, who expectantly wait for the Church to speak out on behalf of the downtrodden. The silent majority were more easily subdued than the vociferously violent minorities that cause high profile trouble. Parliamentarians pay more attention to belligerent troublemakers, well knowing that the media are keen to report any confrontation against the authorities, which invariably results in prioritised, yet sensationalised, reporting. Seen from inside the car (spiritually), I knew that the ***Cross of Christ*** was the key to every problem of the shoppers and the gangs. I enjoyed the freedom of Christ's *shalom* (peace), a serenity and a joy that could not be experienced by non-believers. I was able to rise above my earthly circumstances despite living in a world governed by unrighteousness. The security of the ungodly will disappear like the morning dew, whilst believers await the joys to come in the Kingdom of God. These words of prophecy were received:

> ***"Oh foolish fallen man, why have you moved far from My righteous law? Why have you not used your wisdom to find Me? Why have you chosen to go your own way knowing that you cannot escape from My world? I offered you freedom but by the consequence of your actions you have chosen to live in bondage and imprisonment. Your leaders, promising much but producing little, have deceived you in their haste for stature and power. Profligate spending, by nations of limited financial resources, on weapons of destruction***

and weapon systems to deter any acquisitive neighbour, in a competitive race no nation can win, has impoverished every nation. The richer nations have exploited and impoverished the poorer nations without consideration, for which behaviour I hold them responsible. The consequence of spiralling sin results in the laws of nature, that I imposed on My creation, in this instance the law governing entropy[136] being applied as a balance and a brake. Oh foolish fallen man, I offered you freedom to worship Me and to receive My blessings in return for your obedience. You have ignored My promises of blessings, yet at times of misfortune you have been quick to accuse Me of capriciousness. You have run from Me in your haste to find freedom, determined to enjoy your selfish pursuits. You cannot escape My judgement, any more than you can hide your thoughts or deeds from Me. I have decreed that righteousness and justice for the people of all nations should be of paramount importance to the more enlightened nations. Surely you must realise that I do not take sides in times of conflict between equally unrighteous nations. I am also impartial over political agendas and economic systems. Your national leaders have impoverished My creation by passing popular but ungodly amendments to laws that were decreed by Me, allowing society to descend deeper into iniquity. My exhortations, and consequently My purposes and promises, will be fulfilled as I have decreed. Very soon the Kingdom of God will be established fully on Earth, when I return to reign over all the nations. My people who know Me and who are obedient to My commandments have wisely and rightly put their trust in Me. I hear their prayers of supplication, against injustice and unrighteousness. Am I a fleshly father who would deny his children their urgent petitions? My heralds have already lifted the trumpets to their lips to announce My

[136] Entropy is a thermodynamic statistical measure, amalgamating good order with disorder (energy unavailable for useful work) in constant operation in a closed physical system that undergoes change: the greater the disorder, the higher the entropy. All systems and elements in the universe tend to disintegrate into a lower structure of order, less well organised and more disruptive owing to increasing disorder. Evolution is based on the opposite stance of simple systems becoming more sophisticated or more complex through natural adaptability to changing circumstances.

arrival. All people throughout the nations should tremble at the prospect of the coming judgement. Says the Lord your God."

On the 31st of October 1917, whilst the outnumbered and outgunned 400 Australian Light-Horsemen charged and over-ran the well-entrenched enemy at Beit Sheba, the British Cabinet were signing official documents, confirming the provision of a homeland for Diaspora Jews in Palestine, by enacting the Balfour Declaration signed by Arthur J Balfour, the British Foreign Secretary on behalf of the British Government. This confirmed an agreement in principal made earlier, between Lord Balfour and the Jewish scientist Chaim Weizmann. Weizmann had invented acetate, a synthetic propellant for shells used during the First World War. Without this discovery being made available to Britain, she and her allies would probably have been defeated. The territory agreed as a Jewish homeland extended over both banks of the River Jordan, covering 43,075 square miles. A decision was arrived at the meeting of the Allied Supreme Council in San Remo in April 1920, to recommend to the 52 member countries of the League of Nations, that Britain should be granted a continuation of the Mandate to protect the interest of the Jews in Palestine. In 1922 Britain sanctioned the formation of Trans Jordan, carved out of Palestine, providing a home for world Jewry, whilst not displacing the resident Palestinians. This action cut Palestine to 10,615 square miles, 23% of its (mandated) size. I now understand that the policy of offering comfort for the Jews was a cynical ploy to persuade the League of Nations to support the mandate of Britain in administering Palestine, which ensured that British interest in the area was internationally approved, whilst keeping control of the Suez Canal, through granting a superficial sovereignty to King Faud of Egypt. Britain cynically reneged on the terms of Article V of the Mandate, by partitioning Palestine (I suspect on advice of the Royal Institute of International Studies[137] amongst other 'capitalist exploiters'), but the British Government must shoulder the blame.

[137] On the 29th of July 1921, a group of European and American bankers and political figures formed themselves into an international 'Council of Reference', whose prime objective was to manipulate and control the movement of money throughout the world. Three of the four main centres of operation were located in Europe. In Britain the organisation was called the Royal Institute of International Studies, in France the Centre d' Estudes de Politique Etrangre, in Germany the Institut fur Auswartige Politik, and in America, the Council of Foreign Relations. Today its members are executives of the World Bank, as well as the International Monetary Fund (IMF) and the World Trade Organisation (WTO).

The Judeans, in 606 BC, were sentenced to 2,520 years of exile for losing their ***patriarchal*** fervour (606 BC plus 2,520 years, brings the year to 1914. It is significant that the First World War started in 1914, 2520 years after the Babylonian exile; perhaps this was the fulfilment of the ***times of the Gentiles***? The First World War was not confined to professional armies, but relied upon the conscription of private citizens in order to face an enlarged theatre of battle. I believe this war was the war that Jesus was speaking of in Matthew Ch 24:7, when ***patriotism*** was demanded by all nations to enforce conscription. The war in which family members will feud amongst each other will occur later into the remaining years of pre-Rapture history. The Jews were released from exile, but not from further persecution. The slaughter, in 1929, of 69 Jews in Hebron by rioting Palestinians occurred without reprisal by Britain, dismaying but alerting the Jews as to Britain's bias. Until this massacre there had been a continuous presence of Jewish families in Hebron since biblical times. Prior to the commencement of the Second World War, the British Government acted disgracefully towards the European Jews in preventing their every attempt to settle in Israel. British servicemen followed War Office Orders in forcing the, often unseaworthy, craft carrying the European Jews to Palestine, back out to sea. These pathetic scraps of humanity often had insufficient food or medical supplies, and sought only the right to live in the homeland of their forefathers. Many Jews died when their boats finally sank whilst trying to dock in some other country that they hoped might demonstrate mercy regarding their plight by allowing them entry. Death by drowning was preferable for families, than the prospect of return to the regime of the ***Third Reich***[138].

During the Holocaust the British Government had full knowledge of the crimes perpetrated against the European Jew, and, although in a position to publicise the suffering, chose not to inform America of the inhumanity being executed. Once Hitler's armies began to conquer Europe, the male Jews (many of whom had been forcibly repatriated) were shot or starved to death when they could no longer work as slaves, whilst their wives and children were asphyxiated in

---

[138] Chillingly, but necessarily, I must point out from Revelation Ch 20:13, that those people who died in watery graves will be present in God's courtroom, to accuse those who were accomplices to their murder, through supporting or conforming to ungodly practices. I believe that the desperation of 'boat people' around the world, witnessed over 30 years on our tv screens, has been in order to draw the world's attention to a parallelism of the righteous judgement of God on every nation. Especially those nations enjoying a 'safe' environment who have not considered the needs of the majority of an imprisoned world as 'their' problem, and have not seen third world poverty and godless leadership as reason to agitate for a greater humane response to such ignorance.

gas chambers. The Foreign Secretary Anthony Eden and the Home Secretary Herbert Morrison of the coalition government were anti-Semitic, but, out of a sense of decency, they did send the decoded German High-Command's letters[139] to the War Cabinet. PM Winston Churchill decided not to inform the USA of Hitler's plans of mass extermination of whole families and communities of Jews. He also resolved not to carry out bombing raids on the railway lines that were transporting the cattle-trucks of Jews to the death-camps. Such a succession of air raids could have been accomplished quite easily, and would have delayed mass extermination. The memory of the inhumanity meted out to European Jewry by the Nazis, in the death camps, and the wholesale slaughter in the gas chambers during the Holocaust has faded, but the spectre remains today. However, it is reliably reported that the names of every Jewish family in Palestine was recorded, and every Jew was to be transported back to the death camps of Europe, in the event of Germany winning the desert war. Britain granted sovereign power of what became known as Trans-Jordan to King Abdullah of Jordan in 1946, who changed the name of this misappropriated piece of real estate from Trans-Jordan to Jordan in 1950, and illegally annexed Judea and Samaria renaming the area as the 'West Bank'. The Egyptian *Wafd* party supported the Allies during the Second World War, when Britain failed to deliver on the promises made to grant full independence; the Muslim brotherhood incited embarrassing resistance causing Britain's withdrawal of troops in 1947. A revolution followed, and by 1952 the *Wafd* party were in power, finally overthrowing the puppet monarchy in 1956. In 1947 the UN divided the remaining 23% of Palestine west of the Jordan into a second Arab State occupying 11% of the area, leaving the Jewish State an area of a paltry 12% of the area proposed by the League of Nations. The Jews had no alternative but to accept the tiny piece of land, renamed Israel, and to agree to share their ancient city of Jerusalem as the capital of Palestine. This was purely further deceit by the British Government who displayed undisguised bias towards the Arabs, handing over control of fortifications to the Arab Legions (located strategically on the mountain tops), and seconded military officers as advisors, at the same time supplying the Arab militia with weapons, ammunition and instruction in combat training. During this largesse, the disarming of Jewish nationals and the forbidding of any training manoeuvres of the *Hagannah* defence

[139] The Government Decoding Unit, based at Bletchley Park in Milton Keynes, using the Enigma computer, cracked any codes devised in Germany, and their results were swiftly passed to the War Office.

force[140] was enforced. It appears to me that the British Government colluded to over-ride UN decree to provide a homeland for world Jewry. This whole course of events was unjust and unrighteous, and was politically motivated. Much more infamy has been uncovered and reported in the book by Richard Breitman titled ***Official Secrets***.

The climax of the indifference of the British Government shown towards the plight of the European Jews occurred at this time, when 4,500 emaciated survivors of the Holocaust, who were passengers on the ship Exodus, which was attempting to ferry European Jews to Palestine, was denied docking facilities in Haifa. Whilst in the bay approaching port, the boat was rammed seven times by British naval vessels. The skipper managed to anchor the Exodus, but this enabled armed British sailors to board the ship, and enforce obedience to their will on the passengers and crew. Two refugees were shot, and died of their wounds, whilst other passengers were clubbed into submission. The Exodus was then escorted to Cyprus and interned; the dismayed Jews were providentially finally allowed to complete their *aliyah* upheld by the UN. Although Britain had been commissioned by the UN to administer law and order during the rebirthing of Israel. In two World Wars Jews and many colonials dwelt peaceably in Britain whilst contributing to the war effort. Many Jews laid down their lives, serving their adoptive country, but the majority of their progenies still feel badly treated and alienated. It is ironic that Argentina was one of the favoured hiding places for escaping German war criminals, but those who helped them escape, and those, whose blood was shed, or property stolen, will see justice imposed in God's final judgement. There will be other accusers and accused in that final courtroom scene; some whom were involved in the sinking of the Argentinean warship, the General Belgrano, in 1983[141].

Since the beginning of the 20th century, the nations that extended a welcome towards refugees in providing homes, education and employment, have found that, at times of internal recession and high unemployment, racial discrimination by a minority of xenophobic nationals erupts into civil disorder. Any employed person from a 'foreign' ethnic background has been resented and subjected to racial abuse by the endemic nationals; particularly if the 'foreigner' appeared to enjoy a better standard of living than the racists experienced. Initially the Jewish race provided the scapegoat, but inevitably,

---

140 The Hagannah were a mishmash assortment of ex-militia Jews who had fought on the side of Britain and its allies during the Second World War.

141 The Belgrano was torpedoed in its own territorial waters before Britain officially declared war on Argentina.

the ethnic cleansing witnessed around the world today is the direct consequence of the Holocaust. The wish to eliminate the Jewish race has now overflowed its gruesome boiling pot. I believe that God has allowed ethnic hatred to manifest among the tribes of the nations, resulting in terrible carnage as retribution for the unwillingness of the nations to provide shelter for European Jewry, prior to and during World War 11. The nations continue to offer unrestrained vociferous protestation, that Israel must concede even more land to the Arabs. What an unfair solution! Israel is treated as a pariah nation, a social outcast, by most of the 185 member states of the UN, and receives a very bad press from the world's media.

Following the invaluable support to the British Military Services during the Second World War the Karen tribesmen of Myanmar (Burma) were given similar assurances to promises given to European Jewry during the First World War. General Bill Slim said of their support against the Japanese: "***The Karen are no fair-weather friends.***" Britain has reneged on its obligation to honour promises of support to the seven million Karen people, 40% of whom are Christian, to establish their own Independent State. The military junta are relentless in their inhuman policy of mass genocide (ethnic cleansing). The Karen have sought sanctuary in Thailand, but are in danger of forced repatriation to Burma, with the certainty of extermination.

America in the Dock

Following the Second World War President Harry Truman, had initially been eager to offer substantial solace to world Jewry for the inhumanity practised against their race, by petitioning the UN to support his plan to provide a homeland in Palestine for world Jewry. In reality this action was a formality, for many Russian Jewish families had lived in the land of Israel since the 1880s. Mr Truman succumbed to pressure from senior State officials to be less vociferous in his support for a Jewish homeland. He continued to work quietly, but forcefully, behind the scenes, and was successful in bringing together an *ad hoc* committee of the UN who conducted a survey on 25th November 1947 of the likely voting at the UN General Assembly for the establishment of a separate partitioned state for the Jews[142]. Mr Truman persuaded the **UN** to carry out a vote, which resulted in the nation of Israel being approved on the 29th of November 1947. I do not intend to write of America's fall from grace, it is well documented[143].

My reader will be aware that, in recent years, the **UN** has repeatedly passed resolutions condemning Israel's insensitivity towards the Palestinians' claim of ownership of the Temple Mount, which successive governments of Israel emphatically reject. A recent resolution by the UN General Assembly voted 148 to 1 that it was illegal for Israel to govern the international City of Jerusalem. The 22-member Arab League is a very powerful contingent of the 56-member Organisation of the Islamic Conference (OIC). The OIC in turn forms the core of the 113-member Non-Aligned Movement, a remnant of the Cold War era, that still represents the Third World countries, and dictates the agenda at most Conferences. At a **UN** sponsored conference, on racism in Durban in September 2001, the agenda was predictable for the Arab/Islamic bloc commands a majority of votes in most **UN** proceedings. Some 3,900 registered non-government organisations (NGO's) signed a draft petition accusing Israel of '***systematic perpetration of racist crimes, including war crimes, acts of genocide, and ethnic cleansing against the Palestinians***'. The document set forth a recommended "plan of action" for the UN to follow, that effectively called for the dismantling of the '***racist***, ***apartheid State***' of Israel, urging enforcement of the Fourth Geneva Convention of 1949, to include a 'protection force' for Palestinians and the dismantling of the 'Jewish Israeli colony'. It also endorsed the 'right of return' for all Palestinians,

---

142 The recorded tally of 25 votes in favour to 13 votes against the proposition was insufficient for success, as a two-thirds majority was necessary for adoption. Mr Truman warned Israel's first PM, David Ben Gurion of the likely outcome. Israel resorted to covert 'encouragement' to Mr Truman's initiative. Mossad (Israel's State Intelligence Service) had compiled a comprehensive dossier of Nelson Rockerfeller's financial dealings with the Nazis, and the involvement of USA officials and the Vatican, in providing escape routes into South America for senior members of the German High Command, to escape their facing the War Crimes Tribunal. Ben Gurion confronted Nelson Rockerfeller with this damning indictment, and in return for Israel agreeing to suppress the information contained in the dossier, Ben Gurion was promised that the Latin American members of the UN would switch their votes to ensure a successful outcome. The final vote cast on the 29th November in support of a homeland for the Jews, through the partitioning of Palestine, was 33 for (which included the Russian bloc) and 13 against, with 10 abstentions, which was sufficient to ensure Israel's rebirth.

143 John McTernan and Bill Koenig in their book ***Israel. The Blessing or the Curse*** have written of America's rebellion against God's laws in much the same regretful way that I undertook concerning Britain. Internationally recognised Pastor David Wilkerson of New York has written and spoken in much the same heartbreaking vein.

and called on the world body to revive UN Resolution 3379 equating Zionism with racism, to force repeal of Israel's Law of Return granting citizenship to Jewish immigrants, and to establish a war crimes tribunal to '***prosecute Israeli racists***'. The government representatives of both Israel and the USA withdrew from the Conference in protest, which I believe resulted in the immediately triggered inhuman decision to terrorise America in reprisal.

At the heart of the UN hq in New York is a multi-faith meditation room ('off limits' to the public); in which is contained a four foot high black stone, on which initiates can concentrate their attention, when in existential meditation. This black stone appears to me to be a facsimile of the ***Kaaba*** Black Stone in the central shrine in the Great Mosque at Mecca, and confirms nothing more than the ***worship of idols made by man*** (Isaiah Ch 40:18-20). The incitement from ***bellicose imams*** for a holy ***Jihad***, with promises of rewards in heaven from *Allah* for destroying first the Saturday people, and then the Sunday people, (the Jew and then the 'Christian'[144]), through an unholy *intifada*, has resulted in terrorism by suicide bombing in Israel, on an unimaginable scale. Muslims are taught to regard dying as a *shahid* (a martyr for Islam), as being a glorious privilege. A suicide bomber who destroys 'infidels' is guaranteed instant joys in paradise. The most persuasive, gentle Muslim is in the minority; most who follow that faith would murder opposition as vociferously incited to do by their imams, who find sufficient material in the Koran to support their views. Subjugation or elimination of alternative life-styles is deeply imbedded into the psyche of the ***Muslim extremist***. ***Holy wars*** were a religious inheritance 'bequeathed' by the Crusaders to Muslims from the time of Mohammed.

I share the indignation of American people, over the atrocity of the twin-tower's destruction and understand their wish to retaliate, but revenge is a human reaction and is despised by God. Devout Christian and Muslim zealots, who would choose to be martyred for their faith; would never bow the knee to a foreign god, or a human being insisting on being worshipped as a god. I am greatly distressed to prophesy that there will be a devastating earthquake in America, and other natural disasters, which may well lead to a greater loss of life than in the World Trade Centre horror. This could suggests that God has turned His back on ***believers*** in America; but this is not so. God would

[144] This statement is supported by Daniel Ch 10:13, when both the Archangels Gabriel and Michael had been detained in fighting the evil spirit behind the king and prince of Persia respectively. That same evil spirit is abroad today, which may be determined from Revelation Ch 9:11, where the name of angel of the Abyss is given in Hebrew and Greek. (see also the identification made with the same 'Persian' spirit in Chapter 7).

never turn His face away from ***believers*** in any land; but ***God has never upheld unrighteous nations***. I have been praying for mercy, however God will not be pigeonholed into conforming to human wisdom or desires. Unfortunately the Muslim will believe that any natural disaster occurring in America is the will of *Allah*, fully ignoring the natural disasters in Muslim countries! The Arab nations are the descendants of Lot, and of Esau, who married the daughter of Ishmael, Mahalath (Genesis Ch 28:9). The Islamic Arab nations, through denying American 'imperialists', and protector of the Jews, access to 'their' land, from which to establish a ground base, (an essential requirement to any invasion), or even the right to use 'their' airports, and perhaps refusing '***the enemies of Islam***' the right to over fly 'their' airspace. Such denial will strengthen the resistance of other Islamic nations, by their uncompromising stand against the 'imperialists' and will gladden the hearts of Muslims of other nations. America will it know it is in an unwinnable war only when is refused support by Islamic countries.

In America's retaliation through the bombing of Afghanistan, in order to overthrow the Taliban government *Mujaheddin*[145] (holy warriors), who refused to hand over fanatical extremist Muslim, Saudi Arabian millionaire, Osama bin Laden (whom the Taliban admitted harbouring), a hornet's nest has been disturbed. America is facing a many headed Hydra in a battle that they might subdue but cannot win, and which the costs of containment will prove prohibitive. Inevitably the Taliban called all Muslims in every nation to a ***holy Jihad*** against the enemies of Islam, despite the assurances of the Western governments that the battle is only against terrorists, and not a religious crusade against Islam. It is inevitable that America will decide to depose Saddam Hussein of Iraq, as part of their drive against all 'terrorism'. The whole world is expecting bin Laden (or even

---

[145] The leader is Mullar Mohammed Omar, whose movement swept to power in 1994 on the overthrowing of the Communist Party following the withdrawal of Russian troops (in 1990). The Taliban are of the Pashtun ethnic group that at 38% of the 88 ethnic groups living in Afghanistan, are the majority race. A recent internal radio broadcast by Mr Omar, urged his country to "***Stand firm in the forthcoming holy war, as defenders of Islam***". Even if his regime is toppled, or bin Laden is killed, the battle lines have been drawn, the religious war will continue until the New World Order imposes peaceful co-existence. Bin Laden released a video within hours of the attack on American civilisation swearing that the USA will never taste security and safety until peace reigns in Palestine, and before all the army of infidels are driven from the land of Mohammed. Bin Laden is stating that America deserves punishment, no – he means destruction, for supporting the Jewish race. I hate writing his name down for it gives publicity, if not credence to his philosophy.

a lone fanatic[146]) to detonate one of Russia's missing nuclear suitcase bombs in America. Bin Laden, as a young man, was trained in warfare by the CIA to fight from Afghanistan against Russia. His organisation ***Al Qaida*** has trained most of the international terror groups that perpetrate bombing outrages on American and Israeli Embassies and military barracks in countries across the world. America's 'most wanted' list, headed by bin Laden, are leaders of terrorist groups wanted for their involvement in the attacks on the U.S. embassies in Kenya and Tanzania in 1998, in which 224 people were killed. Included on the list of heads of terrorist groups is Imad Fayez Mugniyeh, head of Hizbullah's operations overseas. Mugniyeh is wanted by the US in connection with the hijacking of a TWA flight from Beirut in 1985. He is also believed to have been involved with the 1983 bombings that simultaneously destroyed the US and French military barracks in the Lebanese capital, killing almost 300 people. Mugniyeh is held responsible by Israel for the bombings of the Israeli Embassy and a Jewish Community Centre in Buenos Aires that left 119 dead in the early 1990s. Mossad believes that Mugniyeh masterminded the 'twin towers' bombing in 1993, in which six people were killed. These terror organisations seek to impose their extremism on stable Islamic countries, through destroying the infrastructure, and by the assassination of opponents. Their objective is to impose the Islamic faith over the whole world, even if it causes the ignition of an international religious war.

In 1977, as a damage limitation initiative, President Carter signed executive order No 12148 to create the Federal Emergency Management Agency (FEMA). The FEMA command centre was installed underground at Mount Weather in Virginia. In the event of any nuclear catastrophe or civil disorder America would be administered from this bunker. The chief of FEMA civil security division is on public record as saying: ***"A new frontier is in place for the prevention of dissident groups from gaining access to US opinion or a global audience during times of crisis."*** There has been many reports that since the 'defeat' (?) of Saddam in 1991, his espionage agents have been infiltrating armed militia into America through the borders of Canada and Mexico. These reports are 'hushed up', but the

[146] Such an example may be seen in the story of the horrific revenge exacted for the wanton liquidation of the Branch Davidians. In 1995 the Murrah Federal Building was dynamited by former US army sergeant Timothy McVeigh, who had placed canisters filled with the nerve gas Sarin, in the truck used in the attack, resulting in the deaths of 168 people. The heat from the explosion incinerated the gas leaving only a charred residue, otherwise many more deaths would have resulted, and Oklahoma City would have been uninhabitable for a century!

Anti-Terrorist Forces based at Houston are known to have investigated some illegal Islamic activity, accidentally stumbled upon by members of the public. The conclusion of the US Commission on National Security held in 1999 was that America would become increasingly vulnerable to hostile attacks, and that Americans would likely die on American soil, ***possibly in large numbers***. It was recommended to President Bush on 31st January 2001 that a National Homeland Security Agency be created, which is the wish of the law-abiding, easy going but vulnerable citizens of America. Any act of reprisal by America will inevitably be protested against by the Arab nations as anti-Islamic and supportive of Israel.

Chapter 6

OPEN OUR EYES LORD

Conrad Adenauer, founder member of the Christian Democratic Union Party (CDU[147]) declared that Germany had a divine mission to unify Western Europe under one overall parliament[148]. Former CDU leader and Chancellor, Helmut Kohl, shares the vision of his predecessor. Mr Khol stated his intention to enforce a totally binding treaty, with no escape clauses, for EC Member States. At their summit in Helsinki in 1999, the 15 European Union (EU) leaders decided to form a rapid-relief force. It has been said that the formation of this 'Force' is to circumnavigate the North Atlantic Treaty Organisation (NATO) as a whole, and America in particular, when it is believed that politics may cause a delay or a veto of action, which is perceived by the EU arbitrators as against their best interests[149]. The EU are proposing to implement an all-embracing International Law based on the Convention of Human Rights, for the protection of Europeans from religious exhibitionism and exploitation by any 'fundamental' pressure group. The Bill seeks to subject every organisation having an affiliation to any religion, that administers hospitals, schools etc, including their supportive charities, as 'public authorities', subject to the same rules and scrutiny. The objective of this legislation being to standardise services of worship in buildings authorised for worship, enforced through Statute Law, in each of the countries under EU jurisdiction.

---

[147] The CDU is the political wing of the Vatican, and influential throughout Europe.

[148] Former Russian President Mikhail Gorbachev was the main speaker at a five-day forum held in Los Angeles (during 1995), entitled ***The State of the World***. He spoke of a global metaphysical civilisation, speaking a universal language, trading with a universal currency, with freedom to worship any god of one's choice, under the one roof, at individual or multi-faith services. Gorbachev wanted all services monitored to ensure no seditious speeches were made.

[149] The formation of a '**Rapid Relief Force**', is to free the EU from the need to seek the agreement and cooperation of the UN or NATO to any response the EU may wish to make over a particular situation. I am certain that because of the diverse political interests of a the number of nations involved, political manouverings take up so much time at UN and NATO meetings that the EU must often feel that the specific problems they want addressed are not dealt with at all, or not promptly enough. The Force is envisaged as having the capacity to deploy anywhere in the world 60,000 personnel within 60 days, for up to a year, backed by a large combat air and naval force. A senior EU official has said that member countries have pledged the finance for 100,000 soldiers, 400 aircraft and 400 assorted special capability ships. I received revelation that the EU will prove to be part of the demonic rule that will finally be overthrown at the Second Coming, when unredeemed capitalism and faith in other religions will be demolished by Christ's rule.

Denominations established over 5-10 years or more will be allowed to conduct services within the boundaries of the EU's ambit.

During 1994 the UN funded a report entitled ***Our Global Neighbourhood,*** detailing universal social and distributive justice. A proposal was made that the General Assembly of the UN should pursue the consensus reached on 'global governance'[150], with a strong commitment to democracy and a fairer distribution of the world's resources initiated by the UN. A follow-up conference was held in October 1998 at which Britain's PM Tony Blair drew the attention of the delegates to the collapse of national economies throughout the world. He called for an independent international committee to be formed, which should be empowered to deal with international social and economic issues. A spokesman from the corrupt monarchical country of Indonesia, added his exhortations for international intervention. The USA delegate requested the officials of the IMF and the World Bank to consider how they might support the issues raised by Mr Blair to administer the economy of Indonesia.

Allegedly the governing body in Indonesia, which has the largest Muslim population in the world, surreptitiously invited a militant Islamic terror group, *Laskar Jihad*[151], trained by bin Laden, to terrorise the Christians of Indonesia into recanting through intimidation by mutilation and murder. Indonesia is spiralling into terminal decline as disorder degenerates into chaos. Vice-President Hamzaah Haz is an extremist Muslim cleric, if he ever gets to be President of Indonesia,

---

[150] 'Global governance' replaces the now politically incorrect method of identifying 'global governance', or 'New World Order'.

[151] The most conservative of reports is than 10,000 Christians were murdered in the Malacca Islands of eastern Indonesia, in May 2000, by an army of well-armed and well-trained Muslim militia of 15,000 Laskar Jihad. Repeated savage attacks, destroying Christian family life and homes, and the burning down churches, took place. It is well documented that the captured were laid spread-eagled on the floor, and under the threat of death, for refusal to recant, were cut with the one blade, without antiseptic cleansing, and then herded into the sea as their only medication. The Barnabas Fund issued a report that a 3,000-strong army in December 2001 was closing in on thousands of Christians who for safety have left their villages, and gathered together as refugees in the town of Tentena. They are under pressure to return to their villages, but the Muslim extremists will not allow any Christians to reside in areas that were 'cleansed'. I am writing of a total breakdown in law and order, which will soon become evident. It is a constant fear of mine that Muslim extremist might well similarly slaughter Christians in other mainly Muslim countries if they refuse to convert. It is necessary for me to feature the horrific attacks on the Sudanese Christians since 1983 resulting from the country's Islamic government imposing Sharia Law. Thousands of Christians and animists have been through the enforced ceremony of conversion, which stripped of flowery language, means instant circumcision unhygienically and inhumanly administered, without medical supervision or after care.

then there will be major trouble. The loss of the former so-called colony of 'Christian' East Timor has rankled the Islamic nation, which has opposed the two years of UN intervention in restoring democracy to the island. It does not need the mind of a rocket scientist to work out that one answer to Indonesia's economic woes is to employ the nation in an invasion of a 'Christian' country. I foresee a fanatical regime plotting with an Islamic government of Malaya[152] to overthrow the democracy of Singapore in a pincer invasion. I have heard recently that a prophetic figure in Australia has prophesied that Australia would be invaded by Indonesia. How on earth can the 20 million people living in Australia resist an attack from a nation with ten times as many people? Civil disorder, due to ethnic and religious intolerance, and collapsing economies, is having commercial ramifications throughout the third world. The 'domino effect' of a religious war will lead to the collapse of the world's economy.

The UN have decided that there is a need for an International Court of Law to prosecute any dictator who authorises mass destruction or deportation of an ethnic or religious group living in any nation. Such a dictator will be brought to trial for his inhumanity. Xenophobic hatred is not restricted to religious intolerance, or the colour of one's skin. The plight of the refugee, the violation of human rights, the lack of adequate education, and the welfare of the poorest people of the nations, are the concern of all mankind, and should be properly and speedily addressed. The global protectionism of patents and rights that is practised by every multi-national company, along with tax avoidance, is criminal and evil[153]. The communication explosion[154] has arisen through the advent of satellite cameras and computers. Today we live in a global village where the events in one nation are instantly reverberated around the globe to every other nation. There is therefore merit in the Commission's proposals, for problems in any part of the world to be dealt with by an international

---

152 The Malayan government in December 2001 sentenced to death by hanging, three members of the Muslim extremist group (Al-Ma'unah), and a further 16 members to life imprisonment. This group of fanatics were seeking to impose Shariah law on their more moderate fellow countrymen, through an armed revolt: a popular ploy of the Al Qaida trained terrorists.

153 The UN has calculated from research that £480 billion is lost to the poorest nations through global protectionism by multi-national companies, £68 billion for the cost of spurious excuses of tax evasion, and £69 billion in respect of exploitation of agricultural policies. These limitations have been eroded by extortion and bribery, often condoned by self-seeking administrators.

154 At the press of a button computers can now communicate in more than 400 languages. Financial, legal, and educational documents etc can all be translated and processed instantly.

police force. One can understand the logic of a global taskforce being available, to stifle any insurrection against stable government. However history proves that human intervention by external forces in the affairs of another nation can never succeed.

Early in 1999 the countries of NATO, in their determination to halt the ethnic cleansing of (Muslim) Croatians and Albanians domiciled in Serbia, decided to bomb 'Greek Orthodox' Serbia into submission. The intervention has been completed for humanitarian reasons, but harmonious relationships between the two people groups will never be restored. Hatred can be contained, but not overcome. President Yeltzin of Russia may have been caught unawares by NATO's intervention in Serbia, but I suspect that NATO leaders were gambling that Russia was not in a strong enough economic position to support her former protégé, and was rightly upset over the attack, having been assured by President Clinton only months earlier that NATO would never cross national borders to impose sanctions against the former Soviet Bloc nations. Once the suppositions of the Western nations were confirmed, the General Assembly felt confident to publish (in April 1999) a new strategic doctrine entitling NATO to impose its own moral imperatives worldwide. Violent systematic attacks against people groups, territorial encroachment by force of arms, the abuse of human rights and other infringements, ***if deemed appropriate***, could result in military intervention being undertaken by NATO. If my cynical interpretation is correct, then '***appropriate action***' is a politically correct way of saying '***interfered***' with. The Secretary-General of the UN, Kofi Anan, remarked in Sweden on the 25th May 1999, that: "***There has been a gathering momentum in international thinking, moving towards direct interference, where humanitarian principles and rights of any ethnic or religious grouping governed by any nation's jurisdiction are not protected by the civil authorities from repeated acts of violent disorder. Such disorder includes the burning of homes and murder carried out by fanatical fundamentalists, then, if the leaders do not accept the UN's appeal to be invited to assist in restoring order, the UN may choose to override the leaders refusal.***" NATO acted pragmatically over ***not*** interfering with Moscow's authority to smother the resistance of Muslims in Chechnya who wished to break away from Russia, which I suspect had something to do with the logistics and expense of long-range bombing, with perhaps extended involvement, and the moral high ground conceded. I predict that it will not be too long before Israel is '***interfered***' with, by the UN, to enforce the internationalising of Jerusalem.

Some writers of apocalyptic literature believe that the supreme committee of the Illuminati, or the ***Bilderberger Group***[155]*,* or the ***Club of Rome***[156], will be the manipulating puppeteer pulling the strings behind the soon to be established New World Order, which was prophesied in Revelation Ch 13:7 as coming to pass during the Great Tribulation. Some members of the WTO, and EU officials, will undoubtedly become part of the leadership of New World Order. Those who lead an international government are a law unto themselves, not answerable to higher authority. Through collusion and coercion and by the clever use of 'spin-doctors', feeding misinformation and propaganda to the world press, events will be manipulated to justify their action.

I am praying that just as the animals and the first-born sons of the Hebrew families were spared prior to the Exodus from Egypt, there will be provisions made for sustenance and protection supplied by God for His people, during the Great Tribulation. Christians may be largely unaffected during the 'Day of the Lord' and have a sufficiency of food to share with their non-believing neighbour (bridesmaid[157]). Yet I am conscious of the parable of the wise and the foolish bridesmaid (who are those 'pagans' who haven't accepted Christ), with each one being personally responsible for one's own provision. There is in Matthew Ch 25: 1-13 the injunction that the unprepared were rejected by the bridegroom, and were responsible for their own rejection by their unpreparedness. Every reader ought to seek God's revelation over what action one should take to store provisions during the Great Tribulation. I do believe that Christians with the internal ***gift*** of '*faith*', as opposed to the external ***fruit*** of '*faith*' can expect God to provide sufficient sustenance to share with others.

I can identify with Lord Shaftesbury's passionate statement made towards the end of his life: "***I do not think during the last 40 years I have lived one conscious hour that was not influenced by the thought of our Lord's return***." I am similarly captivated, whether awake or asleep, by the colourful thought of the imminent Second

---

[155] The Bilderberger Group is a powerful group of industrial magnates, bankers and politicians, selected from various nations, who initially met together at the Hotel de Bilderberger in Oosterbeek, Holland, in May 1952, to plan the necessary steps to be taken apolitically to unify their nations.

[156] The Club of Rome was formed in 1968 with 75 members of outstanding ability, recognised throughout the world as experts within their field of reference. The purpose of the '***Club***' was to dictate to national governments policies the '***Club***' advocated.

[157] There are four good examples of God's supernatural provision in the Bible, 1 Kings Ch 17:14, 2 Kings Ch 4:3-6, Matthew Ch 14:17-21, Mark Ch 8:6-9. God will feed His people at this time, as He provided for the Israelites in the wilderness, prior to them entering the Promised Land.

Coming. The heady atmosphere of witnessing the ushering in of the Prince of Peace and His Kingdom excites me. If my reader could imagine the uncertainty of living on the slopes of an active volcano, or in an area where stormy seas during high tides may inundate the land, threatening total annihilation, then that is the most vivid description of my anticipation of the Second Coming. I am apprehensive of the transition that will change my ageing body into an imperishable one. However in a similar way to the uncertainty of survival from an impending disaster, I know that the outcome will be eternal joy. The elect will be immediately 'Raptured' with Christ at the '***Revealing***'. The fleshly bodies of those who are alive at Christ's descent from heaven on to the Mount of Olives will be changed in an instant into an imperishable body that does not deteriorate. They will reign together with all those who have died into Christ, throughout the millennium.

My understanding of the acceptance and heeding of all the signs of the 'Rapture', or the Great Tribulation and the Second Coming, is that believers should not want to hold on to anything or anyone in this world, or be regretful over unfulfilled ambition, but rather should accept that the God of all the Earth will do right for those who love and trust Him. All who totally rejoice in Christ's return will be more than compensated for whatever has been left behind. I believe that Jesus' reference in Matthew Ch 24:19 to pregnant women[158], and nursing mothers praying that they will not have to flee on the Sabbath or in the Winter, is a timely reminder that we will not know the hour or the day of the Lord's return in retribution. It is inconceivable that parents of young children will find their offspring not being better blessed following the Second Coming, than they are currently.

I believe in a continuous (partial) ***unseen*** (but not secret[159]) Rapture, because the thief on his cross was told that he would be in paradise with Jesus that very day (Luke Ch 23:43). Also in Matthew Ch 27:52-53 reference is made to holy men rising from their tombs, whom I believe had been converted through Christ's ministry but died before Jesus' atoning sacrifice. I believe that their ***Translation***, and that of the repentant thief into heaven, was awaiting Christ's resurrection, when they too would have been Raptured joining the

---

[158] I cannot believe that following the Rapture pregnancies will be terminated on reception of our new bodies. I do believe that those who have lost a foetus or a baby during pregnancy or delivery will meet with the person that God had fashioned in the womb, but they will be in the prime of their adulthood, just as Adam and Eve were.

[159] Samuel Tregelles, a member of the Brethren Movement, first expounded the belief in a secret Rapture in 1830. The Movements' founder J N Derby accepted Tragelles' view, and the Schofield Reference Bible has popularised this non-biblical concept.

assembly in heaven in worship (Revelation Ch 5:13). Theologians have written of the Rapture as the 'second exodus'[160], reflecting a mirror image of the first exodus from Egypt, with the Israelites arriving in Saudi Arabia three days after starting out. Perhaps a continuous ***unseen*** Rapture of the dead commenced, or some other mystery occurred in the heavenlies, during the fiftieth year following restoration to the land, of which mankind has not been made aware. That nothing ***apparently*** took place is not evidence that nothing of spiritual significance happened. It seems to me that the fiftieth year of the regathering of Jews into the Promised Land, was perhaps highlighting either a hidden Rapture, or was reinforcing the immediacy of His ***Second Coming***.

In April 2000, Jew and Gentile celebrated Passover and Easter over the same days, for the ***third*** year in succession. I believe these '*coincidences of conjunction*; highlight the ***third*** millennial birthday of Christ which took place in 1996. Also on the ***third*** day of the wedding in Cana, when Jesus performed His first miracle, He declared that His time had not yet come; Jesus' day of judgement is now upon us! It is written in Hosea Ch 6:2:

> *"After two days He will revive us; on the third day He will* ***raise us up****."*

What I am pretty certain of is, that the final trumpet fanfare prior to Christ's feet touching Earth once again will herald the ***completion*** of the Rapture, and the reign of Christ with the martyred saints of the '***first resurrection***' (Revelation Ch 20:4-6). The appearance of the 24 elders of Revelation Ch 4:4, with the multitude of souls who had been slain during the Great Tribulation (together with the martyrs who had been slain in previous years, who will be under the altar, Revelation Ch 6:11), refers to a continuous period of time ***encompassing*** the whole of the Great Tribulation, when martyrs will be created ***daily***, through being persecuted even unto death[161] for their faith. Jesus did not establish a political (or ecclesiastical) kingdom on Earth, nor did He replace the Gentile Church in superiority over Israel, upon the fall from grace of the Jews. In the same way that not all

---

[160] It is possible that only Jews who have died, both believers and non-believers form this *second exodus*. The first exodus did not happen *in the twinkling of an eye*, nor will the second. I believe that believers will be 'Raptured' individually *in the twinkling of an eye,* **but not all of God's chosen will be taken at the same instant of time**.

[161] During the Second World War, many Europeans risked death by hiding Jews from the Nazi executioners. I believe this assistance will be repeated during the Great Tribulation, which will be one of a number of ways through which Gentiles will become martyrs. Those Gentiles who are caught by the authorities providing refuge for Jews will be martyred.

descendants of Israel are Israel (illustrated by Romans Ch 9:6), so not all who are baptised into a denomination, as an extension of Christ's body, are redeemed into 'new life' (a ***born-again*** existence) in Christ.

Clearly from Zechariah Ch 14:16-17, the 1,000-year reign of Christ follows the slaughter of the armies attacking Israel, as detailed in Ezekiel Ch's 37-38. All Gentile nations will then be subjects of Christ's rule, and the leaders will be compelled to attend the Feast of Tabernacles in Jerusalem, under penalty for non-attendance of suffering water restrictions in their homelands (Zechariah Ch 14:19). I drew attention in footnote 58 to the significance of the 2,300 evenings and mornings of Daniel Ch 8:14 leading to the Second Coming. Between the 13th of September 1993 (the date of the signing of the 'Oslo Accord'), and New Year's Day 2000 AD there were exactly 2,300 evenings and mornings! It is significant that 2000 AD was the Chinese 'Year of the Dragon'. It is written in Revelation Ch 13:1:

"And Satan (alias the dragon) stood on the shore of the sea."

Satan will have summoned his false christ to assume office at this time. I recognise the power of the tidal wave as synonymous with the ***Beast out of the Sea***, (aka the ***man of lawlessness*** or the ***final antichrist***, Revelation Ch 13:1-2), and the ***Beast out of the Earth*** (the ***false prophet***, Revelation Ch 13:11-17), able to perform miracles, introduced into ***authority*** as the flooding of lands from rainfall. I believe the two men that complete the trinity are already in office, but will not be appointed to their unholy function until after Israel is next invaded. On numerous occasions, both Arafat and other senior PA officials have assured Arab audiences that the Oslo Accord is only temporary, and not a binding permanent peace agreement. Arafat cited as precedents the *Khudaibiya* agreement. The accord signed by Salah a-Din with Richard the Lion Heart, as a temporary agreement until he was in a position to make further lasting incursions into the 'Christian' lands. In the Palestinian Arab newspaper Al Quds on May 10, 1998, Arafat was asked: "***Do you feel sometimes that you made a mistake in agreeing to Oslo?***" Arafat replied: "***No...no. Allah's messenger Mohammed accepted the al-Khudaibiya ten year peace treaty with the more powerful Koreish tribe***, which Mohammed reneged on two years later, when in a position to defeat his enemy.

Follow the seven 'abundant' years of uneasy peace that existed during the 'Oslo Accord' negotiations, the world can expect to enter into seven lean years of famine. George Curle, in his book ***The Times of the Signs***, believes from the evidence of his research that an unknown day in 2005 for the Second Coming is pointed to from several different sources. The EU has completed its budget plans until 2006. The Euro currency has been in circulation since January the 1st 2002[162], it probably employs the recently produced microchip called "MEW", just 0.4 millimetres in size, but capable of storing security codes which can be woven into paper money, and used for identification and surveillance tracking. Initially everybody will trade through the use of a personal debit card, but later, only those people who have accepted an identification mark on their body will be allowed to purchase and sell goods. A new policy of the marking of the body for personal identification to control all forms of bartering will be introduced, on the earlier policy being not suitable for total surveillance. The world powers will probably choose to implant a microchip under each person's skin, as an alternative to any physical marking, to appease Christian protests, because, even though 'those in authority' may not be Christians, they will be aware of the biblical warning contained in Revelation Ch 14:11. Believers will refuse any voluntary implant, but governmental law will eventually impose compulsory implants. These draconian measures are alarming, and need the overview of a pastor shepherd, to determine how the flock in their charge respond to the challenges against their beliefs[163].

During the 49th year of restoration to Israel, a unique star formation formed in the heavens over Jerusalem on the night of the 14-15th September 1997, Virgo (the virgin mother) was crowned with a constellation of 12 stars as she gave birth to the new moon (under her feet). The original image had been of Christ's birth, and his parents fleeing to Egypt until King Herod died in 4 BC, but that had been an imminent warning and not a sign of a 3½-year period of satanic activity. This new star sign announced the Second Coming (prophesied in Revelation Ch 12:6), in explaining the arrival of the red dragon (Satan) who relentlessly pursues the new-born child

---

162 Europe's income base is a little less than America's, but because Europe trades more (25% of gross domestic productivity (GDP) as opposed to America's 20%), its worldwide impact will be as great. The US has a trading deficit of US$140 billion and rising to an accumulated deficit of almost US$2 trillion, whilst Europe has a surplus of US$100 billion. Both these statistics suggest Europe will once again emerge as the dictatorial power throughout the world.

163 My understanding is in line with God-breathed biblical prophecy. It is what God said in Genesis Ch 41:32, which convinces me that the Great Tribulation will be similarly activated following God granting clear interpretation of events for watchmen to sound the warning. This is probably the reason why God gave Joseph revelation and interpretation over a number of years, as he has done with the revelation received by others and myself. The interpretation of Pharoah's dream by Joseph is recorded thus "***The matter has been firmly decided by God and He will do it***."

(the ***Messianic Jew***), and proclaimed the start of the biblical, '***about one half-hour***' period, of Revelation Ch 8:1, during which the worshippers in heaven contemplated the forthcoming wrath and prayed for God to exercise His mercy. The pursuit of the Messianic Jew persisted for 3½ years, and ended in 2001, when in accordance with Revelation Ch 12:17, Satan decided to attack the whole nation of Israel through Islamic fanaticism in the form of a second *intifada*, with an increase in suicide bombings against the Israeli public, which will undoubtedly be compared with the suicide attacks, that have been carried out against the American public. I received revelation at the Wailing Wall at *Rosh Hashana* 2000 that the second-stone throwing *intifada* would follow, but develop into a full-scale armed conflagration (in the 49th ***sacred*** year 29th September 2000-16th September 2001), which would escalate into the invasion of Psalm 83 during the 'sacred' fiftieth year (*Yovel*).

Chapter 7

GOD'S MEASURED FOOTSTEPS

Red moon eclipses are a rarity and have always been identified with the Messianic hope of the Messiah's reign on Earth (the Messianic millennium). Such lunar eclipses are pointers to the three apocalyptic references in the Bible:

- the first prophecy is written of in Joel Ch 2:28-32
- the second in Acts Ch 2:17-21 repeats Joel's prophecy
- the third is in Revelation Ch 6:12-17.

The red moon effect is caused by a veil or shadow (known as the *penumbra*) passing between Earth and the moon, at a time when the moon is travelling through the umbra. If the moon passes through the centre of the umbra, the total lunar eclipse lasts for two hours (the blotting out of the sun at Jesus' death lasted for three hours, Luke Ch 23:44, marking that the event was especially significant). In 1996 on the evening of *Pesach* (Passover, the 3rd April), which always falls on the 15th of the Hebraic month of *Nisan*, a ***red moon*** lunar eclipse occurred over Jerusalem. A repeat of the lunar eclipse occurred on *Succoth* 1996, the first evening of the eight-day festival celebrating the summer harvest, on the 15th of *Tishrei* (the 26th September). A further red moon eclipse occurred in 1997 on *Succoth* (the 17th of October). It is significant that three lunar eclipses in *Nisan* and *Tishrei* 1996 and 1997 sandwiching the fiftieth year of 'return to the land' mirrors the two ***solar*** eclipses encompassing the births of John the Baptist in 7 BC and Jesus the Messiah in 6 BC. On the 13-14th *Adar* (the 23rd March 1997), the day preceding the two-day Festival of *Purim*[164] a total ***solar*** eclipse occurred over Jerusalem. I believe that the world entered into the ***third*** millennium on Ascension Day (the 14th May) 1996, following the 2,000th anniversary of Christ's birth as the ***servant*** king.

Owing to an instruction received whilst in Jerusalem during my 1993 assignment, I booked a holiday in Eilat for a family Christmas holiday in 1994. On the Christmas Eve I took my family to the Church of the Nativity in Bethlehem, and later that afternoon, when visiting the Wailing Wall, I prayed and listened to God, who confirmed that all the

---

[164] This festival is also called the Feast of Lots when Jews across the world celebrate the anniversary of the day their ancestors were delivered from the first planned Holocaust. The Comet Hale Bopp reached its closest point to planet Earth in 2,380 years on these two days. On this occasion it will not be Queen Esther who will save the Jews, nor any other human agency, but the hands of the Messiah Himself and the evidence will be undeniable by even the most antagonistic God hater.

revelations given to me were from Him, which heartened me. Whilst the aeroplane returning us to Eilat was setting its course, I had a panoramic view of the lights of Jerusalem beneath, and of the city of Amman in Jordan a few miles distant. I received a *word of knowledge* that it would be a relatively simple matter for a fanatical organisation to hijack an aeroplane and destroy the Al Aqsa mosque, and the worshippers inside in a suicide 'missile' attack, a possibility under serious consideration by right wing Jewish fundamentalists. I was horrified at the thought and dismissed it from my mind[165]. I heard the words recorded in John Ch 12:35-36:

> *"You will have the light a little longer. Put your trust in the light while you have it, so that you may become sons of light."* (paraphrased)

I recalled a vision I had received in 1990.

> I saw a barbed-wire boundary fence, with two single strands strung between two wooden posts (the 'fortification' looked a bit like a low-current electric fence for restraining cattle). The fence would not deter a foot-soldier, let alone a tank. I knew the fence to represent the communities of unwalled Jewish settlements and towns that God would defend against the attacking enemy. I watched the fast approaching dark clouds billowing up filling the whole horizon, and felt strangely disquieted. I sensed that I was being told that the lights of Jordan and other nations would be supernaturally snuffed out like a candle. I heard a voice saying: "***Trust in Me you people of Tiberius and Jerusalem.***"

That night (Christmas Eve) I received an aural vision, which was repeated on Christmas night:

> I knew myself to be in Jerusalem; I could hear what I knew to be petrol bombs and hand grenades exploding setting houses alight. I could hear people screaming and the chatter of machine-gun fire. I pleaded to God that this scenario must not be fulfilled, but I was not given any reassurance that the government were in control. I was told that God was going to

[165] I remembered the power-cut I had witnessed a month earlier whilst staying in Tiberius, when the whole region was plunged into darkness by a violent uncontrollable act of nature; an electric storm, which claimed the lives of more than 500 people as it ploughed its path through Egypt and Israel (of which I amplified in Chapter 7 of my autobiography).

raise a man with the 'spirit of Samson' to power; he was Binyamin Netanyahu[166], who would call the people to prayer.

As the *schmitta* year of 2000 approached, I heard Jesus telling me to present myself at the Wailing Wall on *Rosh Hashana* and *Yom Kippur*, at which time I would be given revelation. I made a reservation at Christchurch in the Old City, (where I normally stay), and duly arrived in Jerusalem on the 23rd of September 2000. I attended my assignment at the Wailing Wall, on the anniversary date of the *schmitta* year I had experienced in Israel seven years earlier[167], when (in 1993), it was revealed to me that the world would enter the Great Tribulation shortly after the ending of the next *schmitta* year, but prior to the expiry of the fiftieth sacred diamond jubilee year. Whilst I was in Tiberius, I was alerted to the eruption of the forthcoming civil disorder, through a tv clip showing the leader of the Likud Party Mr Ariel Sharon, exercising the right of every Jew (established by Moshe Dayan symbolically handing the keys of ***usage but not sovereignty*** back to the Islamic authorities on the liberation of the Temple Mount in 1967), to visit the Dome on the Rock, in accordance with his previously announced intention. Scuffles did occur at the time of his visit, but nothing of much significance. On the following day, the first day of *Rosh Hashana* (Friday the 29th), the Grand Mufti of Jerusalem (Ekrima Sabri (appointed by Mr Arafat), speaking at the Al Aqsa Mosque, called for the shedding of the oppressor's blood. In the subsequent riots four Arabs were killed, 100 injured and 58 arrested. Many roadblocks were installed, and some areas were put out of bounds. In obedience, on Sunday the 1st of October, at 9:00AM, I walked to the Temple Mount. Military vehicles, carrying army personnel with automatic weapons, and policemen carrying full body shields and truncheons were continuously overtaking me. I spent an hour firstly praying and then

---

166 I shared this vision with the folk in my Prayer for Israel (PFI) group following my return to Britain on the 29th December. Following the Israeli General Election of 1997, I reminded my PFI group of the words I had prophesied 29 months earlier, which had been fulfilled. Although Mr Netanyahu was subsequently deposed at the following election, I believe he will return to office as PM.

167 I believe it to be significant that the tortuous route that the taxi in 1993 took to avoid any 'troubles', in order to board an earlier flight to the UK was repeated, as was my need to return home earlier than scheduled (I have devoted Chapter 7 of my autobiography I have written of all my early experiences in Israel, which is helpful in understanding my great love of the Jewish peoples, especially of those still part of the Diaspora. It is my belief that Christians should support financially as well as prayerfully the ministries that provide the funds to transport Jews to their natural homeland, and then provide the comfort that we are urged to in Isaiah Ch 40:1.

just watching the Temple Mount fill with ever increasing numbers of uniformed militia, ready to face down any rioters. God spoke to me:

> ***"You are witnessing the first minor skirmishes in a major insurrection that will escalate into the final [international religious] war between Isaac and Ishmael, in which the whole world will become embroiled. There will be a respite, but it will only be of short duration. An invasion by Arab mercenaries living in other nations will soon follow. Initially Islamic nations will support the Palestine Arabs with weapons and financial aid. Militant fundamentalists living in Islamic nations will incite the more peaceable Muslims to demand their national leaders to declare war on My chosen ones. Following Israeli action that will be perceived internationally as an inhuman response, the nations will conspire to impose sanctions over the Government of Israel, and declare My holy city of Jerusalem an open city, and an armed occupier will once more rule in Jerusalem. But take heart, for these occurrences are ordained by Me and will lead to My Son's return to rule and to reign, and to judge the nations. It is time to unblock deaf ears and open blind eyes. It is time to beat ploughshares into swords, but do not despair, for the battle belongs to Me. I will respond to the challenge of My enemies, who have enslaved My children and stolen their land and possessions. With a sweep of My hand I will swiftly restore their inheritance, whilst devastating My enemy. You have been given an increase in spiritual awareness, because you have proven obedient to your calling. Do not be afraid of the opposition raised against you. Despite the opposition, you will not be silenced in your testimony. Says your Lord."***

Later that morning I took a taxi over the Mount of Olives and through Jericho on my way to Jordan, to visit friends. Evidence of the rioting in these run down Arab communities was present on every street.

During the eight days I spent in Jordan, I saw much evidence for support of the Palestinians; they were days in which King Abdullah received both Mr Arafat and later General Moamar al Gadaffi of Libya. I witnessed public protests and some disorder, but mostly the blockaded roads were detoured around, through the insight of well-ordered service corps. I imagine that owing to Jordan's long border with Israel, the discussions between these leaders may have included a possible invasion, of Iraqi land forces through Jordan. I returned to Israel by air, and stayed in Tel Aviv for three nights. I am certain that Jordan will allow land forces from Saudi Arabia and/or Iraq through its borders to launch a concerted attack on Israel, which will result in Jordan's total devastation. A bus on which I was travelling in Tel Aviv was routinely stopped by the police and searched for explosives, a necessary vigilant action in Israel. Parcels or carrier bags filled with high explosives[168] have often been left in crowded market places or buildings. On Thursday the 12th of October I returned to Jerusalem in order to attend the Feast of Tabernacles Conference. In my hotel room I watched on tv a horrific live report of bestial scenes surrounding the death of two Jewish army reservists, who had been taken into police custody in Arab controlled Ramallah. Since that time I have constantly relived the picture of that murderer grinning devilishly and waving his bloodstained hands to the cheering crowds below. Having spent a restless night, reliving the tv reports of the previous evening, I awoke with the instruction of the Lord, ringing in my ears, to visit the Wailing Wall this day of *Yom Kippur*. I read in the newspaper of the 'Voice of Palestine' Radio Station, through their alarming unsubstantiated propaganda sound bites, inciting their listeners to violence. Palestinians no longer watch CNN and BBC satellite tv news channels, because their coverage is perceived as pro-Israeli, a philosophy encouraged by Islamic extremists. As I walked into the old city I was aware of vigilant IDF militia, in their pairs, stationed in every street, within sight of the next pair of armed soldiers, questioning all passing Arabs, and advising the populace to return to their homes. All citizens are aware of the Muslim fundamentalists penchant for strapping themselves (or a vehicle) with explosives, and becoming human time bombs, prepared to further the cause of those who incite them to martyrdom, in order to receive specifically promised benefits in some imaginary heaven by blowing themselves and their targets into kingdom-come. '*Brain-washing*' by Arab *mullahs* extolling martyrdom as pleasing to *Allah*, guaranteeing a special place of recognition in

---

[168] In the months following the outbreak of this intifada, many such 'plants' have failed to detonate, or the vigilant public has been able to forestall danger to life by alerting the bomb squad to disarm many bombs, but vigilance cannot lead to complacency. In the final analysis only the godhead can provide protection.

heaven is engrained in the Arab psyche[169]. On this occasion international tv camera crews were everywhere on the Temple Mount, and helicopter gun-ships hovered overhead. At the Wailing Wall the Lord spoke to me:

> ***"I have summoned you here to witness at first hand man's inhumanity towards his neighbour. You were told at the instigation of the false Peace Accord that only bad fruit would be produced. The ramifications of each escalation will reverberate throughout the Arab nations, and demands of reprisal will become more insistent. The peacemaker will be howled down, and pacifists will be considered enemies. Those who control international funds will engineer economic crises, but these events will escalate outside the control of those who believe themselves to be conducting events. Be certain that your redemption is at hand. Says your Lord."***

Unconfirmed reports that a war was almost brought about on the 22nd of February 2001, when President Saddam of Iraq ordered six armoured divisions to proceed to Iraq's border with Syria, towing launching equipment capable of firing ground-to-ground missiles into Israel. According to Israeli and American intelligence sources, the Syrian Government had agreed to allow passage to this invasion force. Hizbullah had also been given permission to execute a long-range rocket attack into northern Israel, to coincide with a similar attack by Hizbullah from Lebanon. Saddam was threatened with retaliation by small neutron bombs, capable of destroying his advancing forces. Nevertheless, Saddam (the master of brinkmanship) continued to move his forces into position like chess pieces. American and British aeroplanes were 'scrambled' from the Turkish airbase at Incherlik and from a US naval Aircraft Carrier in the offshore waters, and bombed the town of Mosul, meeting stiff resistance. Thirty-five ground-to-air missiles were fired, and a further bombing raid was aborted. It should be remembered that the USA and Britain are acting without UN authorisation, in their continuous attacks on Iraq, a policy that has inflamed Islamic anger. In any event the final order to fire missiles into Israel was not given, although Israel was left in a

---

[169] America is concerned over the success that has been achieved by the martyrs, particularly as American servicemen and installations have often been the target (America is hated by Muslim Arabs almost as much as the Jew). In Yemen on October 12th 2000, a human bomb crippled the USS Cole, since that time a videotape featuring bin Laden, acclaiming the success of the mission, and inviting other Muslims to carry the war into the enemies camp is regularly transmitted. It is impossible to guard against such fanaticism.

state of high alert. Not all ten Arab nations were involved on this occasion, but I believe that a further escalation will occur during 2002.

Saddam has postulated that four million Iraqis have volunteered to assist the Palestinians in defeating the approximately two million Israelis of fighting age. The Israelis recognise that they are too weak to withstand ***any*** sustained invasion. Yet, during their anguish, they will cry out to God to deliver them from another Holocaust, and His forgiveness will deliver the Jew from blood-guilt (in a single day, Zechariah Ch 3:9). Although Israel is guilty of pride and rebellion and the shedding of innocent blood, she will be exonerated; as she was on entering Canaan (Israel had to stand against seven tribes on that occasion as well). Israel's guilt has finally been pardoned because the sins of the Gentiles are an even greater abomination in God's eyes[170]. The thirtieth year of Israel's parliamentary control over the whole city of Jerusalem, on its liberation, occurred in 1996. Also, from 1997 Messianic believers completed 30 years of continuous service to Jesus (the priesthood of Christ) in the Promised Land since the liberation of the Temple Mount (the sanctuary of Mount Zion).

Sallai Meridor, Chairman of the Zionist Executive, and the Jewish Agency, speaking at the Zionist General Congress in June 2001 said "***despite the current intifada, almost 35,000 new immigrants have made aliyah to Israel, since September***". It would seem that the returning Jews have received a spirit of joy and forbearance if not yet the promised new heart. It is a fact that Muslim families generally have twice as many children as Jews. However there is no disguising the fact that immigrations were 30% lower than the previous year. Tourism suffered badly due to the constant bomb and bullet attacks, and the economy is on its knees. It is thought that, if the Lord tarries, and, unless there is a major change in the worlds' political position, by the year 2020, there will be equal numbers of both Jews and Muslims in the land.

Thirty is the age at which Jews entered the priesthood (as detailed in Numbers Ch 4:3-4). There were, in 1996, 12 Messianic congregations assembling in Jerusalem, each one of them growing through vigorous evangelism. By January 2000, this figure had risen to 50, and one year later 80 Messianic groups were meeting in Israel. Statistically, in recent years, the Jewish race has

---

[170] Along with many other countries who have relaxed state legislature, in the latter half of the 20th century, Israel has condoned the killing of more babies in the womb through abortion than were killed though the holocaust. I have read statistics that claim that in Israel 500,000 pregnancies have been terminated since 1948 and that a further 5,500,000 Jewesses throughout the world have endured an abortion, which I suspect, is fallacious.

experienced a proportionately higher rate of conversion to Christ than all other races. Messianic believers ***living in Israel*** calling on the name of Jesus expect God's intervention, ***during*** if not ***prior*** to this invasion. It is written in Jeremiah Ch 50:20 that in the ***latter days,*** God said He would dwell with His chosen people ***eternally*** (Joel Ch 3:21). In Joel Ch 2:18 it is written:

> *"Then the Lord will be jealous for His land* (Israel, the holy land and Jerusalem, the holy city, are the only two named places God claims as His), *and take pity on His* (chosen) *people."*

Hosea Ch 14:4, 8 agrees:

> *"I will heal their waywardness and love them freely, for My anger has turned away from Judah and Ephraim."*

In Matthew Ch 23:39, Jesus was not speaking of *every* Jew living in every nation, calling on His name for deliverance. Jeremiah Ch 3:14-18 supports my reasoning:

> *"I will choose you, one from a town and two from a clan and bring you to Zion."*

A combination of Genesis Ch 17:5-9, Leviticus Ch 25:23 and Psalm 105:11 may be paraphrased as follows:

> *"The land of Canaan is given to Abraham and his seed, Isaac his son and Jacob his grandson and every generation of their seed after them."*

I foresee the ten nations of Psalm 83 joining in a conspiracy to support the Palestinian Arabs[171]. The prophet Asaph's agony of mind was caused by a military alliance of ten nations attacking Israel, at some time in this first decade of the 21st century. No history book claims that all these nations have combined to invade Israel in earlier years. The people groups of the Edomites, the Ishmaelites, the Moabites, the Hagrites, the Gebalites, the Ammonites, and the Amelekites, listed in the Psalm, were semi-nomadic. Their ancient boundary stones were often moved (see Proverbs Ch 23:10), and their people intermarried. The people of Philistia and Tyre, mentioned in the verses 7(b) were formerly sea-faring people, who have been absorbed into the Muslim milieu of ancient Mesopotamia, which today includes the people of Lebanon, Syria, Iran, Iraq, Saudi Arabia and Turkey.

---

[171] I believe that the invasion of Psalm 83 by the ten plotting nations surrounding Israel in their support of the Palestinian Arabs, may well be the people groups of Ezekiel Ch 36:2-7, in which it is declared that the plotters will be struck down by God's intervention, because they rob the Jews of the wealth of their land, forcing them into an impoverished position. This invasion may be the invasion of Ezekiel Ch 38-Ch 39, but I have not received revelation over this issue, but Ezekiel Ch's 29 and 30 do suggest that it is the friends of (Muslim) Egypt who are to be put to God's sword.

Gaza is a Philistine city and the City of Tyre is located in modern Lebanon. The last two nations listed, together with Egypt, had at some time all been part of the Assyrian Empire.

In Isaiah Ch 19, the curse against Egypt may well be due to their leaders duplicity, over the forthcoming invasion. Egypt will either be suffering under the effects of a plague, or retribution will arise from nuclear fallout causing the invading forces to rot whilst they live. Whatever the arising punishment brings, it will at least cause five cities to swear allegiance to the Lord Almighty. The passage continues in stating that the whole of the Muslim population of Egypt and all of the former lands to Assyria, which are part of those invading countries in which Ishmael settled, convert to Christ!! I believe that a plague of retribution for the catastrophic invasion will occur during the following seven months (or are these months the seven years prophesied of in Ezekiel Ch 39:9, in which the weapons of the enemies are used for fuel?). The infected dead bodies of Israel's enemies will be collected and buried in Jordan, which I believe to be one of the nations from where the invasion of Israel will originate. Ezekiel Ch 35 clarifies that Edom is to suffer, whilst Ch 39:11 says:

> *"In the valley east of the sea the inhabitants of the land* (Jordanians), *will bury the dead in order to cleanse the land."*

The purpose of this purification is to avoid any defilement of the Jews, which implies that the Jews are to be restored as priests. To whoever the task of witnessing is given, supernatural powers will be wielded by them (Revelation Ch 11:3-12). During their ministry recognition and respect will be enjoyed by the Jewish race in every land, a period during which ten Gentiles will seek the guidance and companionship of every Jew (Zechariah Ch 8:23).

Many church leaders will need to understand my interpretation of the symbolic picture language of the Book of Revelation (which of course although historical is also describing future events), in order to teach their congregations positively of reassurance of their eternal security, providing they stand firm until they die. Other than the first three chapters, the book is not written chronologically. The various references to the seven angels, seals, trumpets, plagues, and bowls of God's wrath, could be seven parallel events, occurring simultaneously. I believe I have pieced the likely scenario together fairly accurately. First the seven Churches of Revelation Chapters 2-3 may also be interpreted as representing seven ages of Church life, and many books and sermons have been offered expounding various views. David Yonggi Cho separates them as below:

1. Ephesus means-'*to relax*, or *let go of desires*'. 33-100 AD

2. Smyrna means-'*crushed myrrh*'. 100-312 AD
3. Pergamum means '*marriage*' (State religion). 312-590 AD
4. Thyatira means '*continued sacrifice*'. 590-1517 AD
5. Sardis means '*those escaping*' (from Catholicism, or from the flames) 1517-1750 AD
6. Philadelphia means '*brotherly love*'. The missionary expansion through the now enlightened body of Christ 1750-1905 AD
7. Laodicea means '*the right of laity*' (experimental-the expansion of the non-conformist groups of churches) 1905-2000, and then the 'Rapture'.

John had difficulty describing Muslim invasions, and the use of gunpowder, of which there was no knowledge in the days in which he lived. In Revelation Ch 6:12, John described the effects of a nuclear holocaust, in the only way he knew how, as an earthquake. Isaiah, in a parallel passage, was describing the devastation to the vegetation following the destruction of Damascus after a nuclear explosion (foretold in Isaiah Ch 17). I believe that before The 6th of September 2002 a nuclear retaliation will be made by Israel, following a rocket attack on northern Israel from Lebanon, where the Popular Front hq of the Hizbullah, and much of the Syrian army is located[172]. This will exacerbate the call by the surrounding Arab nations of Islamic faith to collectively invade Israel, fulfilling Psalm 83. Only in the two passages quoted are the words recorded '***Like chaff before the wind***'. Such reaction is a feature of a nuclear explosion, which scientists say releases a huge amount of soot, that shades out the Sun's light from the planet, perhaps for a two-year period over which time rain would carry the impregnated particles of carbon, as acid rain, to Earth. If such bombs were liberally released throughout the Earth, then it may be expected that '***one third of the Earth***' could be destroyed (Revelation Ch 8:12).

Other symbolic passages need to be interpreted, in order to explain how I reached my conclusions. For example Revelation Ch 9:5-10 speaks of a fixed period of 5 months (5 months of 30 days = 150 days of years), of a mounted militia, that strikes like scorpions, distinctive through their wearing of 'golden crowns'. This description of the

[172] President Bashar Assad of Syria has elevated himself to Commanding Officer of all troops of ***occupied*** Lebanon. He can do this for he is the power behind the throne Lebanon. He has recently been appointed for a two-year seat on the UN Security Council. The seat was not opposed, which, in view of the support Syria has given to terrorist groups, is startling and alarming! I am convinced that the five permanent members of the UN Security Council, and those other ten nations, who occupy seats by rotation, will recommend that an armed peacekeeping force be stationed in Jerusalem, to protect the Arabs; NATO will support this resolution.

invading hordes identifies the attackers as the Saracens, a desert people whose headdress was a distinctive yellow turban. The Saracens were followers of Mohammed (*c*570-632), who was the false prophet paralleling John the Baptist's ministry, as one '***calling out in the desert***'. In 630 AD, having initially overcome the Koreish tribe, who ruled the area from the City of Mecca, sought to recover all other occupied lands. The Mohammedans devastated the Greek Orthodox Churches of North Africa over the period 613-763 AD. The 150 years of unstoppable tidal waves of attack, similar to the 150 days of the Great Flood that had deluged planet Earth, could have referred to the hordes that were spoken of as being horse mounted troops numbering 200 million (perhaps a second allusion to the earlier Great Flood). In Revelation Ch 9:16, we are informed of a better-armed and disciplined, more astute enemy commanded by Salah a-Din (1138-1193 AD), a Kurdish born Seljuk Turk, and Sultan of Egypt. His armies were filled with religious fervour to recapture the lands that Alexander the Great had defeated. The Seljuk Turks, who in Revelation Ch 9:16-19, are identified as wearing a much more colourful breastplate, used cannons and rifles in their warfare, which is why John wrote in verse 17 of three plagues of fire (the result of the use of gunpowder). The ability to strike in opposite directions suggests that their core strength lay in their motivation, whilst being equally able to attack in overwhelming numbers in any direction. The illusory picture of horses having a sting in the tail was to inform readers of the Book of Revelation, that the Seljuk Turks (who developed into the Ottoman Empire) would rapidly expand westwards into Europe and eastwards into Asia and the Orient. The period of the Seljuk's power, until the Ottomans overran Greece and Spain in 1453 AD, was ***c400 years***. This is the biblical period that was written of as arising for '***this very hour and day and month and year***' in Revelation Ch 9:15, which interprets as ***c400 years***. The Mesopotamian tribes were a loose confederation of nations, centred on Iran. Osman 1 (1259-1326AD) united the tribes, and founded what became, the Ottoman Empire *c*1300 AD, centred on Istanbul (formerly Constantinople). It should be noted that it was God who ordered the release of the four angels, who represented the four Arabian horses of the apocalypse chained in Mesopotamia (which means 'between'), at the Euphrates and Tigris Rivers. Proverbs Ch 21:30-31 makes it clear that the four horses are released at God's instruction.

The Ottoman Empire continued (as a declining power since the 17th century), until the Sultan of Turkey sided with Germany at the outbreak of World War 1. Their defeat resulted in the emerging oil States asserting autonomously sheikdoms. Since 1967, when the last Greek king, King Constantine 11 was deposed, the more fanatical Muslims have worked to overthrow what they perceive as the Christian influence and impudence against their god *Allah.* America is seen as the Great Satan by most Muslims, because of the acquisitive materialism exhibited, by many of the despotic and nepotistic leaders of Sheikdoms, having received from American largesse into 'Western ways', and also because it was President Truman, who initiated the legal right of the Jews to establish the Israelite nation in their former homeland. This has increased the anger of the uneducated proletariat that the Sheiks rule over, which bellicose imams always highlight. Presidential successors have supported the Israelite regime despite the worldwide protests, inflamed by a biased media, over the 'inhuman' treatment of Palestinians living in Israel. Many third world nations have become Islamic, and many other stable and more emancipated of Muslim regimes are being intimidated, in the face of death-threats, by armed terror groups of Islamic extremists to introduce *Sharia* Law. Many Muslim clerics nurse ambitions of holding government office, with a view of imposing a strict adherence to the Muslim faith, and of 'Islamicising' their nation.

I believe that this current third invasion against Christianity is being launched because the Muslims are certain they can now overcome Western imperialism, which modern-time Christians would call 'Western humanism', which has developed out of Greek Hellenism. The democratic governments of the all-powerful Western Alliance have (unsuccessfully) sought to impose their powerful 'protectionism' over impoverished peaceable people of other nations. It should also be noted that it is the Persian spirit of *Pontifex Maximus*, which is Satan on his release from the abyss (Revelation Ch 9:1-3), which is the spirit behind the savagery and cunning of extremist Muslims. Many peaceful Muslims will turn to Christ, once God, in defending Israel against the ten surrounding Islamic nations, is recognised as the Almighty protector of His people. In Ezekiel Ch 18:7 the reader is told that the Ethiopians will carry a 'gift' to Jerusalem, having suffered at the hands of an invader. I believe that this 'gift' will be taken to Jerusalem as a tribute, following the defeat of the ten Arab nations. The 'gift' is probably the copy of the Ark of the Covenant that was bequeathed to the Ethiopian nation following the liaison between Solomon and the Queen of Sheba[173].

I believe that for the first 3½ years of the Great Tribulation, at the commencement of the seven years the two witnesses of Revelation Ch 11 (who may be archetypes rather than individuals) will commence their unique ministry, and they will be revealed ***before 6th September 2002***. I first thought the two witnesses might be Enoch and Elijah, two men who did not die but instead were carried into heaven. I later wondered if the two representatives might be '***people groups***', perhaps the Messianic Jew (as sons of the Covenant), and his elder half-brother Ishmael (the Christian Arab who was not the child of the promised inheritance, Genesis Ch 21:10). Another candidate might be the suffering Coptic Church of Egypt. Perhaps the Ethiopian believers will be represented, for they have suffered greatly in their discipleship over the generations. In the 8th century AD, the Muslims built the walled city of Harah in Ethiopia. It is still regarded as the fourth most holy place, behind Mecca, Medina, and Jerusalem; there are 99 mosques in this city. In the 19th century, the Ethiopian royal family became Christians through the missionary work of the LJS, which meant that many of their subjects accepted Christ. Colonel Gadaffi of Libya has said, "***Ethiopia is a Christian island surrounded by a sea of Islamic nations***". I believe that Islamic fundamentalists will shortly be 'cleansing' Ethiopia. We will have to wait and see, just whom God appoints. It is stated in Revelation Ch 11:12-13 that at the resurrection and Rapture of the two witnesses, 3½ days (years) following their deaths, 7,000 people will die in an earthquake, and a tenth of the city of Jerusalem (which I assume will be the part rebuilt as the capital of Palestine) will be destroyed. This rising to life of the two witnesses, together with the elect marks the end of the second woe (Revelation Ch 10:1-Ch 11:13).

It is written in Jeremiah Ch 31:38-40 that Jerusalem and the rebuilt necklace towns outside the old city walls would never be violated

---

[173] I wrote in my autobiography that there had been two separate waves of repatriation, 'Operation Moses' in 1986, and 'Operation Solomon' in 1991, during which time the descendants of Jews of the Babylonian exile made *aliyah* to Israel. I had stayed on Lake Kinneret in a hotel adjoining a hotel full of happy immigrants who laughed and smiled continuously, especially the children when they were getting into or leaving the school busses. Many Ethiopians had accepted Christ and now a decade later the Israeli authorities are trying to take away their citizenship, under the guise that its alright to be an atheistic Jew, but if a Jew turns to Christ he rejects his ancestry! Needless to say, the Ethiopian Jew over the years must have converted many of their animist neighbours to Christ.

again[174]. This passage suggests that Israel is ***persuaded*** to allow an armed 'peace-keeping' force a right of entry. Zechariah Ch 13:8-9 states that two-thirds of the population of Israel will die, presumably when the nations of the world will be gathered together to fight against Jerusalem, which will be occupied, with half the population of the city going into exile (Zechariah Ch14). On the occupation of Jerusalem by the New World Order[175], the two witnesses will be made an example of and killed. From Zechariah Ch 14:2-15, it can be anticipated that on occupation, Israel will suffer great distress at their enemy's hands. I believe that this ***occupation*** of Jerusalem will follow 3½ years after the invasion of Israel by the ten neighbouring Muslim nations.

Many books on eschatology have concluded that ten European nations will support the Pope's claim to be appointed as Governor or Custodian of the Temple Mount by the international government of the New World Order, to protect the Vatican's oversight of 'religious shrines'. He will only later be recognised as the ***final antichrist,*** or the '***man of lawlessness***'. Whoever is appointed as '**Custodian of the Sanctuary**'[176] will be given authority to enforce an international law of tolerance, allowing every person's right to follow the religion of their choice, without hindrance by followers of other faiths; thereby overcoming the problem of *religious persecution* by the leaders of the New World Order, in its decision to impose a representative governor in Jerusalem in what will become an international city. In future years the writer, publisher (or owner) of this kind of '***seditious***' book you are now reading, will suffer extreme penalty.

---

[174] Jeremiah could only have been referring to the final period of history, for those settlements have not been rebuilt in any earlier period of history.

[175] Amongst these nations supporting the New World Order who overcome Israel will be the kings from the East, invited to cross the Euphrates River, owing to its having dried up (Revelation Ch 16:12). They will join with the other kings appointed by the Beast from the Sea. During their 'one hour' reign, the invaders will cause devastation in Israel. Only God knows the duration of the occupation of Jerusalem, prior to the Rapture.

[176] It has recently been revealed that former Israeli PM Shimon Peres wrote to Pope John Paul II in May 1994, offering to relinquish sovereignty of the old city of Jerusalem to the Vatican, in order to encourage the emergence of a confederation between the religious aspirations of the PLO and Jordanian Arabs, as well as Jews and Christians. An ***'agreement in principle'*** was reached, to bequeath political and religious authority of the Temple Mount to the Vatican, at which time Jerusalem was to elect both a Palestinian and a Jewish mayor. Whilst holding office as PM, Yitzak Rabin pledged a town (mainly populated by Arabs located on the outskirts of east Jerusalem), to be recognised as the Palestinian capital and to be bequeathed by Israel in exchange for allowing certain areas of Judea to be retained by Israel for 'security reasons'. One of these two former premiers must have consulted with the UN, the Vatican and the Anglican Church, concerning the detail of this proposal, for it is of public record that all parties approved of the plan.

From Mark Ch 13:14 I anticipate a mirror image of Antiochus Epiphanes' desecration of the holy place on Mount Moriah ***not in the temple, but on the sacred place*** (Mount Zion or the Temple Mount). The ultra-Orthodox Jews living in Israel, firmly believe, as their rabbis have told them, that the Messiah's arrival on Earth, ***for the first time***, will occur following the rebuilding of a fourth temple. The ***false prophet*** will order the erection of the ***abomination, that causes desolation*** (an image that speaks, probably in the form of an electronic statue of the antichrist) alluded to in Daniel Ch 9:27, and Matthew Ch 24:15. All mankind will be forced to venerate the beast (Revelation Ch 13:12-14), which God will allow, well knowing that Satan will possess his own appointed servant the antichrist in due time (Revelation Ch 17:16-18). He will exercise authority and power (as prophesied in Daniel Ch 8:23-26).

Other authors have written that during the Great Tribulation the world is to be divided into ten economic regions, and further administratively subdivided into agricultural and manufacturing mini-regions, in a '***strategy for survival'***. If this (unworkable) plan is implemented, the nations that produce sufficient food to feed their population may not initially suffer as badly as those nations that rely on supplies of imported food. My understanding from Revelation Ch 6:5-6 is, that the rich and influential individuals, and perhaps even the wealthier nations that are self-sufficient in the growing of crops, will sustain their citizens initially. But later in every nation shops and manufacturers will cease trading as ordered supplies cease to arrive, leading to mass unemployment. This will surely be approaching the very end of time, when the beast will try to impose the marking of the body, as a control over individual bartering. Based on Revelation Ch 8:12, it would seem that a nuclear war precedes the eagle of verse 12 issuing the warning of the final three woes, which are the three angels of Chapter 14, who fly around the world. The last angel issues a warning to the citizens of the world (in their own language), on the pain of eternal death, not to accept the marking of the body.

A heavenly trumpet will be blown at the Rapture of all the elect from every country, (1 Corinthians Ch 15:52-54), on Christ's descent from the clouds onto the Mount of Olives, probably on the occasion of the earthquake of Isaiah Ch 24:18-20, and Revelation Ch 16:18-20 taking place. The effects of the earthquake will be experienced all over the world. Ezekiel Ch 38:19, states that every wall will fall (which I assume means that, nowhere on Earth will there be homes left standing at this climactic of times). It may be at this time that the terrestrial cataclysmic disturbances prophesied in Joel Ch 2:1-2,10,

30-31 or Revelation Ch 6:12-17 will occur. It should be remembered that 3½ years would have passed, in which the lands of the surrounding nations will remain fallow (due to God's plague of retribution, together with the effects of any nuclear warfare in the fulfilment of the attack of Psalm 83). The completion of the third woe (of Revelation Ch 8:13) falling on the unbelieving world will occur, at the confrontation at Armageddon, prior to Christ's millennial reign; a partial description of which is written in Revelation Ch's 15-19. I believe it is right that every preacher and teacher, having read this book, should begin to preach on this greatly neglected part of the counsel of God, to reassure their flocks that God is in control of all events. It is God that dries up the River Euphrates enabling passage for the armies of the kings of the East. It is God who puts the hook into the mouth of the peoples of the North, bringing them to fight against Israel, and it is God who summons the antichrist, the false apostle and the armies of the kings of the West to attend the feast of the birds at Armageddon. All born again believers will realise that salvation has come through the suffering of the Jews, since Christ's vicarious death for all. The Jews are a race protected by God, having been chosen for special servanthood.

I had received a repeated vision of a tidal wave striking a heavily populated coastal community, warning me of a coming calamity. In July 1998[177], a 9 m tsunami (a series of long, high sea waves caused by a disturbance on the ocean floor), close to the shores of Papua New Guinea, created a seismic disturbance of 7.1 on the Richter scale. Seismologists have said that a disturbance of this magnitude was not sufficient to generate a major tsunami. This undersea landslide struck, giving no time to escape this powerful and destructive wave, which inundated several villages almost one mile inland. I was reminded again of the flood of Islamic invaders, figuratively written of in the Book of Revelation. A radio broadcast reported that 70 people were known to have died and that 1,000 were missing. I sensed a check in my spirit on hearing this and received a '*word of knowledge*' that the number of deaths would multiply. The final death toll exceeded 2,000. However I am fearful of even greater tsunami at sea in the near future, which will result in a greater loss of life. It has been reported that in the 1998 flooding of China, arising from torrential rainstorms, the number of deaths was of similar

[177] I sense that 1998 was the year when the bad fruit of the unholy fruit started to fruit; partly because 3 x 666 =1998, but because this year followed on the heels of the special star sign of 1997. As mentioned elsewhere, it was at this time that Messianic Assemblies in Israel started to fruit in multiplying numbers.

proportions. The national religion of Papua New Guinea is Shamanism[178], although many nationals have converted to Christianity. Both of these countries are currently experiencing revival, which will have infuriated Satan!

God's spiritual laws have been finally breached, allowing the flooding of the world with every kind of pollution caused by mankind's abuse of the environment, marked by the attack on the World Trade Centre, and the increase of indiscriminate attacks against people of every religion in many nations. The Holy Spirit of God will ***increase*** His protection over those who are, or become, disciples of Jesus Christ[179]. Yet at the same time God will ***allow the release of evil and lying malevolent spirits***[180]. The conspiracy between the two beasts and Satan will endure throughout the period of the Great Tribulation[181]. The symbolic imagery of the rider of the four horses of the Apocalypse of Revelation Ch 6, illustrates that it is not the ***rider*** who changes, but the colour of the horses he rides, as the severity of his power on the world's population is increased. The white horse depicts the initial absence of war, the red horse, the start of war, the black horse, scarcity and famine, and the pale horse (whose rider is lastly revealed as Death and Hades), disease of epidemic proportion. This pictorial illustration demonstrates that the antichrist will be increasingly merciless during the Great Tribulation.

I do not want my reader to cease supporting any long-term projects that their church leadership, in answer to a revelation from God, may be investing much time in prayer and application over. All projects undertaken will need to be based on overt evangelism and love for the community during the Great Tribulation. Jesus will not allow vacillation of the responsibility of Christians, because it would be inconsistent of the Godhead towards those Christians of previous generations who had not seen Christ returning on the clouds, but who, until they expired, had proclaimed and lived out their faith. Jesus will not tolerate indolence by those who waste these last days in dissipation or sloth (Luke Ch 21:34-36). I would urge every Christian to extend themselves for one final burst in response to the exhortations to finish one's

---

[178] A belief held by many peoples in northern Asia that good and evil spirits could be influenced or controlled by the shamans.

[179] During the Great Tribulation, God will increase the manifestations of His Holy Spirit, and of miracles. If He did not, there would not be any hope of salvation for the countless number of martyrs who surrender their lives during this time.

[180] See the story of the ***lying*** spirit entering the prophets in I Kings Ch 22:21-23, and of the ***evil*** spirit that visited King Saul in 1 Samuel Ch 16 14:14-23, both sent by God.

[181] This false trinity is not one of unity, for Satan hates the Beast who has attracted much of the world's worship, leaving Satan unacknowledged (Revelation Ch 17:16).

personal race strongly (1 Corinthians Ch 9:26). Gather around your leaders to encourage them, especially if you are certain they are godly men, shepherding the sheep of their flock to the best of their ability.

I believe that I am to remain on Earth through the latter part of the Great Tribulation to encourage the Church and the Jews to rely on Christ's provision. I am apprehensive about this commission, but I will be obedient to God's commands, as indeed other Christians who move in the prophetic, and who have received a similar call to my own, have told me they intend to be. Frankly I believe that this book is delivering an oft-times repeated prophetic message, but perhaps for the final time. Salvation does not depend upon one's patriotism for one's country, or loyalty towards a denomination, but on one's personal walk with God. The saints will be 'Raptured' with Christ into the Heavenlies, where they will be given their millennial assignment. The millennial rule will be shared between both believing Jew and Gentile, wearing their newly received imperishable bodies.

Prior to undertaking a journey of prolonged absence from one's family and friends, it is usual to make plans well in advance. The procedure is the same when a person approaches the end of their mortal days. The elderly complete their wills, to verify how their assets are to be divided, and often reassure their loved ones that they will be reunited in the afterlife. The fear of the Lord is upon me, as I lie awake on my bed during the watches of the night, and I pay homage to the Creator Redeemer. My heart, soul and spirit revere Him. I can no longer remain silent concerning that which He has given to me to speak aloud about. It is futile to resist Him. It is foolishness for me to rage against Him, for only in obedience lays contentment and fulfilment. I am reminded of Jeremiah Ch 20:7-10:

> *"Oh God you deceived me, overpowering and governing my thoughts. When I speak in Your name of violence and destruction, I am ridiculed and mocked by both priests and scholars who are widely read and sit in the seats of the elders. I have tried keeping silent because I want to be accepted by my peers as a legitimate servant of God. I hate being insulted and reproached each and every day. Your words are like fire in my bones. I can no longer hold back the explosive words You have hammered into me as sticks of dynamite. Your servant speaks".* (paraphrased)

These verses exactly state my own sentiments.

I am no guru, or John the Baptist living a simple stoical life. If anything, I am an epicurean, for I enjoy the good things of life, and cannot sit in splendid isolation meditating on my oneness with the universal soul of creation. I know that God has made me as I am, and is maturing me into what I will one day become. I do believe that it has been necessary for me to write this book for the same reason as the man, blind from birth was born so afflicted; which had been ordained in order that the work of God might be ***displayed in his life*** (John Ch 9:3). I had hoped to complete this book without writing of the gift of '*miracles*' and '*healings*' of the Holy Spirit, which have often accompanied revelation received by me, seemingly to verify the prophecy as being truly from God. My reluctance is out of fear of becoming proud over the gifts that God has entrusted to me, for I am well aware of my weaknesses and inadequacies. The Lord has prompted me to include a sentence on this subject, because many of this generation's proclaimed prophets are not visionaries and do not experience confirming supernatural miracles in support of their oracles. I do not wish to generalise, for I realise that this statement is as ill informed as sweepingly saying that any prophecy without accompanying signs is not valid. Yet it can be clearly read in the Bible that prophecies were often accompanied by miracles, as have several of my own prophecies. God has graced me by giving me the ***gift*** (as opposed to the fruit) of '*faith*', and He has allowed me to be used in saving sinners from eternal death, and delivering others from phobias and demons. I have witnessed God's grace in raising the dead, opening blind eyes and healing the sick. I know that God has anointed me as a prophet, despite the reluctance of those who know my background to accept me into this office, because of familiarity. It is as Jesus said, "***a prophet is without honour amongst those who have never considered him as worthy***". I am sorry that I have to speak out in this way, to an ecclesia that judges (discerns? I do not think so) rather than encourages. In 1 Corinthians Ch 14:1 it is written:

> *"Eagerly desire spiritual gifts, especially the gift of prophecy."*

But the ***ministerial anointing*** of prophetic utterance is hugely different from the ***gift*** of '*prophecy*' that we are all urged to covet. I am not God's friend, as Moses was, like all other prophets I receive (as one of a number of God's servants) my messages in riddles (Numbers Ch 12:8). However I am aware that I have been given a scroll to eat that sours my stomach. God says in Revelation Ch 10:6-11:

> *"There will be no further delay. You must prophesy again about many peoples, nations, languages and kings"* (paraphrased)

Once a man has received a vision from God, he cannot be anything other than totally focused and obedient to that which he has been given to do, and he cannot hold back any of the Counsel of God revealed to him. I have the example to comfort me of Jonah, who was angry with God because he believed God had always intended to delay the time of judgement of Nineveh and the Assyrians. Jonah's sin was in not wanting to see God grant mercy to the Ninevites, because he did not want to be accused of being a false prophet, on their delayed judgement! Jonah was well aware of the Assyrians' hatred of Israel, and did not want them to receive the same grace granted to himself. If God has revealed to me all that I have written of only as a warning for the reader to repent, so be it. 1 Corinthians Ch 14:8 states:

> *"But if the trumpet does not sound a clear call, who will get ready for battle?"*

I have tried to be even-handed with the extra biblical material I have drawn from, and have stated that I do not accept every written word that the authors of the books I have made reference to are ***gospel truth*** (even the Bible is contradictory in some parts[182]). The ***Source*** behind the Scriptures is infallible even if the redactors are not. I do not boast of the spirituality demonstrated in my life, rather I boast of how the Holy Spirit has changed my nature and entrusted me with godly assignments. It seems that the more readily obedient I am, the more I am blessed by being used as a channel of His love.

Some prophecies I have made have been fulfilled since publication of this book, or it's second edition:

- the handing over of Bethlehem by Israel's government to the Palestinians before Christmas of 1994
- the election of Mr Netanyahu to the premiership of Israel
- the initiation of the meltdown of the world's financial administration 'mystery Babylon'
- a major invasive action on American soil, by an extremist Islamic organisation

Some of the prophecies still awaiting fulfilment, but clearly waiting God's sanctioning are:

- an invasion of Israel by the Arab nations surrounding Israel.
- an invasion by Indonesia on a 'Christian' country, having ethnically cleansed the homeland.
- the ethnic cleansing of Ethiopia.
- the imposition of a 'Caesar', to administrate the Temple Mount on behalf of the New World Order, in a shortly to be declared 'international' city of Jerusalem.

[182] Compare 2 Samuel Ch 10:18 with 1 Chronicles Ch 19:18, or 2 Kings Ch 24:8, with 2 Chronicles 36:9.

- the death before *Hanukkah* 2002 is completed, of a plotter to the division of Jerusalem, and the deaths of other leaders, who spun their webs of deception on their intentions.
- the complete and final destruction of the former glorified empire of Babylon.
- a nuclear attack on Damascus.
- a devastating earthquake in America, within a succession of other natural disasters.
- the 'ten toed' EU government that will place micro chips into all paper money, later introducing a cashless society, and the marking of the body to control trading.
- the re-election of Mr Netanyahu to the premiership of Israel.

He who is obedient to the Lord will be strengthened in the days of turmoil still to come. I pray that the Holy Spirit has enriched you as you read this book. Amen.

SUMMARY

18th of March 4001 BC	Planet Earth was formed at the first Spring Equinox.	Page 3
606 BC	Daniel and his three friends (representing Israel) deported.	Page 51
539 BC	Cyrus gave permission for Judah to return.	Page 57
536 BC	The return from Babylonian exile	Page 52
7th of June 334 BC	Greek army defeated the Persian army at the Battle of Hellespont River. There were 2,300 years between 334 BC and 1967 AD, when the final king of Greece, King Constantine 11 deposed.	Page 44
167-160 BC	Antiochus Epiphanes' reigned in Judah for 2,300 days.	Page 65
14th May 6 BC	The date given by Clement for Jesus' birth	Page 59
613-763 AD	150 years of the Saracens revolution and destruction of Greek Orthodox churches throughout North Africa.	Page 154
1055-1453 AD	The Seljuk Turks, who became part of the Ottoman Empire, occupied the whole of the lands in which the Greek Orthodox Church had established itself on the foundation of the empire of Alexander the Great, over 398 years	Page 154
1914 AD	2520 years after 606BC was the start of the First World War	Page 39
14th May 1948	Law of Return in Israel passed 2,520 years x 365.25 days=2483.8 years after 536BC	Page 59, Page 61
14th May 1996	Ascension Day, third millennium since anniversary of Christ's birth	Page 153
14-15th Sept 1997	The 49th year following 1948 AD, the unique star formation of Revelation Ch12:6	Page 150
1st Jan 2000 AD	2,300 days after the signing of Oslo Accord (13th September 1993). See Daniel Ch 9:27	Page 148

Glossary

%	per cent
°	Degrees (angle of, or temperature)
AD	Anno Domini (After Christ)
	also known as
Aids	Acquired Immune Deficiency Syndrome
AOG	Assemblies of God
asl	above sea level
BBC	British Broadcasting Corporation
BC	Before Christ
c	circa (about the time of)
CIA	Central Intelligence Agency
cms	centimetres
DNA	Deoxyribonucleic Acid
EC	European Community
EU	European Union
EDLS	Equidistant Letter Sequence
FBI	Federal Bureau of Investigation
FEMA	Federal Emergency Management Agency
FEPA	Federal Emergency Preparedness Agency
GDP	gross domestic product
ICEJ	International Christian Embassy of Jerusalem
IDF	Israeli Defence Forces
IMF	International Monetary Fund
JWs	Jehovah's Witnesses
Kgs	kilograms
lbs	pounds (weight)
MP	Member of Parliament
mph	miles per hour
ms	metres
NASA	National Aeronautics and Space Administration
NGO	non government organisation
NIV	New International Version
NKJ	New King James
OIC	Organisation of the Islamic Conference
PFI	Prayer for Israel
PLO	Palestinian Liberation Organisation
PM	Prime Minister
psi	pounds per square inch. used to quantify the weight of atmospheric pressure at ground level
Rev	Reverend
SDA's	Seventh Day Adventists

TV	television
UCLA	University of California of Los Angeles
UDI	Unilateral Declaration of Independence
UN	United Nations
UFO	Unidentified flying object
USA	United States of America
WTO	World Trade Organisation

Biblical Terminology

Biblical year	360 days
season (a)	90 biblical years
Elect (the)	believers in God
time (a)	360 biblical years
Great Commission (the)	The preaching of the Gospel throughout the Earth
Great Tribulation (the)	The end of time period lasting seven years immediately preceding Christ's Second Coming also recognised by many as the '*time of Jacob's Trouble*'.
Promised Land (the)	Land of Canaan given by God to Abraham
Rapture (the)	Catching away in the air of the elect (the believers in Christ)
Second Coming (of Jesus)	Christ's return on the Mount of Olives to reign on Earth

Jewish Terms

Aliyah	to 'go up' to the Promised Land
Menorah	a seven branched candelabrum
Midrash	a collection of oral homilies
Shalom	Christ's peace
Shofar	the horn of any kosher animal
Talmud	the primary source of Jewish religious law
Tanach	Old Testament
Teshuvah	repentance after sin (starts on *Elul* 1 through to *Tishrei* 10)
Torah	the first five Books of the Bible.
Yeshua HaMashiach	Jesus Christ the Messiah

Hebraic Months

1 *Tishrei*	September/October
2 *Heshvan*	October/November

3 *Chislev*	November/December
4 *Tevet*	December/January
5 *Shevat*	January/February
6 *Adar 1*	February/March
7 *Nisan*	March/April
8 *Iyyar*	April/May
9 *Sivan*	May/June
10 *Tammuz*	June/July
11 *Av*	July/August
12 *Elul*	August/September
13 *Adar 2*	Held approximately every 2½ years

Jewish Festivals

Hanukkah	Feast of Dedication or the Festival of Lights
Pesach	Feast of the Passover
Purim	Feast of Lots
Rosh Hashana	Feast of Trumpets, or New Year's Day
Shavuot	Pentecost, or Feast of Weeks
Succoth	Feast of Tabernacles or the Feast of Booths or the Feast of the Nations
Yom Kippur	Day of Atonement
Yovel	Sacred fiftieth 'diamond' year

Bibliography

Breitman, Richard. *Official Secrets.*
Penguin Press

Bullinger, E. W. *Companion Bible. (The)*

Chumney, Edward. *Seven Festivals of the Messiah. (The)*
Treasure House PO Box 310, Shippensburg, PA 17257. USA.

Compton, Piers *Broken Cross. (The)*
Veritas Publishing Company PTY. Ltd. Australia.

Crombie, Kelvin. *For the Love of Zion.*
Hodder and Stoughton,
Mill Road, Dunton Green, Sevenoaks, Kent TN13 2YA.

Cornwell, John *Hitler's Pope : The Secret History of Pius XII.*

Curle, George. *Times of the Signs (The)*

Diprose, Ronald E. *Israel in the Development of Christian Thought.*
Istituto Biblico Evangelico
Italiano, Via del Casale Corvio, 50 00132 Rome, Italy.

Drosnin, Michael. *Bible Code. (The)*
Weidenfeld and Nicholson,
London

Faid, Robert W. *A Scientific Approach to Christianity.*
New Leaf Press, Inc. PO Box 726,
Green Forest, AR 72638, USA.

Faulstich, Gene. *History Harmony and Daniel.* & *Witness for Jesus the Messiah.*
Box 3043, Spencer, Iowa 51301, USA.

Hislop, Alexander. *Two Babylons (The)*
Partridge.

Hunt, Dave. *A Woman Rides the Beast.*
Harvest House Publishers, Eugene, Oregon 97402, USA.

McTernan John & Koenig Bill Israel. The Blessing or the Curse.
Hearthstone Publishing. Oklahoma City. Oklahoma USA

Mitchell, Roger & Mills, Brian — *Sins Of The Fathers.*
Sovereign World Ltd,
PO Box 777, Tunbridge, Kent

Pembor G H. — *Mystery Babylon the Great.*

Rambsel, Yacov. — *His Name is Jesus.*
The Mysterious Yeshua Codes.
Yeshua-The Name of Jesus Revealed in the Old Testament.
Frontier Research Publications Inc, Box 129, Station 'U' Toronto, Ontario, M8Z 5M4, Canada.

Rees, Professor Martin. — *Just Six Numbers*
Weidenfeld& Nicholson. London.

Rohl, David. — *Legend, The Genesis of Civilisation*
Century. Random House UK Limited.

Satinover, Dr. Jeffery — *Truth Behind the Bible Codes (The)*
Sidgwick & Jackson.

Washburn, Del and Lucas, Jerry — *Theomatics*
Stein and Day; N Y New York 1997.

Wiseman. P. J. — *Ancient Records and the Structure of Genesis*,
Thomas Nelson, 1985

Wright, Fred. — *Words From the Scroll of Fire*,
Four Corners Publishing, PO Box 32310, Jerusalem 91322 Israel.

Wyatt Archaeological Research — Videos and newsletters from 713 Lambert Drive, Nashville, Tennessee 37220, USA

Yallop, David. — *In God's Name.*
Corgi Books, Transworld Publishers Ltd, London.

Index